Southern Excursions

Other Books by George Garrett

FICTION
King of the Mountain
The Finished Man
Which Ones Are the Enemy?
In the Briar Patch
Cold Ground Was My Bed Last Night
Do, Lord, Remember Me
A Wreath for Garibaldi
Death of the Fox
The Magic Striptease
The Succession
An Evening Performance: New and Selected Stories
Poison Pen
Entered from the Sun
The Old Army Game
The King of Babylon Shall Not Come Against You

POETRY
The Reverend Ghost: Poems
The Sleeping Gypsy and Other Poems
Abraham's Knife and Other Poems
For a Bitter Season: New and Selected Poems
Welcome to the Medicine Show
Luck's Shining Child
The Collected Poems of George Garrett
Days of Our Lives Lie in Fragments: New and Old Poems, 1957–1997

PLAYS
Sir Slob and the Princess
Enchanted Ground

NONFICTION
James Jones
Understanding Mary Lee Settle
The Sorrows of Fat City
Whistling in the Dark
My Silk Purse and Yours
Bad Man Blues: A Portable George Garrett
Going to See the Elephant

Southern Excursions

Views on Southern Letters in My Time

GEORGE GARRETT

Edited by JAMES CONRAD McKINLEY

LOUISIANA STATE UNIVERSITY PRESS

BATON ROUGE

Copyright © 2003 by Louisiana State University Press
All rights reserved
Manufactured in the United States of America
First Printing
12 11 10 09 08 07 06 05 04 03
5 4 3 2 1

Designer: Barbara Neely Bourgoyne
Typeface: Adobe Minion
Typesetter: Coghill Composition Co. Inc.
Printer and binder: Thomson-Shore, Inc.

Library of Congress Cataloging-in-Publication Data

Garrett, George P., 1929–
   Southern excursions : views on Southern letters in my time / George Garrett ; edited by James Conrad McKinley.
     p. cm.
   ISBN 0-8071-2850-3 (alk. paper)
   1. American literature—Southern States—History and criticism. 2. American literature—20th century—History and criticism. 3. Southern States—Intellectual life—1865– 4. Southern States—In literature. I. McKinley, James. II. Title.

   PS261 .G37 2003
   810.9′975′0904—dc21   2002013639

The paper in this book meets the guidelines for permanence and durability of the Committee on Production Guidelines for Book Longevity of the Council on Library Resources. ∞

For Suzy

—J. C. M.

*For my colleagues and comrades
in the Fellowship of Southern Writers*

—G. G.

Take away William Faulkner, John Crowe Ransom, Allen Tate, Robert Penn Warren, Eudora Welty, and Katherine Anne Porter, and the shining modernist era in the United States would dim like a flashlight in the wee hours of a Boy Scout Jamboree.

>—Fred Chappell,
> " 'Not as a Leaf': Southern Poetry and the
> Innovation of Tradition"

Alas! for the South, her books have grown fewer—
She was never much given to literature.

>—J. Gordon Coogler

The excursion is the same when you go looking for your sorrow as when you go looking for your joy.

>—Eudora Welty,
> *The Wide Net*

Contents

Preface, xiii

🕮 ESSAYS

Anarchy and Family: A Few Words About the Southern Tradition, 3

A Summoning of Place, 7

An American Family History (We Eavesdrop While a Family Tells Its Private Stories): Review of *The Hinterlands* by Robert Morgan, 29

A Life Without End: Two Novels About World War II by William Hoffman, 35

Liberty and the Southern Tradition, 45

Part Scam: *The Encyclopedia of Southern Culture*, 53

A Voice for the Voiceless: Review of *My Drowning* by Jim Grimsley, 60

Jesse Hill Ford's Play, 66

William Price Fox's *Dixiana Moon*, 71

Forest of the Night: A Declaration of Independence, 77

The Man Who Wrote the Movie: Faulkner and the Public Arts, 86

William Goyen's "Ghost and Flesh, Water and Dirt," 94

New Market: The Cost and Waste of the War, 98

The Death of Regional Writing, 102

Soil of Hope: New and Other Voices in Southern Fiction for the Nineties, 108

The Ordways by William Humphrey, 111

Cassandra Singing by David Madden, 116

Crime and Punishment in Kansas: Truman Capote's *In Cold Blood*, 119

SHORT REVIEWS

The Commonplace Book of William Byrd II of Westover, edited by Kevin Berland, Jan Kirsten Gilliam, and Kenneth A. Lockridge, 135

The Fabulous History of the Dismal Swamp Company: A Story of George Washington's Times by Charles Royster, 138

A Consuming Fire: The Fall of the Confederacy in the Mind of the White Christian South by Eugene D. Genovese, 141

"No Wonder People Got Crazy As They Grew Up": *Bastard Out of Carolina* by Dorothy Allison, 144

Eneas Africanus by Harry Stillwell Edwards, 147

A Way of Happening: Observations of Contemporary Poetry by Fred Chappell, 150

Gaining a Foothold in Old Jamestown with a Sovereign's Tightly Held Funds: *Big Chief Elizabeth* by Giles Milton, 154

The Sharp Teeth of Love by Doris Betts, 157

The Big Ballad Jamboree by Donald Davidson, 161

White People: Stories by Allan Gurganus, 164

It's True South with a Sense of Humor: *The Sharpshooter Blues* by Lewis Nordan, 167

Kate Vaiden by Reynolds Price, 170

The Collected Stories of Reynolds Price, 172

A Visitation of Spirits by Randall Kenan, 176

Nashville 1864: The Dying of the Light by Madison Jones, 179

The Thanatos Syndrome by Walker Percy, 182

Celebration by Mary Lee Settle, 185

Wolfe in Wolfe's Clothing: *O Lost: A Story of the Buried Life* by Thomas Wolfe and *To Loot My Life Clean: The Thomas Wolfe–Maxwell Perkins Correspondence*, edited by Matthew J. Bruccoli and Park Bucker, 188

Peter Taylor: A Writer's Life by Hubert H. McAlexander, 191

Bow to the Bull's-Eye: *To the White Sea* by James Dickey, 195

A Letter from Earth, 198

INTRODUCTIONS

Introducing Wendell Berry, 205

Introducing Reynolds Price, 208

Foreword to *The Liberation of Lord Byron Jones* by Jesse Hill Ford, 210

Introduction to *So Red the Rose* by Stark Young, 215

Foreword to *The Long Roll* by Mary Johnston, 223

Foreword to *Cease Firing* by Mary Johnston, 229

Foreword to *Dream Garden: The Poetic Vision of Fred Chappell*, edited by Patrick Bizzaro, 236

Introduction to the Modern Library Edition of *Snopes*, 239

INTERVIEWS

Life into Art: A Conversation with David Huddle, 247

Buzzards and Dodos: George Core (Editor of the *Sewanee Review*) Talks with George Garrett About the Quarterlies, 266

An Interview with Paxton Davis (1925–1994), 275

THREE TRIBUTES

William Goyen, 285

Peter Taylor, 288

Paxton Davis, 290

EPILOGUE

Southern Literature Here and Now, 295

Acknowledgments, 303

Preface

Southern Excursions is a selection of previously uncollected, representative pieces—essays, reviews, and speeches, etc.—by George Garrett concerning the state of southern letters. It is important to know that these are examples lifted out of a larger context: although Mr. Garrett's principal endeavor has been as novelist and poet, during the years represented by the work in this collection (roughly from the 1960s to the present) he published seven books of criticism and wrote many more as-yet uncollected pieces concerning a variety of literary subjects and writers, among them John Updike, Anthony Burgess, Barry Unsworth, John Ciardi, Kurt Vonnegut, Frederick Buechner, James Jones, Joanna Scott, Russell Banks, George V. Higgins, James Gould Cozzens, Stephen Millhauser, Anthony Hecht, and many others, including for example the great film director Sam Peckinpaugh.

However, the scope of this particular collection, *Southern Excursions,* is limited to writing that examines Mr. Garrett's deep interest in the literature of his native South. In three of his previous books of literary criticism, *The Sorrows of Fat City* (1992), *My Silk Purse and Yours* (1992), and *Going to See the Elephant* (2002), Mr. Garrett has collected major essays on such leading southern writers as William Faulkner, Robert Penn Warren, and Shelby Foote, but *Southern Excursions* is intended to be more inclusive, treating many deserving but perhaps lesser-known southern writers past and present.

As I culled through the boxes, folders, and envelopes of typescripts, magazines, books, clippings, and handwritten manuscripts (pages and pages of Mr. Garrett's inimitable fountain-pen scrawl on yellow legal pads) which I had been given to work with, I sorted my selections in what at first was nothing more than an intuitive manner. I grouped together essays and in-depth, essay-type reviews, short reviews, introductions (both from published works of literature and from events at which George introduced the guest of honor), interviews, and tributes according to the type of work, and then rearranged them within those groups.

George Garrett has had a long and varied writing career. In 1961, when he published his second novel, *Which Ones Are the Enemy,* he was just over thirty years old; by then he already had six books behind him, including his brilliant collection of short fiction, *King of the Mountain.* In the forty-one years since then, he hasn't let up. He has published stories, novels (including the acclaimed trilogy of Elizabethan novels—*Death of the Fox, The Succession,* and *Entered from the Sun*), poetry, and criticism, written plays and screenplays, edited anthologies, and has taught creative writing at some of the best programs in the country, including Hollins, Michigan, and Bennington, and, most recently, he held the Henry Hoyns chair at the University of Virginia (where I was lucky enough to have been one of his students). I'm proud to be associated with Mr. Garrett and with this book, which gives to the reader a sense of where southern writing has been in the twentieth century and the possibilities of where it can travel in the twenty-first.

—J. C. M.

ESSAYS

These are not strictly essays, I suppose, not in the conventional sense of the term, anyway. They are representative pieces of essay length, originally written for various books and magazines—reviews, lectures, critical pieces, and even a travel article—where I was allowed a little more space and elbow room than one can usually expect.
　—G. G.

Anarchy and Family: A Few Words About the Southern Tradition

Not counting the newest of the new and the youngest of the young, we have three living generations of southern writers, although we have lost many strong voices, including Robert Penn Warren, Walker Percy, Andrew Lytle, Cleanth Brooks, Peter Taylor, and Eudora Welty. Shelby Foote perseveres (at this writing), and all of the above have earned more than regional honors and recognition.

When you think of all these, together with so many others, a surprising number, at one end of the living tradition and, at the other, the writers representing their own generation, one has a genuine sense of the continuity and variety of the southern literary tradition in our time. Missing—but their long shadows remaining—are a crowd, a cloud of the elders and witnesses who link the great flowering of southern writing in the twentieth century to its historical and literary past: first and foremost, of course, William Faulkner, who mapped the territory for us even as, in many different forms and strange contexts, he influenced and changed the literature of the wide world and all its babbling languages; the great and influential Agrarians and Fugitives—Tate and Ransom and Donald Davidson and Caroline Gordon and Brooks and Warren, and, of course, their own pupils, people like James Dickey and Randall Jarrell and Madison Jones; remarkable independents, people like Thomas Stribling and Stark Young and John Gould Fletcher; and the first generation of women who made their way, and often their living, as writers—Ellen Glasgow and Mary Johnston and Elizabeth Madox Roberts and Evelyn Thomson and many others, not the least among them being Margaret Mitchell. And none of this should slight or ignore the no-longer separate and equal traditions of black southern writing, from, say, Richard Wright and Ralph Ellison (who sometimes identified himself as a southern writer and who was a member in good standing of the Fellowship of Southern Writers) to younger voices like those of Percival Everett and Randall Kenan. This listing, however hopelessly inadequate, at least serves to offer the sense of a thriving and traditional enterprise. Which is a point taken for granted by our younger writers. The point is, and truth is, that we all know each other—the work, anyway. There is great independence, and even a certain anarchy within the southern tradition, but there is also a strong sense of family.

Another thing not often mentioned by our own critics and writers, not because it is taken for granted but rather because it is so sensitive and runs the risk of giving real offense, is the split within the family of southern letters that is directly a result of the Civil War and the loss, for the better part of a century since then, of major publishing centers in the South. Ever since the Civil War, the southern writers who had any kind of national ambitions or aspirations, or the writers who worked in special forms—the drama, for example—whose principal centers of commerce and appreciation are elsewhere, have been forced to live up to an alien image of what the southern writer is supposed to be and to say; and, behind that, the subject itself, the truth presented in approved and certified southern literature, must conform to an outsider's image.

Long training in and acceptance of the forms of good manners and tact have prepared the southern writer for a certain amount of role-playing in both life and art. Role-playing on both sides, for example, was and probably remains a crucial element in the complexities of race relations in the South. Similarly, role-playing among southerners, including any number of southern writers who have chosen to move and to live in the North, is nothing new. To an extent, we have all sold out, some minimally and only for the sake of survival, others more seriously and for the sake of . . . *success*. Remember some of what Faulkner wrote in his introduction for the Modern Library edition of *Sanctuary*? "I began to think of books in terms of possible money. I decided I might just as well make some of it myself. I took a little time out, and speculated on what a person in Mississippi would believe to be the current trends, chose what I thought was the right answer, and invented the most horrific tale I could imagine and wrote it in about three weeks." Shades of Bret Easton Ellis! Of course, there is much more to the Faulkner story than that. It has become an *exemplum* of artistic integrity. Most of us have exercised and demonstrated much less integrity. And this needs to be understood. Should I be bold and name names? Should I show that much integrity? Not bloody likely! But let this much be understood: that to the extent that southern writing is apt to be, on a national scale, commercially or critically successful, it is also likely to conform to imposed or, at any rate, distorted and generalized stereotypes. These days, there is always a clear and present danger that southern literature will fall victim to terminal cuteness. It is also always a possibility that southern literature will die of a surfeit of liberalism.

Although we have seen the arrival and expansion of good, if small, southern publishers (Algonquin, Peachtree, Blair, Pelican, among others), we must not look to southern publishers to change or ease these problems. For they too must prosper nationally to endure and must play their role as seriously as any ambitious or desperate individual. Southern publishers cannot afford to take many chances. Not yet. . . .

And within the South we have to admit to some other kinds of roleplaying, deviations from the strict and factual truth. Think how many among us (again no names, no sir) insist on claiming a more genteel and aristocratic lineage than any facts can be mustered to support. Or, sometimes within the same family, we lay claim to more rowdy depths of redneck, cracker culture than even our best friends would allow. More recently, we have developed two light variations on this theme, both aesthetic: the worldlier-than-thou, hard-nosed cynics, and then the aesthetes who, though they may come deeprooted from the deep boonies, try to allude as knowingly as any Manhattan sybarite to the vintage wines of the world, to great foreign cities and foreign philosophers and artists. I have a poet friend who firmly maintains that an absolute test of the fraudulent is that contemporary American writer, of any kind, who summons up the image of Akhmatova and kidnaps her into his own poem or story. My poet friend may be right. In any case, there are southern writers who have done exactly that.

Meanwhile, the novels being written by southern novelists are lively and various; and the range and energy of these novelists, who have been busy and productive in large number throughout and since the twentieth century, show no sign of shrinking or diminishing. If, as so many critics have gleefully predicted, the novel falls over dead, it won't be the fault of the southerners.

Another point needs to be made. Except for some literary criticism, we do not make enough of the very real contributions of southern writers in the fields lumped together as "creative nonfiction." I am thinking of the highly individual essays and articles of people like Roy Reed, Roy Blount, Hal Crowther, Sam Pickering, James M. Cox, Pat C. Hoy, and John Shelton Reed. And it is in that field that we find, on the grandest scale, the greatest single literary work attempted and achieved by any American author of our time—*The Civil War: A Narrative* by the southern novelist Shelby Foote. The late Walker Percy aptly called it "our *Iliad*." In every detail, large and small, it is a magnificent alchemy of fact and art, worthy of all the tradition and variety of southern letters that came before it and, like the overwhelming achievement of the life work of William Faulkner, becomes an integral part of the tradition, and by example and by challenge, becomes an invitation to the future. Foote says something of the same thing himself in his "Bibliographical Note" to Volume II of *The Civil War,* writing that, among his many sources, "Mark Twain and Faulkner would also have to be included, for they left their sign on all they touched, and in the course of this exploration of the American scene I often found that they had been there before me." Foote joins them as one of the precious few who point the way forward.

(1991)

A Summoning of Place

Most of the important things about the place of place in fiction have been said before and said better by my betters. And so it is probably outrageous, bad form all around, to write about place again, to try to recapitulate the persuasive arguments so ably advanced that they are by now our unspoken assumptions, matters of faith and belief. Yet, precisely because one so seldom examines or even questions one's unspoken assumptions, it might be useful to reconsider my own life and work, how my private practice coincides and connects with the public assumptions that I accept and honor without thinking much about them.

For my own good reasons, I have tried to avoid too much self-consciousness as a writer, thinking, superstitiously perhaps, that I might somehow inhibit or at least limit myself and my work by too much self-study. That's a proposition that might well prove to be true; but here I am in my seventies, someone whose past is a good deal longer and stronger than any imaginable (or maybe even desirable) future. From this point of view, it would seem to be a more serious inhibition not to be able freely to look back and consider the road behind me, the road already taken. It is not necessary to stake claims or to make claims about that work. The work will simply have to speak for itself.

Over the years, I have written novels, short stories, poems, and some other things (plays, movies, biography, essays, criticism, and journalism).

Not that it makes that much difference, because, beyond my tacit acceptance of the working rules of the road and some safe-driving tips for each of these forms, I think, of them all, large or small, lighthearted or heavy, as chips off the same block. Which is to say that I think that the writers I most envy and admire and honor leave their signs on all they touch, and that, as Auden says somewhere and I here have to paraphrase, even a limerick ought to be something a man facing a firing squad or death from cancer could read without contempt.

There is something that, enjoying the pleasures of hindsight, I had not noticed before because I was not looking for it. Looking back now, it seems to me that I took advantage of the variety of work I was doing to play off one form against another. That is, for example, that when I was writing more-or-less realistic fiction, stories and several early novels, colloquial in style and matter-of-fact in mundane detail, I was, at one and the same time, composing verses that were more-or-less formal, metrical, and rhymed. Later, when I was deeply engaged, for thirty-odd years, creating an Elizabethan Trilogy and searching to understand their language and then to echo and to translate it, a slightly more elevated, even elegant level of speech, all through those days, while not completely abandoning my other habits (in either fiction or poetry), I wrote looser if not "freer" verses focused on less "poetic" subjects and sources. These things seem to have depended on each other.

Just so, one cannot escape from the good and bad habits of the age, its customs, conventions, and stereotypes. One acts and reacts within the literary context of a real world with real values, though many of these values, over a lifetime, prove to be as transient and insignificant as hemlines and the length of haircuts.

Places matter greatly in the art and craft of making literature. I said places plural, because I think now, after stumbling through the twentieth century and into this one, that plurality in and of itself is something that tends to separate us from the world of our parents, grandparents, and ancestors. Most of us in those days were born in one place, lived out lives in that place, came at last to be buried there. Other places were mostly imaginary, though our imaginations were fueled and sometimes fired by the tall tales of drifters and passing strangers, the reports of some few travelers who had left behind this place only to return later with the good news or bad news of a wider world and all its various and sundry places. And there were always the wars, close by or often very far away, that gathered up our young men and took them off to alien places where many died and from which many, often maimed beyond repair or recovery, hobbled home to take up (gratefully) their old lives in the homeplace. These veterans could have told us a tale or two, but most often they didn't. What had happened to them was beyond their power to describe or evoke. Silence was the golden rule. Later, as in, say, the case of the aged veterans of the Civil War or World War II, they mellowed enough to begin to share some of their memories, memories colored and distorted by nostalgia and blessed forgetfulness.

Of course, for me and all Americans there is always the great leap sideways, that long voyage over from old countries to the newfound land, a migration that continues, for better and for worse, to this day. But for those of us whose people came here earliest, it was an enormous change of place, beginning with the dangerous passage across the wide sea and, for the lucky survivors of those voyages, arrival at and then living and dying in bleak, hard-scrabble settlements on the edges of a vast, dark, brooding wilderness.

Would we now be witness to the overwhelming migrations of today, from all directions from ancient and distant civilizations, if that were the inevitable end of their journey? Who knows? But I kind of doubt it.

Recently I read an accounting, synoptic to be sure, of the amazing travels and travails of an English sailor, Davy Ingrams, in the middle of the sixteenth century. Left behind on a beach in Yucatán by Sir John Hawkins (Sir John had some men ashore but had to flee for his life to save his ship and crew from superior Spanish forces that suddenly appeared on the scene), this fellow escaped the clutches of Spaniards and Indians alike and set off, briskly at first one likes to imagine, in a generally northeast direction, hoping to get to Newfoundland just as soon as possible. He had sailed on fishing vessels to Newfoundland and knew that fishermen and other adventurers congregated there in the high summertime. He had no idea how far away from Yucatán Newfoundland might be. A few years later, after walking all the way across the continent, he arrived at Newfoundland, found a vessel that would take him aboard and eventually returned to his homeplace in the West of England. There, after a while, some authorities (in the modern terminology) "debriefed" him. He told them all that he knew and could remember—the basic problem being that anybody tough enough to walk across the whole American continent for several years, all by himself, though he was often given hospitality by Indians . . . and sometimes not, anybody who could do that might not, most probably wouldn't, be a highly sensitive observer. He climbed big mountains, he crossed the wide rivers, he lived through hard seasons. He came home. It was soon apparent to his official questioners that the fellow had very little to add to their knowledge of the secrets of darkest America. When they began to look sidewise, to shrug to each other, and to yawn in his face, Davy began to make up things that might arouse their interest: multicolored sheep and monstrous rabbits, miracle plants and crops, tribes of two-headed Indians, buckets of silver and great lumps of gold—the usual things. They eagerly copied down his testimony, and some people even elected to believe it.

Imaginary places, emerald cities at the end of yellow-brick roads, have always been part of our sense of place.

Sometimes imaginary history, and at its heart an imaginary sense of place, not only haunts our lives with ghostly voices and echoes but is, finally, stronger, even more accurate than the cut, shuffled, and dealt world of hard facts. Having lived long enough, I have inevitably witnessed things, *experienced* them, that later, in the hands of others, as past history, were rearranged to suit the pleasure and purposes of "objective" observers, historians who, never deviating from factual "accuracy," nevertheless have turned the truth completely upside down. It is in this sense that narrative history, even fictional history, can be as important as factual history. Born to one place, for generations we almost always lived and died there. Our ghosts spoke to us in the common language of presences, with the common logic of poetry. We knew our past, chiefly by word of mouth, in our skin and bones, though our knowledge of the facts might be more than a little sketchy. We could love it or we could hate it or both at once, but we could not easily leave it. Or, if we did manage to move on, as many did, we left our hearts behind in the homeplace, often feeling a little ashamed of ourselves, as if we had failed in our bounden duty.

All that changes in a mere historical blink of an eye. Complex forces set us Americans off a-wandering to many places. Meantime, our homeplaces changed radically before our very eyes—many shriveling and shrinking into a shabby insignificance, others growing, "developing" into huge, crowded, disorderly suburban and city places that share not much more than a name with the original place and its vanished inhabitants.

Among writers, the first great generation of modern American masters—Faulkner, Hemingway, Fitzgerald, etc.—had to contend with this. Many moved on and about for the rest of their lives. Others, particularly the southerners, stayed or regularly returned home where, even amidst the shrinking and shriveling, or the lunatic expansion, they could feel at home. That was the last literary generation of Americans that truly enjoyed that choice. We, who followed after, are close enough to them to feel a nostalgia for the lost (or fading) place they once and for all summoned up for us. We tend to be sentimental about it. They were not. Nostalgia and sentiment are not true love. No *caritas* there. To do their work, Faulkner and Welty and Warren and Foote and Settle and all the rest had to love the place. Deeply.

I doubt seriously that we will again see that kind of love shining through American writing, not exactly in the same form anyway. We will live to see something else, something different, maybe even some things quite wonderful, but never that true, unconditional love again.

One of the many drastic changes in American late-twentieth-century literature has been the association and affiliation of our writers with our academic institutions. For the first time since the great years of the monasteries, a large number of serious writers are kept by colleges and universities as teachers and performers. This began just before World War II but accelerated and expanded rapidly in the 1950s. It follows that the writers went to the places where the jobs were. Some found homes and tenure. Most of the others became academic nomads. Many, myself among them, imagined this to be a kind of temporary condition, one we would shed as soon as possible for careers as full-time writers. Failing that, in fact as well as imagination, I have only recently retired from thirty-odd years of full-time teaching, broken occasionally by free or study years here and there. Thus I have lived (never mind considering short or long visits) in Middletown, Connecticut; Rome, Italy; Houston, Texas; Charlottesville, Virginia; Princeton, New Jersey; Roanoke, Virginia; Columbia, South Carolina; York Harbor, Maine; Miami, Florida; Charleston, West Virginia; Lexington, Virginia; Ann Arbor, Michigan (twice); Charlottesville (again); Tuscaloosa, Alabama—not counting some early times logged in New York City, first in the Village, then on 115th Street. A fairly typical record, I reckon, for a writer of my generation.

And so it is that, in my lifetime, place has become plural. We have "places," real and imaginary. We have those places where we have worked well and whose qualities, as we know and understand them, seem to bring out the best in us.

For example, I have not written a single word of fiction set on the coast of Maine—where I lived year-round for several years, where I still return yearly, where I wrote more than half of my novels and collections of stories. Wrote them mostly in one particular place—at a zinc-covered worktable set by a couple of small windows in a long, narrow boathouse, itself fixed on a rock-and-earthen pier, jutting out into the York River. It is a place that has been first in my wife's family, now in ours, for five generations. Behind the boathouse, set on a little slope, the old house (1780) faces the river too. Tidal, the river is always moving, and the boats moored out there, fishing boats, lobstermen, and, in summertime, the yachts and pleasure boats of summer people, move in and out also. Gulls fish, cry out, roost, and fly.

And one writer managed to get a good deal of work done there without writing a word of fiction about it. Others there have worked well too. Mark Twain upriver half a mile, Sidney Lanier, Thomas Nelson Page, William Dean Howells, and May Sarton, and now Ann Beattie, among others, in the area, in the neighborhood.

What I have said, though, needs to be slightly modified. If I have written no fiction about the place, I have in fact done a play (*Enchanted Ground*) for readers' theater and for local performance, about the place and some of its history. And, I now notice, I have done any number of short poems whose setting, firmly in that place, is as much the subject as anything else.

As, for an obvious example, this little poem, what I would call a "watercolor":

MAINE MORNING
Where clear air blew off the land,
wind turns around and the sky changes.
Where there was burning blue is pale gray now,
heavy and salty from the cold open sea.
And the long groaning of the foghorn
saying *change . . . change . . . change . . .*
like a sleeper dreaming and breathing.

Tide turning, too, with the weather.
The lobster boats swing about to pull

against moorings like large dogs on chains.
Gulls cry like hurt children and disappear.
And I think, surely it is a magician,
bitter and clever, who has pulled this trick.

That old magician is laughing in the fog,
and the cries of wounded children fade away
while the bellbuoy sounds farewell . . . *farewell* . . .
daring the dead to rise up from dreaming,
to hold their lives like water in their hands.

Some years ago, speaking to the North Carolina Historical Society (a talk entitled "Why They Left Home and What They Were Looking For"), I touched on the kinship of that place and my work. I said to them that much of the work, almost all of the writing of my trilogy of Elizabethan novels, was done in that rickety boathouse set on an earth-and-rock pier jutting out into the York River in York, Maine. This place was once the site of the first town pier with its warehouse and with the village marketplace conveniently and directly behind it between the boathouse and where my house stands. There I sat in my boathouse on the place of the first pier in the first village that was settled in what was then called the Palatinate of Maine, governed, from a great distance, by Sir Ferdinando Gorges—who was, as these things happen, a cousin of Sir Walter Ralegh.

We know that for one reason and another Europeans had been coming to the coast of Maine, most often to the off-shore islands but sometimes inland as well, for a much longer time than anyone has yet reckoned. Certainly the English were coming here in the early years of the sixteenth century for the sake of the seasonal fishing and to set up fishing camps, some of them quite elaborate and as solid as little settlements; for exploring also and for some trading with the local Indians. Sir Ferdinando, ruler of the Palatinate, decided on what became York as the appropriate site for the first permanent, year-round settlement in Maine. It had already been cleared and somewhat tamed. There had been a village there inhabited by some agricultural Indians. Sometime around the end of the sixteenth and the beginning of the seventeenth centuries, more or less coincident with the end of the reign of Queen Elizabeth, the Indians simply vanished. It was speculated that they had died from disease or during one of the innumerable and unquenchable tribal wars.

It was a likely place, then, clear and empty of its people when, in the early seventeenth century, Captain Christopher Levett sailed the *York Bonaventure* through the tricky, rocky mouth and safely into the calm harbor of the York River (in those days called the Agamenticas), looking for an appropriate place to plant a settlement. He recommended this one: "There I think a good plantation may be settled, for there is a good harbor for ships, good ground and much already cleared, fit for the planting of corn and other fruits, having heretofore been planted by the Savages who are all dead. There is good timber and likely to be good fishing."

And so they came here and have been here ever since, the original families—the Bragdons and Blaisdells and Moultons and Sewalls and Stovers and so forth. My boathouse is insured by Bob Bragdon, himself directly descended from Arthur Bragdon who came to York in middle age from the English town of Stratford-on-Avon, where it is quite implausible to imagine that he did not have at least some memories of that place's second-most honored and famous citizen.

The history of York is not entirely uneventful. On the day after Candlemas in 1692, a large band of Abenaki warriors attacked the village at dawn, killed many men, women, and children, and carried off more than half the inhabitants. Two garrison houses withstood the attack. One of them, Captain Alcocks's, was located roughly a hundred yards downriver from my boathouse. Captain Alcocks reported as follows to Captain John Floyd, who brought some troops (too late) to the rescue from nearby Portsmouth: "All gone. Everything we built and planted, every mark we made on this place is gone. There is nothing left but bloody corpses and cold ashes."

For the next decade or so, the survivors all slept for safety in garrison houses, and they planted crops and rebuilt their village. A lot of it stands there to this day.

By the way, the first encounter with the Abenaki war party occurred at first light when a young boy, checking a line of traps, came upon a great pile of their snowshoes. He was shortly captured but lived to tell about it. He was the third Arthur Bragdon of York, Maine.

Also an aside: I remember that the old women of my family, keepers of tribal lore, sometimes spoke of ancestors of ours who came in the seventeenth century to live in Portland (Maine) just up the coast a ways from York Harbor. These people, they said, were seamen and their families. One of them, captain of a vessel, drowned at sea when the ship was lost. Sometime in the eighteenth century, they moved away, to the South as it happens. I do not know the name of my Portland forefathers. The women who could tell me are long gone. But I think that they were named Holmes. In any case, the memory that some of my family had been here in Maine from earliest days helped to make Maine a kind of homeplace for me.

I mention these things to make the point that after all my reading and research, all my travels and sightseeing in England and Scotland, I ended up writing my Elizabethan novels in as good a place as any I can think of for the summoning up of old ghosts. It was not, is not, a haunted place, really, but it surely is a kind of enchanted ground. And there were bright moments for me when I felt the bristling energy of that enchantment, moments when I felt the presence of others as close as my elbow, ghostly presences as palpable as any shadow, including my own, moments when, out of the shadows, I seemed to hear voices speaking to me.

As for those Elizabethan novels and the old country, the story is fairly simple. Except for a look at the white cliffs of Dover from the crowded deck of a troop ship and later a few days holiday, I was never in England (in fact) until after I had brought out the first book of the trilogy, *Death of the Fox*. For *The Succession* that followed, I spent a good deal of time, by car and on foot, following in the footsteps of my characters, looking not so much at the houses and buildings and artifacts, though I certainly looked at them where I could, as feeling the ground under my feet, walking and wondering how this may have felt for those for whom (the times as well as the places) it was home. It was a foreign place, to be sure, but it was *my* foreign place.

I was stationed in Trieste, courtesy of the U.S. Army, and I have lived in Italy, once for more than a year in Rome, and have visited there whenever I could, logging more time and mileage than I have in England, Scotland, and Ireland. Out of the Italian experience has come one novel, *Which Ones Are The Enemy?* (1961), an army story set in Trieste (written in Middletown, Connecticut), a couple or three short stories, and a scattering of poems. While living in Rome, courtesy of the American Academy in Rome, I wrote my first novel, *The Finished Man,* set in central Florida, my home and birthplace. Like many other American writers, I had to leave home for Rome (or somewhere) to begin to rediscover my original place in the world. I had to go elsewhere to find out where I had already been.

Here is a "Roman" poem from that time, a quick sketch or candid snapshot of the impact on a visiting (American) stranger:

NIGHT POEM: ROME
When the great gray European dark
settles on the city like a spell,
the streetlights haloed, the old people
huddled in doorways, eyes alert,
and my heart sags in a net of veins
like a rock in a sling (for History
is the giant here, stretches and straddles
the dark continent), and I walk home
and would go on tiptoe if I could
so as not to break anything,
not to kiss dust from anybody's lips
or change anything from stone to flesh,

then, by God, I see the lovers,
the Roman lovers on the walk,
leaning together, he whispering,
she listening, laughing, so close
you can't separate their shadows.
O Noah's pairs of all creation
couldn't please me more! I hurl
my heart against the night
and hear the astounded giant fall.
And I rejoice. I fumble with a key
and open doors. I kiss my wife
and hold my children hostage in my arms.

Another word or two about living in Rome. Looking back, I now think that only living there like that, surrounded by that glowing, ruined, immemorial city, would have permitted me the active leisure to imagine (in a state of complete practical ignorance) that I could invent and create, together with some others, an international literary magazine—the *Transatlantic Review,* named after Ford Madox Ford's celebrated (and defunct) magazine, a copy of which none of us had ever so much as seen before. But we did that, putting out the first issue early in 1959, in and from Rome. Used our own money, such as it was (not much), together with the very generous support of Joseph McCrindle, literary agent and, in the best sense, amateur and entrepreneur. We presented it to him, and he kept it going well for about twenty years, head-to-head competition with the elegant and slowly fading *Botteghe Oscure* and with George Plimpton's little hobby, the *Paris Review*. For a while, with offices in London and New York, we were the leading English-language literary magazine in the world, widely circulated (and with a magnificent and eclectic list of contributors) everywhere in the world—except in the United States, where our circulation was typically modest.

All that is another story for some other time and place.

The reason for doing it in Rome was that we were there and that we had found, out in the high ground of Frascati, overlooking the sunny sprawl of Rome, an Italian doctor who loved English and its literature and who, coincidentally, owned a printing business. His outfit offered us a deal and printed the first couple or three issues.

I would go out to Frascati, hanging onto the back of a motorcycle owned and operated by the Irish poet John Patrick Creagh. We would pick up proof, settle down at a café table with a view of Rome, armed with pencils and a carafe of the white wine for which that town is justly famous, to proofread. The first two issues are, needless to say, riddled with proofing errors.

Back in the city, Fellini was shooting *La Dolce Vita* (or, as it was then titled, *La Vita Dolce*), and some of our *Transatlantic* people, notably Desmond O'Grady, are in that movie. In the "Steiner sequence," concerning the arty side (and suicide) of the "sweet life," you can see a copy of the *Transatlantic Review* on Steiner's table—if you don't blink.

This recollection is sponsored by the notion that, of all places I have lived, Rome alone demanded some kind of direct and immediate response. I was writing a first novel about politics in Florida. The magazine became for me, as it was, I think, for my comrades in arms, an answer and a salute to the ancient and modern stones of this homeplace (one of them, anyway) of our embattled Western civilization.

As for Trieste, that beautiful port city on the Adriatic, I was a soldier there, stationed near the village of Padricano up on the Yugoslav border (in those days). My *place* was the U.S. Army, but there were powerful literary vibrations.

You could not go down into the city to the main PX without passing the Berlitz school where Joyce taught for years and worked on *Ulysses* and other things. His brother, Stanislaus Joyce, was teaching at the university in Trieste while I was there. You could not leave the city, going west along the coast, without passing by Duino Castle, where Rilke listened for angels. Two of my favorite Italian/Triestine writers, the poet Umberto Saba and the novelist "Italo Svevo" (Ettore Schmitz), had lived there and had written in the local Italian dialect, which was the first Italian I learned.

In one sense, the real subject here is memory. Memory and place are hopelessly entangled, memory exposed to hard-edged facts that sometimes directly contradict memory. It seems to me that there are at least three kinds of memory—one that is private, your own secret word hoard of facts and fiction; public memory; and somewhere in between, but perhaps more powerful than both, lies family memory, what we can recall from the experience of kinfolk we know and have touched, those we have witnessed.

Thus, for example: as a baby I was held up high by one of my great-grandmothers for a family photograph. She lived as a girl and as a young bride on a very large, remote, and isolated plantation near Apalachicola, Florida, before the Civil War. She well remembered looking out of her window over wide flat fields at dawn and seeing scattered tree stumps begin to move around. The stumps were, in fact, Indians, not up to any harm or mischief, just checking out the lay of the land.

That was the Florida frontier six generations ago.

Another example. In my childhood, we had a maid who often brought her mother, a very old woman it seemed to me then, with her. This woman had been born in slavery. She told me stories about those slavery days, and she taught me, though I have long since forgotten most of them, some songs and games and skip-rope rhymes from that gone time.

All these stories, and others, became a part of memory.

Of course, there are always some documents as well. Such as the "autobiographical notes" of Hardy Greeley Garrett, my grandfather's brother on my father's side, who came to central Florida in the 1880s to make his way in the booming real-estate business:

People came from all parts of the United States and a great many from England to buy property in Florida. It was so easy for them to believe that they could make money raising oranges that it became a kind of craze. . . . Many people were afraid to wait until tomorrow to buy for fear that nothing would be left or that they would have to pay a higher price. There was another side to this picture. The natives had lived lives of seclusion and seriously resented any and all invasions. It was their country, and they did not welcome outsiders. Judge Spear, who lived about six miles west of Orlando on the south end of Lake Apopka, told me that when he first lived there his nearest neighbor lived six miles away. He met this neighbor one day and found him so overcast with gloom that he asked him what the trouble was. 'I'll have to leave this country. They're crowding me out.' It turned out that another family had settled where Orlando is now, about six miles from both Judge Spear and his neighbor.

Another time and place, speaking to the Florida Historical Society in Orlando, I described myself as "someone for whom the Orlando of the 1930s and '40s is more vividly present than this bright and shiny hotel ballroom and the bright and shiny world outside just beyond the windows where massive towering bank buildings, vaguely brutal and Babylonian, brood over this city by day and by night. . . . There was a time, lasting a decade from the end of the 1920s to the beginning of World War II, when it would have been distinctly disadvantageous to flaunt such prosperity around these parts, when even the (secretly) rich professed and pretended to be members in good standing of the genteel poor. It was a time I hiked and biked and hunted and fished all over what is now this large city and most of Orange County. I would have sworn that I knew every inch of it, but I got lost today trying to find my way to this hotel."

World War II was a time of great change for central Florida. Thousands and thousands of men from the army and the Army Air Force came to train to fight in the war they later won (see James Gould Cozzens's *Guard of Honor*). It was a very exciting time for a teenager. I remember the very young RAF pilots, veterans of the Battle of Britain, coming to our house on Phillips Place for Christmas dinner, 1941. They smoked all the time, drank and laughed a lot. Their eyes had the old thousand-yard stare that I had so far only seen in the eyes of uncles who had fought in the First World War. They were daredevils, those young pilots, and a surprising number of them crashed and were killed hereabouts just when it seemed that their most dangerous days were behind them.

Here is another sign of the turn of the tide during World War II, the beginning of the end of sleepy old, shady old Orlando: My mother was standing at a corner on Orange Avenue, the corner next to Ivey's Department Store, waiting quietly for the traffic light to change. Next to her, also waiting for the light, was an officer of the Army Air Corps. Suddenly, loudly and directly overhead and very low, an airplane, clouds of smoke pouring out of it, sputtering and staggering (if a plane can be said to stagger).

"Lord have mercy!" My mother exclaimed. "Is that plane going to crash?"

The officer standing beside her had already spoken his reply before she realized he was Clark Gable. "I don't know, ma'am," he said in the famous, expensive, and throaty voice. "But I sure am glad I'm not on it."

I elect to date the time of great change in central Florida from the arrival, on the scene and in the flesh, of Clark Gable. First came the war, then Gable, then air-conditioning.

Florida has (so far) been the explicit setting of two of my novels—*The Finished Man* (1959) and *The King of Babylon Shall Not Come Against You* (1996), written in Charlottesville, Virginia, and Tuscaloosa, Alabama, and maybe a dozen or two dozen short stories and a few poems.

Explicit setting? More and more in an interchangeable contemporary landscape our writers are rooting their fictions in an indefinite, one might say *implicit* setting. Partly this is an attempt to avoid the pejorative label of being "a regional writer," as if, at this late stage of our wildly changing culture, that meant anything or made any difference at all. Do these fictions take root, bloom, and flourish? Time will tell, one supposes.

I believe that the summoning-up of place from memory is likely to be different from inspection of the place where one is, in fact, standing and looking. Each point of view has its strengths and weaknesses. Memory is all too often flawed and untrustworthy. Just so, close familiarity breeds not contempt but frequently takes too much for granted.

Another place I have written about in poems and stories, and in one novel, *Do, Lord, Remember Me* (1965), written in Houston, Texas, is the mountain country of western North Carolina. This is the home turf of any number of "Appalachian" writers. One thinks of Fred Chappell, Wilma Dykeman, Robert Morgan, and, just over the border in Virginia, people like David Huddle, Lee Smith, Alyson Hagy and R. H. W. Dillard.

Always a visitor, an outsider, I spent some of my life, especially my youth, in various seasons and for various years, there at my grandfather's farm. It was then and there, under the tutelage of a tall mountain man I always called Uncle Tom, though I have no good reason to think he was any blood kin, that I learned to milk a cow and how to plow a field behind two horses or one mule, what were weeds to hoe and plants to cherish and protect in the kitchen garden, how to kill chickens, with ruthless efficiency and dispatch, for noon dinner, and where to find the best wild blackberries, where the pigs went and could be found when they escaped to a temporary freedom. All those things and more. Now, chances are, I could not again perform even these rudimentary chores. I was proud of myself in those days, and that childish pride became part of the place. What was up early and soon sweating became in memory, and thus in the camouflage of art, a little glimpse of Eden. Lost and gone. Near the end of his long life, that grandfather sold off the farm place and moved back down to the low country of South Carolina to the village of McClellanville, where he had been born and raised (briefly "raised"—for, like so many others in Reconstruction days, he went to work before he was twelve). In his old age, his nineties, he was inspired by his own rage and by the stylish speeches of Adlai Stevenson to go forth and to campaign (a Lost Cause if there ever was one) for him across South Carolina, in person (as they say) and on the radio.

All of the above memory, the whole story, flickers through a single poem I wrote at that time and place, like a reel of movie film running out of control in an empty projection booth:

MAIN CURRENTS OF AMERICAN POLITICAL THOUGHT
Gone then the chipped demitasse cups
at dawn, rich with fresh cream and coffee,
a fire on the hearth, winter and summer,
a silk dandy's bathrobe, the black Havana cigar.

Gone the pet turkey gobbler, the dogs and geese,
a yard full of chickens feeling the shadow of a hawk,

the tall barn with cows and a plough horse, with corn,
with hay spilling out of the loft, festooning the dead Pierce Arrow.

Gone the chipped oak sideboards and table,
heavy with aplenty of dented, dusty silverware.
Gone the service pistol and the elephant rifle
and the great bland moosehead on the wall.

"Two things," you told me once, "will keep
the democratic spirit of this country alive—
the free public schools and the petit jury."
Both of these things are going, too, now, Grandfather.

You had five sons and three daughters,
and they are all dead or dying slow and sure.
Even the grandchildren are riddled with casualties.
You would not believe these bitter, shiny times.

What became of all our energy and swagger?
At ninety you went out and campaigned for Adlai Stevenson
in South Carolina. And at my age I have to force
myself to vote, choosing among scoundrels.

Most southern writers that I know of, at least the last several generations of them, going back to the days before the Civil War, have been townspeople, not farmers. But the society was, for a long time, predominantly agricultural, and almost always a family farm stood as a real place and a place that stood for something. From before Jefferson until here and now, we have looked on the great cities with a farmer's *frisson* of illicit awe, contempt, desire, scorn, and humility. Remember how Jefferson (somewhere in the letters) calls the Yellow Fever a blessing in disguise because it purges the population of the cities. Many of us, at least in my generation, Agrarians and not, gratefully include the family farm as part, if only a ghostly one, of our full sense of a homeplace. Some of us—I think at once of Madison Jones and Wendell Berry—have returned to farming and to writing directly out of the experience. Others, the poets Henry Taylor and Fred Chappell for example, growing up on farms, have kept the place and the experience alive for all of us. That many of the Agrarians of the 1930s didn't know (in an old rural definition) "which end of a horse to feed sugar to" is not strictly relevant.

Many of their points and arguments were, still are, well-taken, if seldom seriously debated.

Would we really call the U.S. Army a place? An *institution,* yes, but a *place*? Why not? Millions and millions of us, especially Americans of the twentieth century, spent years as a part of it. I spent eight years in the active reserve, two of those years on active duty overseas with the 12th Field Artillery Battery (Separate), part of the 351st Regimental Combat Team (TRUST), stationed in the Free Territory of Trieste, then later up on the Danube at Linz, Austria, where the 12th Field was attached to a reconnaissance battalion whose name and number, and even the shoulder patch, I have mercifully forgotten, having only the memory that at its battalion headquarters this unit, originally a Union cavalry outfit, had battle flags from the Civil War and trophies from the Indian wars in the West.

The army, one learns soon enough, is the same place wherever it goes and is located, though it is, or is said to be, a professional army now (read: mercenary) and was still a citizens' army from the beginning until the end of the Vietnam War, it was, is, always will be the same place.

I remember that they often tried to explain things to us in terms of our place in the "Big Picture." Some of my fellow sergeants, good men and true to be sure, believed there really was somewhere an enormous Big Picture, a TV screen as big as the Pentagon or even bigger, where, like crowds of people in a D. W. Griffith movie (*Intolerance*?), we were all to be seen and observed. Someone somewhere out there was in charge and in control, always looking out for our interests, health, and welfare. There was a place (Eden) where the Big Picture was and where everything made perfect sense.

Taking the army as a place (the West Virginia of the American psyche? the Mississippi of the soul?), one also assumed a past. Up close and personal, the men of the 12th Field in Trieste were sometimes fired on (and sometimes returned fire) by various kinds of terrorists and Yugoslavs. A goodly number served in Korea. Some of the older sergeants had good clear memories of World War II. One of them was captured at Kassarene Pass, recovered, then later was wounded and overrun in the Battle of the Bulge. Their past became your past if you listened and learned.

And there was the much larger, longer past, all the way back to the *Iliad.* All of a piece throughout.

For southerners, the army was always a place to be, once in our own army, not for long, but long enough to kill or maim one of us in four and a good many of them, too. You might safely say then, and even now with all its cultivated diversity, that the army is a southern place. It is not a Tom Hanks/Steven Spielberg/Tom Brokaw kind of place, full of mellow old men with their weepy memories and neat graveyards.

We have family memories in between our own and the sad end of Hector, Tamer of Horses. For instance, my Uncle Oliver (my father's side) was not himself a southerner, though we incorporated him when he wrote the final shooting script for *Gone With the Wind.* He went *early* to World War I, spent Christmas of 1917 in the trenches. His unit went into action very early in our part of that war and stayed late; and when, at the end they were pulled out of the line, they were each and all carefully searched for the possession of any loose cartridges, lest someone should take a notion to shoot General "Black Jack" Pershing when they passed in review in a big parade in their honor. Oliver H. P. Garrett had some good stories to tell and even wrote and published some of them. He wrote the screenplay for the first talking film version of *A Farewell to Arms,* the one with Gary Cooper and Helen Hayes and maybe the best film adaptation ever of a Hemingway novel. Oliver's stories were authentic veteran talk. They were always oblique, jokey, and usually funny stories never dealing directly with the inexplicable experience of mortal combat, just the context of it. He was once asked why he didn't write a "war novel." "What is a war novel?" he answered. "Is that like a *life* novel? The Great War was my whole life."

We served and fought in all the American wars—the earliest soldier of the family that I can track down so far was one Gershom Palmer of Stonington, Connecticut, who was lieutenant of a Stonington company during King Philip's War in 1675. We have been at it ever since. The army was, as yapping and barking sergeants were continually reminding us, our home away from home.

Of course, the Civil War, which killed more of us than all the other American wars taken together (so far), was the worst and the one that mattered most. I had four great-grandfathers and one grandfather who walked (or rode) across those killing fields and experienced the slaughterhouse directly. None of them ever said more than a few words about it. Except for one. As irony would have it, the only one who put any words on a page—a private diary and journal for his own family—was the one Yankee of the bunch, Colonel Oliver Hazard Palmer, commander of the 108th New York Volunteers.

He saw action ("going to see the Elephant" was what they called it) any number of times in desperate places, most notably at the Battle of Antietam and the Battle of Fredericksburg. From his notes on the latter, one can learn a good deal about what it was really like. Prior to the passage quoted below, he had led his brigade, following direct orders, to attack Confederate positions on the high ground overlooking the town. To start the assault, they had to begin by crossing roughly four hundred yards of open terrain in the face of "a most destructive, accurate and deadly fire. . . . It was too hot. One third of my Brigade was disabled in twenty minutes and I was compelled to fall back." The brigade was withdrawn into the cover, such as it was, of the town. After which he wrote:

> I remained on the field until nearly dark and until the fighting of the day was mainly over. It was a terribly hot place. The shells were flying in every direction and plowing up the earth all around me, frequently covering me all over as in a whirlwind. The scene was frightful but intensely exciting. New Brigades of fresh troops were forming in line and advancing hoping to be more successful, but I knew they were doomed to disappointment and death. Broken and shattered Companies, Regiments and Brigades were falling back. Dead and wounded officers and men were being borne to the rear, some in blankets, some on the shoulders of their comrades. You would see one here with one arm, another there with one leg trying to get back. Some moaning, some swearing, occasionally a poor fellow trying to save the half not shot away in front would disappear in fragments by a solid shot or amidst the smoke of an exploding shell. . . . About sundown I made my way to town to gather up fragments of my Brigade not knowing what the next day might require. Out of the 1200 men in my command in the morning I could get together at night only 400. It was a sorry sight.

The place, Fredericksburg; the time and place, the Civil War. You have now been there. So can we all if and when we care to.

As luck would have it, or maybe it's not luck, but (in Nabokov's sense and term) as *synchronicity* will have it, I am working on this piece on "A Summoning of Place" in my high attic study in Charlottesville, Virginia, a place, the one place, where I have lived, off and on, for more than twenty years. My attic windows overlook the hedge, the handsome toothpick fence, the huge, shady sweet gum tree (in their back yard) separating my place from that of my next-door neighbor for a dozen years and more—the late Peter Taylor. His widow, the poet Eleanor Taylor, lives there still. It is now Monday, July 2nd, 2001, a cool, bright summer day, clear breezes blowing. Coming after more than a week of hot and humid days, with the temperature in the high 90s, it is most pleasant weather.

As synchronicity will have it, the daily *New York Times* has an essay by the writer Geraldine Brooks, "You Live Differently in a Small Place" ("Arts," pp. B1, B2), part of the paper's ongoing series of star turns—"Writers on Writing." Ms. Brooks's article is pertinent in a number of ways. She identifies herself as having been, until now, a city person at home "in the dense urban tangles of Sydney, New York, Cairo, and London." She has now come to live "in a tiny village of 250 souls in the Blue Ridge foothills of Virginia." A place, whatever its name and wherever it may be, that cannot be far from where I am at work. We are (assuming she is still there at this moment) sharing the same good weather and, to some extent, sharing the same view of the Blue Ridge Mountains lining the western horizon. The central point of her article is to make the case that living in this Virginia village has been an experience that has served to liberate her from some prejudices and preconceptions, and has allowed her to write and finish her forthcoming (next month) novel, *Year of Wonder*, a historical novel set in 1666 in Eyam, "a tiny English village of 250 souls in the year the Bubonic Plague struck." In a larger sense, the piece is a defense of historical fiction in general, defending the art of it against the doubts of Henry James, as voiced in a 1901 letter to Sarah Orne Jewett. Ms. Brooks disagrees with James's arguments and concludes: "It is human nature to imagine, to put yourself in another's shoes. The past may be another country. But the only passport required is empathy."

The past may be another country . . . that is, another place. At some point in the past (James announced it was fifty years), there is a conflation of time and place; and unless we are able to imagine it, the deeper, darker past, inhabited by strangers, is lost to us. Past time becomes an exotic and remote place as far away from and as strange to us as (real or imaginary) China was to Marco Polo.

I spent thirty busy years as an expatriate southerner living, at least part of the time, among Elizabethans and trying to write some news from their time and place to ours. It proved to be at once more pleasure and more challenging than I could have imagined at the outset. One of the most serious problems was to contend with, if not to overcome (impossible), my twentieth-century mind-set. In order to confirm and strengthen our precarious self-esteem and to nurture our hopeful sense of historical superiority, we are ready, willing, and able to distort, even to suppress, any information, and likewise to encourage rare or common misconceptions and misunderstanding in order to defend assumptions and preconceived views. We regularly, almost reflexively, do this with current events and issues. Why would we not seek to do so as well with the imagined and imaginary past?

In her article, Ms. Brooks takes note of this challenging difficulty, honestly noting that, from her globalized, cosmopolitan point of view, from "the dense urban tangles of Sydney, New York, Cairo and London," it was a very strange experience to move to a village in Virginia, after years of living among friends with "like minds and agreeable opinions," and to make friends with alien others there—"I found it hard to be thrust into relationships with supporters of the death penalty or the N.R.A., of prayer in the schools or unbridled property rights."

There it is, exactly there, that the southern writer, a writer out of the southern tradition, has something else to offer, beyond the ritual celebration of the flora and fauna, the weeds and flowers, the winds and weathers of his (increasingly imaginary) homeplace. And that something more is not the mere ability but the habit of accepting the ragged contradictions of our age; understanding, without a need to justify, that we are all of us bundles of contradictory assumptions, beliefs, superstitions; that we have been wrong about so many things and will surely be wrong again; that our tradition, though it be sorely tested, tried by ordeal, is to question the truth and value of the wisdom of "like minds and agreeable opinions." When we summon up our place in the world, we have to call up as well the people who live there.

Finally, however, what can help to save us from the weight and woe of our self-concern is the persistent southern habit of laughter, of skeptical laughter, even at our easy pretensions. I think here of the public service rendered by the *avant-garde* southern writer R. H. W. Dillard, by his satirical, parodic short story "That's What I Like (About the South)." There, taking as his starting point "the defining characteristics of Southern fiction," as defined by the prominent editor Shannon Ravenel, he holds them, each in all, in the light of a pitiless scrutiny. The section under the solemn rubric of "deep involvement in place" is devoted to a richly detailed scene set in (where else?) a 7-Eleven market—"Roy pulls a medium-sized paper cup, red and white with Slurpee written on it in blue, from the torpedo rack of cups by the machine."

The southern place, "real" or remembered and imagined, past and present, is as much haunted by comedy as by tragedy. When we summon up our place and our past, together with a renewed awareness of the ineradicable tears of things, we also hear the sounds of ghostly laughter.

(2002)

An American Family History (We Eavesdrop While a Family Tells Its Private Stories)
Review of *The Hinterlands* by Robert Morgan

A good rule of thumb, always allowing for exceptions, is for a reader not to expect too much from the fiction of a poet. Most modern and contemporary American "literary" novelists began their careers as poets or, anyway, began by writing some poetry, but soon gave up or moved on to the different challenges of creating fiction. From time to time, and more so in recent years, writers known chiefly as poets have taken the fling, trying their hands at the making of prose fiction. Some have managed to produce one or two good books, usually more marked by wit and verbal felicity than strong storytelling or memorable, dimensional characters. There are those significant exceptions, however—for example, James Dickey, Fred Chappell, Kelly Cherry, R. H. W. Dillard, Reynolds Price, James Whitehead, all of these (oddly perhaps) southerners, ambidextrous, almost equally adept at the crafts of verse and prose. With *The Hinterlands,* Robert Morgan's first novel and third book of fiction, Morgan joins this gifted company of his peers. Already established as a poet of considerable reputation and distinction, Morgan has published ten collections of poems and has managed to earn a full share of fellowships and awards, among them a Guggenheim Fellowship, a New York Foundation for the Arts Fellowship, an extraordinary *four* fellowships from the National Endowment for the Arts, the Eunice Tietjens Award of *Poetry* magazine, and the Hanes Prize for Poetry (1991), awarded by the Fellowship of Southern Writers. A native North Carolinian (born 1944), Morgan grew up on a farm in the mountains near Zirconia. He graduated from the University of North Carolina in Chapel Hill, earned an M.F.A. degree in creative writing at the University of North Carolina at Greensboro (where he studied with Fred Chappell, among others), and has taught for some years at Cornell University. His fiction began appearing in a variety of literary magazines in the 1980s, and his first book of fiction, *The Blue Valleys: A Collection of Stories* (Peachtree), was published in 1989.

POET AND STORYTELLER

Like Dickey and Chappell and some of the others, Morgan has demonstrated close affiliations between his poems and his fiction from the outset. Most of his poems have a narrative core; even the simply lyrical poems are ghosted by the shadow of an implied story. And poems and stories come chiefly out of the same experience of the same world—the harshly beautiful, hardscrabble western Carolina mountains. They are composed out of close, detailed, utterly unsentimental observation and experience. Words like *pastoral* and *agrarian,* while accurate enough, seem inadequate, too tame and genteel for the texture of Morgan's world. Here, for example, in the poem "Hogpen," he presents a dramatic and vivid confrontation of hog and man:

>   And he knows you're there always
>   watching through a chink.
>   Suddenly whirls
>   his great weight
>   squealing to the other
>   side, for all his size quick
>   as a cat; stands
>   in mud plush.

Or here, the last lines of "Dark Corner," a poem about a place in South Carolina where, among other things, they made moonshine:

>   Uncle got sent up for moonshine,
>   did time in the Atlanta pen.
>   Long as water runs and corn grows green
>   and fire boils water I'll be making

Judge, reckon on it, he said.
But something there broke him.
Rumor blamed the whippings. He
came back old, a new man.

Something else these lines, even lifted out of context, clearly show—an appreciation for and a mastery of the dialect, the colloquial language, rhythms, and textures of his tribe. Of this language, fellow poet and editor T. R. Hummer has written that it is "a believably living flesh . . . where dignity connects to simplicity, compassion to clarity."

Still, the move from poems and stories to the novel is a large one, one that has confounded many talented writers. Morgan has accomplished it with surprising ease by building on his strengths.

A FUGUE OF VOICES

The Hinterlands consists of two novellas and a long story, separate but linked together in interesting ways. All three are historical and told in the first person by a narrator, in each case a grandparent talking directly not to the reader (listener) but to grandchildren. We only eavesdrop. In the first, "The Trace 1772," Petal Richards begins the story of her life and times in the barely settled mountains in colonial days to answer a question: "The first time I seen your Grandpa?" She tells the tale of how she eloped with Realus Richards to live in the wilderness, to have and to raise a family of her own. The story hinges to an extent on a plot surprise but does not depend on it. It depends much more on the steady accumulation of the details of life in the wilderness reported by a narrator whose purpose it is to pass on the experience as honestly and fully as possible to her grandchildren. She is not unselfconscious about this purpose: "All the people stretching back two or three generations to Pennsylvania and Wales, and back to Adam, are just lost in the fog and the dust. We are isolated in the little clearing of now, and all the rest is tangled woods and thickets nobody much remembers. I always said it's how you enjoy that little opening in the wilderness that counts. That's all you have a chance to do. That's why I'm telling you this story." And what a story it is, a wholly credible tale with wild animals and wild men, both settlers and Indians, with matter-of-fact violence, with stories within the story, signs and portents, folk wisdom, even helpful hints on how to make do with only a little, all of it enhanced by a number of fully realized set pieces—an Easter foot-washing in the settlement church; a nightmarish account of some half-crazed, very dangerous prospectors for gold, with Petal giving birth to her firstborn alone and threatened by a wildcat, in what is surely the finest birth scene since John Berryman's in *Homage to Mistress Bradstreet*.

In "The Road 1816," Solomon Richards, grandson to Realus and Petal, and with a slightly different style of speech for showing and telling, tells his grandchildren a classic, world-class tall tale of how he tried to use Sue, his own starved pig, to find the best route for a road in the mountains. Holding onto the pig's tail with his left hand and carrying a hatchet in his right (to blaze a trail), he is dragged across the country and through a series of improbable but credible encounters—dogs, blockaders (moonshiners), a lone Indian, a pond full of naked women who speak a strange language, a crazed preacher (the Reverend Billy Taylor), a black bear, a desperate family, a lightning-and-thunderstorm that ended as "a frog rain," raining toad frogs, a pursuing wildcat, an ancient man (perhaps Tracker Thomas) and his dog, Powder, a poisonous spider, a secret silver mine, a snake-bit child, to mention only a few. By the end of the adventure, the reader is willing to accept the validity of Solomon's philosophical reactions to things: "I didn't believe much in luck then. But now I'm not so sure. Some things you can't explain except by good luck or bad. Everything just seems a chain of happens."

This day's wild adventures are played out against the courtship of the beautiful Mary McPherson by Solomon, which, we infer, worked out well enough, for Mary is the grandmother of the listening children.

The third narrator, of "The Turnpike 1845," is Solomon's son, David. His listener is a single, specific character—his granddaughter, who is herself a mother with a baby and with her own story, suggested clearly, but untold: "Honey, I want you to be patient. It may look now like you won't ever have another chance to get married. But they will be another boy come to love you, and your baby. You've got to see this through. To see things through is the best we can do. They ain't no escape and I don't believe they is no higher purpose than to finish a task right down to the end without giving up and without turning away from the grief that is give us." Like the other two, though significantly shorter, "The Turnpike" also takes place in the context of a courtship, by David of the beautiful Miss Lewis, daughter of the family he boards with while building a new turnpike through the mountain. It is also a double-barreled story, the main line of action being the frantic (and at times very funny) run for life by David fleeing Old Tryfoot, a three-legged wildcat; the second storyline being the account of how David managed, in spite of almost overwhelming problems, to plan and build the turnpike from the South Carolina upcountry into the North Carolina mountains. In a sense, the high suspense of the escape from the wildcat is, of course, deceptive, for the speaker-narrator is clearly alive and well while telling the tale. It is a tribute to Morgan's art and the dramatized storytelling powers of his narrator and central character that the flight from Old Tryfoot is a riveting account.

MORGAN'S LIVELY ART

It is Morgan's art that breathes life into the separate tales forming *The Hinterlands* and locks them together as one continuous family story. Working as a poet not with fashionable surrealism or the familiar unearned nihilism of so many of his generation, but with the simple ordinary things of "real" life, presented in an accessible, lively, direct, and unselfconscious language, a modest language that does not call attention to itself and accurately fits the voices of its characters and speakers, prepared Morgan for this astonishing first novel. He seems to have learned all the right things, some that have escaped more experienced novelists. One of the great problems of the contemporary novel is the prevalence of passive protagonists, characters to whom things (good and bad) happen. The three narrators—Petal, Solomon, and David—of *The Hinterlands* are passionate and active characters, people who care deeply about things and want to do things. These speakers not only act but, taking advantage of the greatest liberty of first-person narration, they can, without breaking the spell of the story (which is, after all, the story of someone telling a story), interrupt and digress, respond and react to events. Petal wants her house and hearth in the wild country and rejoices in the pure and simple things her life will allow: "People will talk about heaven as some city of gold and pearl, where they sing and play their harps all the time. And some people talk about paradise as a place of pure light and happy ghosts floating around. But I think heaven is whatever you need most of the time.

If you're hungry enough, some hot biscuits and honey seems like all you need of glory. And if you're cold, a warm spot by the fire seems like Abraham's bosom." Solomon knows what drives him: "I was a lad with ideas. I dreamed big dreams. I thought of myself like some boy in the Bible chosen to free his nation." But he has tasted the hard candy of wisdom, too—"Vanity is the weakness of all of us, and the downfall of many. But I don't reckon anybody ever pushed hisself beyond the usual ruts without a certain amount of vanity." David loves trapping in the mountains, a passion he must give up to do his duty as a roadbuilder, his father's son. But we can believe his passion: "I thought of the sparkling pelts of red foxes and gray foxes and coons with rings on their eyes and tails. It was the shining wealth and song of these mountains."

These characters have intelligence, a high level of sensory perception that brings their experiences firmly to life, and have earned a share of wisdom. They laugh and cry, and behind them, Morgan the author judiciously blends humor and pathos without the least wince of self-pity or sentimentality. What develops, little by little, is a classic American story, allowing no doubt or question that these people are worthy and worth spending time with.

Great events of history happen elsewhere—the American Revolution, the War of 1812, the slow coming of the Civil War—and only ripple the surface of these lives. These lives became the American history that matters. Never directly, only by inference and by unspoken contrast, the values of these generations—courage, integrity, hard work, a fundamental decency—challenge our own self-pitying malaise. At a time when the American story is being twisted and revised into a cynical tale of oppression and woe, it is altogether salutary to meet and get to know the people of *The Hinterlands*. For that pleasure, we can be thankful to Robert Morgan, a novelist worth honoring with the hope that he will continue to tell us tales for years to come.

(1997)

*The Army was becoming a life without end.
We would always be at war.*
        —Yancey's War

A Life Without End: Two Novels About World War II by William Hoffman

In the years following World War II, there were any number of outstanding works of fiction which, because they were set in that time and because they were, at least in part, inspired by a desire to bring home the hard truths of the war as witnessed and experienced by its participants, were called "war novels," as if they were a kind of genre like thrillers and westerns and romances. Some of these, like John Hersey's *A Bell for Adano* and Harry Brown's *A Walk in the Sun,* were trailblazers, in that they appeared early, while the war was still in progress. Of course, these early versions, honest and critical as they could be, were partly conditioned, if not controlled, by the rules of home-front censorship at the time (an aspect of those times not often well remembered nowadays) and even by paper rationing, which determined to an extent the length of books and the size of printings. Hersey and Brown and others were honest to a fault, but all of them were also part of the war effort. They knew more than they could ever say. For the gritty reality and absurdity of war, no fiction at the time even came close to the cartoons of Bill Mauldin, a veteran of the 45th Infantry Division whose *Stars and Stripes* newspaper cartoons were published in book form (entitled *Up Front*) at home in 1945. They were part and parcel of the war effort also, though not all the army brass viewed them that way. In an early cartoon, Willie and Joe, ragged and bestubbled, sitting together on a rocky Italian hillside near a dead tree, leisurely working at making a foxhole with their inadequate entrenching tools, M-1 rifles leaning against the trunk of the dead tree, speak to and for all the writers who followed. Willie is saying: "You'll get over it, Joe. Oncet I wuz gonna write a book exposin' the army after th' war myself."

In the years immediately following the war, and continuing on into the 1960s—thus written and published with first the Korean War and then the war in Vietnam serving at once as background and refresher course—there were a lot of war novels, mainly dealing with World War II, written by Americans and for Americans. European war novels, including those by British writers, though treating the same experience, by and large had a different stance. Perhaps because the war was much longer for them and was fought on home ground, meaning that the civilian population was essentially in the front lines, their point of view was not an end to innocence but rather the shapes and forms of overwhelming weariness and the despair deriving from indifference that tormented the survivors. Something of this attitude can be seen in a major work of autobiographical nonfiction, *All the Brave Promises* by American novelist Mary Lee Settle. Ms. Settle served in the British WAAF, and her account offers both innocence at the outset, "when we were young, dashing and lively," and the weight of shrugging indifference at the tag end when "the juggernaut of war . . . was spending itself toward its own death like a great tiring unled beast."

Some of the good American war novels, ones that have stood the test of time, are books like *The Gallery* by John Horne Burns; Norman Mailer's *The Naked and the Dead;* James Gould Cozzens's prizewinning *Guard of Honor;* Paxton Davis's *Two Soldiers;* James Jones's *From Here to Eternity,* and indeed the entire trilogy he worked on for a lifetime, including also *The Thin Red Line* and the posthumous *Whistle;* Joseph Heller's *Catch-22;* and Kurt Vonnegut's *Slaughterhouse Five,* among others. J. D. Salinger is (reliably) reported to have written a large war novel which, in the end, he scrapped, keeping only the opening and closing scenes that became the superb short story "For Esme with Love and Squalor." In between those two scenes, the war is implied and there lies any war novel you can imagine, everyman's war novel. One of our greatest postwar writers, Shelby Foote, a veteran of both army and Marine Corps service in World War II, wrote his war novel, *Shiloh,* set in the Civil War, in costume as it were, a kind of reenactment before that was a habit. Similarly, Stephen Becker, though he has written novels based on his Marine Corps experiences in China, set his principal war novel during the Civil War—*When the War Is Over*.

I mention all these good books, some of them justly renowned, because William Hoffman's two novels dealing directly with World War II unquestionably belong in their company and at the highest rank of the American fiction coming out of World War II.

The first of these and, as it happens, Hoffman's first published novel, *The Trumpet Unblown* (1955), follows the adventures and misadventures of a young Virginia private, Tyree Shelby, from the time he joins his outfit, a field hospital unit in England, through the invasion of Normandy and the rest of the war until his return home. Hoffman's publisher, Doubleday, evidently wishing to emphasize authenticity, accuracy, and, to an extent, its autobiographical elements, subtitled the book on the jacket "A Novel of the Medical Corps in World War II," and stressed the author's personal experience of the war: "William Hoffman made the invasion of Europe on D-plus-3 with the 91st Evacuation Hospital." Told in a straightforward third-person narrative with young and inexperienced Shelby as the center of consciousness, the story moves, as the war itself does, steadily and inexorably from what might now be called "a bad scene" at the outset to the hallucinatory edges of nightmare, staggering finally to an ending when, unable to communicate with his parents and his fiancée, Cotton, unable to begin to tell them what he (and the reader following him like a shadow throughout) has seen and felt, done and left undone, blurts out some truths in a final moment with Cotton, truths that are, we know, facts abstracted from the unspeakable context of the war:

> "What is it, Ty?" she asked, leaning against him.
> "I don't know. Just about everything I guess."
> "You never answered my question."
> "What question?"
> "Don't you like me any longer?" she asked, putting her fine arms around him.
> Shelby looked at her, and for a moment he was tempted. Then very precisely he took her arms from around himself and laid her hands in her lap.
> "You wouldn't want to kiss a fellow that's had gonorrhea, would you?"
> Her eyes widened.

"A fellow who's been in the nut ward of a hospital and should have been in prison?"

"Please, Ty."

"That isn't all. A fellow who's lived with a Kraut whore and been a coward."

She stared at him.

"There's a couple more minor things. A fellow who's lied, cheated, murdered, and just about anything else left in the book."

She sat staring at him until water filled her eyes, then bent her head to her hands and cried softly. He did not move. He watched her cry, and he watched them dancing and laughing under the colored lights.

"I'll take you home," he said to Cotton when she finished crying.

"I don't care, Ty," she said, wiping her eyes.

"You care."

"You're just hurt. It'll get all right."

"I'm afraid not."

"I'll keep on. If you want to, I'll keep on."

"Would you?"

"Yes, if you want to."

As he watched her he filled up inside. He wanted to touch her hair and make believe it could be. But this one last thing he could do right. This he would do for her.

"That' s just the point," he lied. "I don't want to."

Thus Shelby's final act, his first moral act since the experience of the war stunned and corrupted him (and everyone else in the unit, the story), is, in fact, to tell a lie.

The novel is relatively short, quick-moving, at times laconic. The limits of the consciousness and point of view of Shelby work well and positively. He is an engaging character, an innocent, to be sure, unsophisticated and immature, yet possessed of strength of character, physical toughness, a strong sense of honor; and he is easily established as a reliable witness. Through him we gradually come to know the others in the unit, mostly veterans of the earlier campaign in North Africa, restlessly waiting for the war's next stage, the invasion, to begin. To an experienced eye, the unit from the beginning would appear to be out of control, rapidly deteriorating and disintegrating; but from the point of view of the young volunteer, Shelby, it may be strange, not what he expected, but still simply the way things are. What we have is a classic "straight man" in a surreal, comedic (if dangerous) situation. Shelby is kept busy basically fighting for his life and honor against a savage, sadistic brute named Blizzard. We get to know the others, officers and men, in the outfit, including the amazing Petras, called the Greek, who is obviously a precursor of some of the characters in *Catch-22* and (later) *M-A-S-H*, a hustler and a fixer who can somehow arrange everything.

Suddenly, all this life comes to an end as the unit is alerted, packed up, and shipped off to be part of the invasion:

> Colonel Harlan spoke well. He told them the record of the outfit was unparalleled in the ETO and that the most glorious chapters were yet to be written. He told them how proud he was to serve with them. They had had a good and deserved rest, he said, but now it was time to get down to business and their business was war. He told them a training schedule would soon appear and that he expected all noncoms to whip their sections into keen functioning. Then Colonel Harlan closed his speech with a prayer. The last words were, "May God give us the victory."

Once landed, amid chaos and confusion, lost stores and missing personnel, they find a place to set up the field hospital and to be about their business of war. Which is not quite as Shelby had imagined it and not quite as most readers will have imagined or even experienced it either: "Surgery was a butcher shop in which doctors worked without gowns and let sterile technique go, cutting and sawing with sweat pouring off their skin. Metal drums were put by the tables to receive the lopped off arms and legs. The drums were always overflowing." And, as horror and exhaustion wear down Shelby, it grows worse:

> It became a nightmare in which there was no time or reason. Death piled higher and higher, and the world became a place of stumps and torn intestines, of gangrene and men without faces, of giving plasma to men burned crisp like bacon, whose veins were almost impossible to find under the stinking black flesh, of using suction pumps to keep tracheotomy cases from drowning in their own spit, and Ward 4 sounded as if it were full of vipers from the air hissing between the little metal buttons in their throats.

This is the business of war, pages of it, as no one else, really, has presented it—head-on, unflinching: the results of war. Soon, in spite of his shock and fatigue, Shelby becomes fascinated with his job, which, in the confusion, has expanded: "Shelby found himself performing duties that belonged rightfully only to doctors and nurses. Someone had to do them." He begins to study what is going on all around him when he has a chance and time: "He had held the popular idea that surgery was a very fine and precise affair, but the first thing that struck him was how brutal it was. The patients were sawed, hammered, hacked, and wrestled on the tables. When a femur was being set, the patient was thrown around like a side of beef on the block, the doctors and nurses tugging and cursing like roustabouts. He soon lost his civilian's awe of doctoring." Soon enough, everything is routine. The field hospital follows the killing, moves forward and sets up to "wait for the flesh to come in." The war continues, their lives becoming more and more routine. Some of the soldiers go into Paris for drinks and whores, and Shelby loses his virginity. By fits and starts, and with a gradually more evident moral decay, the unit moves back and forth in France, Belgium, Holland; the Battle of the Bulge comes and goes. They come and go and end the war in Germany on the banks of the Elbe.

The inner life of Shelby and the others is deftly summoned and revealed by a whole series of almost surreal events—thievery, rape, murder, betrayals, some of them grotesquely comic, as the men in the unit shed the last vestiges of whatever civilization they had acquired before the war. Long before the war's end, we are at home in a world where the absurdities recounted in *Catch-22* would seem completely logical and fairly mild. One by one, the people in the outfit, those whom we know through Shelby, disappear or come to bad ends. It is peace that breaks them. Shelby finally cracks up, too, in a hospital, and is sent back to the United States where he is almost lost among those he has loved. He imagines telling the truth to his parents: "When I look at you and everyone I see your intestines and smell the way you would stink with gangrene and can never forget how pitiful you and I really are or how easily we can be broken into nothing."

The Trumpet Unblown is a brilliant and passionate book, certainly one of the finest of the novels to come out of World War II. In design and in all the small details, it is superbly well made, superbly written. Part of its power comes from the fact that both its passion and its brilliance are tightly reined in, held in check. The style, sentence by sentence, is matter of fact, direct, transparent even when dealing with the most extraordinary events and circumstances. The contrast, tension, between the calm way of telling and the terrible tales that are told subtly serves to make the impact on the reader all the more powerful. The abrupt cuts from all kinds of comedy to horror and back make both these qualities more emphatic and make the experience more rounded and complex.

Clearly with this, his first novel, William Hoffman proved himself once and for all a major writer with the touch and judgment of a master. That it is not better known, that it was not honored in its first brief season, must be attributable in part to the terrible truths it shows and tells.

A little more than a decade later, with several novels and many short stories behind him, William Hoffman returned to the times and the setting of World War II with *Yancey's War*. This novel is, it seems, a different kind of book in many ways. Almost three quarters of the story takes place at home, on "the home front," accurately evoked, and it concerns in some detail the ups and downs of basic training, Officer Candidate School, and the haphazard, not to say hopeless, training of "the Golden Eagles," a pathetic infantry regiment which (in one of the great, extended, laugh-out-loud comic sequences in our literature) has trouble enough surviving on maneuvers and proves itself to be clearly worthless as a potential combat unit. Eventually, even the U.S. Army is able to figure this out, and in England, prior to the invasion, the regiment is broken up, all that is remaining becoming a laundry unit whose basic duties should keep it far from any frontline action. Unfortunately, near the end of the war in Germany, a simple mistake (not the first, by any means) in map reading puts the unit into a town where it is ambushed and the men are forced to fight for their lives against serious odds.

This section is brief, sudden, brutal (just like combat), and, in spite of various absurdities, not the least bit funny. After a long, steady build-up, a long wait for the American G.I.s and the reader, there is suddenly enough war to last the survivors for a lifetime. There are even moments of credible heroism by these very unheroic men. All that has happened before, all that led them this far, is meaningless, wiped out. It all comes down to a confused and desperate firefight for a few hours in a strange place.

This is a high-risk storytelling, designed (among other things) to dramatize an essential, if often unspoken, truth about war—that in those moments when all the things that have been imagined, feared, trained and prepared for, however ineptly, do come to pass, there is nothing else, before or after, that matters. Paradoxically, in the larger sense that no common soldier in the midst of things can conceive of, these terrible moments of truth don't matter much either. Thus nothing that happens to the unlucky and incompetent laundrymen or their German enemies, a mixture of home guardsmen, young and old, and of implacable SS, though it means everything to them, has any meaning in or effect on the war itself. For all practical purposes, the war is already over and done with even as they are fighting each other to the death.

To tell this story, making all the parts of it authentic, credible, and meaningful (even if the deepest meaning is that it all meant next to nothing), required the highest kind of virtuosity. James Jones had used a somewhat similar strategy in *From Here to Eternity,* devoting the largest part of this story to the peacetime army and its life and problems, all of which vanish or are, anyway, transformed by the Japanese attack on Pearl Harbor. But Jones's story becomes primarily the more traditional story of initiation. Hoffman's story does not contrast America at peace and at war (we are in the war already on page one) but makes the case, *in this case* at least, that there is nothing that can be prepared for and nothing that anyone can be initiated into. Everything comes down to luck and death. "The big picture," much invoked by the army as the place where all the small parts and details come together in some meaningful pattern, does not exist. The result is comedy when nobody really is hurt (the disastrous maneuvering), tragedy without benefit of catharsis when men live and die in acts of war. This is a very hard saying and goes well beyond the stunned pity and pathos at the heart of *The Trumpet Unblown.*

In a literary sense, as a matter of storytelling, *Yancey's War* is more complex and more layered in ambiguities as well. Although the central story is the gradual unveiling and exposure of the life of Marvin Yancey (born Yankovitch), a middle-aged, well-to-do veteran of World War I and a decorated hero from that war, who turns out to be something more and a lot less than he seems to be—a mysterious, if fat and often foolish, figure. Throughout the story, there are disclosures and surprises about Yancey. For example, it turns out that although his medals from World War I are real, the acts of heroism for which he is credited were not. Similarly, at the end of things,

Yancey performs an act of extraordinary heroism, which costs him his life, mainly motivated by overwhelming fear and cowardice. At the naked moment of truth, he becomes a hero only because there is no other choice left for him.

This is complicated, fully dimensional material. It is made more complex and ambiguous because our sole source of information and judgment concerning Yancey is the first-person narrator, young Charles Elgar, of a good old family in Richmond. Elgar has been aptly described by editor and critic George Core as "sophisticated, ironic, and world-weary," to which should be added the adjective *unreliable.* It is not that Elgar isn't trustworthy. He is engaging, easy, at least at first, to identify with. Yancey, seen through his eyes, is a crude, manipulative clown, unforgettable only in his sustained vulgarity and folly. Very gradually, however, without diminishing the validity of Elgar's picture of Yancey, we come to recognize serious flaws in Elgar's character as, motivated as much by revenge as anything else, he does things, including the seduction of Yancey's attractive wife, that render his role as our guide and moral arbiter somewhat suspect. It is not so much that Elgar's perceptions and judgments are *wrong.* By and large, they are acceptable. What is demonstrated is that none of our perceptions and judgments of other human beings, no matter what their source, are good enough. There is always more than we can know. Both Elgar and Yancey perform bravely and are duly awarded medals (Yancey's is posthumous) for their bravery. But a point not quite lost on Elgar is that Yancey's cowardly first reaction, that they should surrender to the Germans, was in fact the course of wisdom and would have saved many lives on both sides. Elgar acts on the perception, which proves to be wrong, that the Germans have executed those of the American men who have already surrendered during the ambush. Elgar's excellent leadership and undeniable courage prove out as utterly unnecessary.

This kind of narration has all the subtlety and power of Conrad or Henry James at their best and finest.

The two books, taken together, have a curious relationship. They are companion stories, each in a sense needing the other for the whole story of the war. There is a little moment in *Yancey's War* when the laundry unit briefly shares some space with a field hospital, probably the one from *The Trumpet Unblown.* They touch on one another and go on about their business and their separate dooms. In terms of action and event, the earlier novel is more shocking in its initial impact. Surely the physical horrors of war and its effects have seldom, if ever, been more directly and vividly described. But, curiously, it is not a world without hope. The world of *Yancey's War,* in and of itself and quite aside from the accident of war, is beyond knowing fully and, except for brief delusions, a hopeless place.

Taken together, Hoffman's two war novels are a remarkable achievement, a full and sufficient statement about World War II from the point of view of a gifted writer who has experienced it and in time come to understand it, including his understanding of the limits of knowing and judging. These are important books, then, among the finest of our time. Even in a world with only illusory hopes, one may be allowed to wish that these books will last for as long as books and stories of our times may matter.

(2000)

Liberty and the Southern Tradition

One of the habitual practices of totalitarian governments and institutions in our past century—a century that has until very recently seen more totalitarian governments than democratic in letter or spirit—one characteristic enterprise of totalitarian groups, institutions, and governments has been not merely the vigorous use of misinformation and disinformation to confuse and deceive enemies, but also the constant revision of the past, recent and remote, to make sure that the past fits with and into present schemes and strategies, ends, and means. Often, at the least, this practice has demanded the serious distortion of both facts and reasonable judgment. Most often it has involved the routine suppression of facts that may challenge and call into question the purposes of the powers that be.

This commonplace totalitarian habit of thought and action has been crudely indiscriminate and sometimes silly, the latter being exemplary of what we might call the "Ozymandias syndrome." By this, I mean to say that no matter how clever the modern propagandists have sometimes proved themselves to be, they lack the subtlety, nuance, and ambiguity of, for example, most absolute monarchs whose power was usually only distantly relative to popularity. The totalitarian powers of our time have, for better and worse, been firmly based on popularity. Stalin, Hitler, Castro, Saddam Hussein, and all the others have depended upon popularity in ways that could never have occurred to, say, Henry VIII or the Emperor Nero. The twentieth-century totalitarian rulers, while they seldom seem to have needed or, indeed, acquired the support of the majority, have nevertheless depended on a firm base of popularity to preserve and maintain their power. Thus we have lived in and through an age riddled with disinformation and misinformation. Together with so much else (physical, intellectual, spiritual), our knowledge is frequently profoundly polluted at the sources.

At exactly this point you are certainly entitled to ask what all this has to do with my title and topic, "Liberty and the Southern Tradition." The relevance is fairly simple: that the history, nature, and character of the South (thus of all southern traditions, including the literary) have been so distorted and clouded by an accumulation of misinformation as to require major rehabilitation before we can think or talk sensibly about the subject. For more than a century since the South was defeated in our most savage and destructive war and subsequently treated (that is, mistreated) worse than any enemy the United States has ever battled, for more than a century the victors have written the history of the South, and the revisionists have also continuously modified that history.

There are so many common errors of fact and judgment, so many distorted stereotypes now honored like public monuments that, except for something like the intellectual equivalent of carpet-bombing, one hardly knows where to begin. Moreover, thanks to the current intellectual climate, there are large areas as dangerous as minefields that are to be avoided if possible.

Still, I can suggest a few things and make a few corrections of misconceptions.

Let us take one of the simplest—the definition and description of the southern people, the inhabitants of the South most of whom became citizens of the Confederacy. Today, the southerner is conveniently described as belonging to a more-or-less homogeneous society and culture, as distinguished from the plurality and diversity of the North. This ignores the present, the several decades since the end of World War II during which nomadic Americans have exercised their extraordinary freedom of mobility to move into the South in huge numbers. Certainly it was not true in the past that the South was a homogeneous population in contrast to the heterogeneous North. At the time of our Civil War, even within the ranks of the white race alone, there was far more national and ethnic diversity in the South than in the North. It was only after the war that immigrants came to swell the ranks of labor for the newly industrialized North.

The diversity of the southern population, from the earliest days of colonization by several nations, helped create a general atmosphere of political liberty and individual independence. Otherwise, because of significant, often antagonistic differences (of this, for example, the carry-over of the quarrels of the Irish and the Highland Scots with the English; or the carry-over of the deeply felt differences between the French Huguenot populations along the East Coast and the Roman Catholics in Louisiana and the Gulf Coast), the growth and stability of political and social units even of the size and scope of the present individual states would have been impossible. The flexibility and authority of English political and social theory and practice, arrived at over the course of centuries of development, trial, and error in that uniquely diverse island setting, made the South a more coherent place than its geography easily allowed, before the Revolution, after the Revolution (during the Revolution, things, not unexpectedly, fell apart), and on up to the time of the Civil War. At that point, the most interesting thing is not the ragged diversity and loose ends of the Confederate States of America but the fact that this new nation worked at all. And, indeed, all in all, building on a constitution that emphasized liberty and independence, it worked well enough. In the end, the war shattered the coherence of the South. Ironically, the rigors of Reconstruction together with seventy-five or eighty years of imposed and enforced poverty brought the modern South—the "New" South of Henry Grady and the "New" South of writers like today's Lee Smith and Barry Hannah (among many)—back together as a whole.

But the main point is that the South, with all its actual diversity and with its multicultural English tradition, developed into a culture and a society committed to liberty and tolerant of individual differences within reason. *Reason* may be the key word there, as in this quotation from Thomas Jefferson, which is carved in stone above one of the doorways into Cabell Hall at the University of Virginia: "Here we are not afraid to follow truth wherever it may lead nor to tolerate any error so long as reason is left free to combat it."

Reason in the South was, perhaps still is, by and large closely associated with manners, with the amenities (manners being described, if not actually defined, as polite and reasonable behavior to others). In a practical sense, a code of good manners can serve to hold together a social unit whose natural tendency is toward disintegration. In a more subtle sense, the requirements of reason and manners honor the essential mystery at the center of every individual. Breaking the code is, then, an attack on the spiritual and central mystery of others. Good manners are, then, serious business. Good manners—the code—are yet another part of the foundation of freedom. The thoughtful southerner recognizes the responsibility of following the code of manners for the sake of freedom.

If you think that because of the emphasis on manners and appearances the South has not been hospitable to its artists, you would be wrong (in my opinion), at least until very recent years. The South has let its artists alone, to sink or swim on their own, not seeking to divert their energies or to enlist their labor in causes. Provided that it has not represented a complete failure of personal responsibility—that is, for example, of the basic family responsibilities—the career of the artist has inevitably been seen as an acceptable one, or, in the words of my grandfather, "as good a way to be poor as any other." Proof of this in writing is evident when I assert that the only major southern writer (up until the present generation) to write much about the difficulty of trying to be an artist in the context of southern society was Thomas Wolfe. That very common subject in Europe and in the literature of the North was for a long time almost unknown in the southern tradition and is still not a major subject of southern letters.

Because of its deep-rooted poverty and because of its aesthetic conservatism, the South has mostly been a good place for artists, and especially for writers, to work, even though the South offered little practical and financial support for the arts.

Within reason, then, the southern writer could be, and usually was, intensely critical of many things about the society he or she (we have had outstanding women writers for all of our history) disapproved of, and he or she had no particular good reason to assert the artist's individuality against the grinding uniformity of the social majority. Part of the charm, the enchantment of southern literature from the earliest days, has been in its *characters,* that is, in the literary celebration of odd and interesting individual characters. There is next to no place, then, for Marxist political or Freudian psychological determinism in southern literature. There is a whole philosophy and a way of life, as well, contained in this one remark by a character named Cherry Oxendine in a story by Lee Smith: "When you get too old to be cute, honey, you got to be eccentric."

In spite of all its clichés and conventions, contemporary southern literature has more variety of form and content than the national literature allows or, indeed, than that of any other nation. (Russia may be the exception, but only after the Soviet Union fell into ruins and fragments.)

Of course, all this discussion of the southerners' love of diversity, of liberty, of individuality tempered by a code of manners and the dictates of reason, all this has avoided the huge question like a large threatening cloud on the horizon—what about slavery?

No right-minded person today would attempt to defend slavery as an institution. But by the same token, there has been such a fog of disinformation and misinformation about the subject that it is almost impossible to discuss or even to imagine it in any depth. Morally, we are clear enough with ourselves. We disapprove of slavery and, whether or not we elect to feel any guilt about it, we tend to disapprove of those generations of our ancestors who allowed it to be. There are limits to this latter, however. For example, Washington and Jefferson have not yet been fully discredited or denigrated, at least by the majority, on account of their being in fact slaveowners. Indeed, paradoxically if you insist, Jeffersonian ideas and ideals were brought to bear to hasten the processes of emancipation and abolition.

There is also the paradox that no matter what the war was, in fact, fought about and no matter what those who were involved in the fighting thought they were fighting for or about (as if that really mattered, we late-twentieth-century survivors can say), one definite result was the end of lawful, institutionalized slavery in the United States. With some notable European exceptions, the rest of the world, including especially Brazil and a large part of Africa and Asia and the Middle East, was slower about getting rid of slavery. When and where they did so, they very seldom spilled the blood of the free for the sake of the slave. And it remains to be said that, in fact if often under other names, involuntary servitude still thrives in many parts of Africa and the rest of the Third World. The institution came to be viewed by Americans as pernicious and wicked, and it was ended in blood. Had there been any kind of serious peace negotiations, a "peace process," between the United States and the Confederacy, it seems probable that some sort of compromise might have been reached concerning slavery. What else was there to negotiate about?

The southern writers coming after the Civil War lived in a time, their lifetime, of defeat and of not so much guilt (though some may have felt guilty, others not) as of a fundamental contradiction. The South was the home of liberty on this continent. It was southerners who held out for and who wrote the Bill of Rights. And yet they fought to the death, and with truly extraordinary sacrifice and bravery, to defend their right to deprive others of liberty.

I do not believe that guilt leads anywhere but to paralysis. I think that fundamental contradictions, and an honest awareness of them, can, among other things, generate the energy for art.

My generation is the last generation of southerners who actually have had any direct, touching-and-speaking contact not only with the survivors of the war but also with survivors of slavery. For the next generation, now edging toward middle age, it is a somewhat more abstract matter, something out of books and school.

All of us coming, as we do, after the Civil War, have shared something (shared, if only a matter of inevitable and individual choice) that you will seldom, if ever, hear about in public or discussed even among ourselves. Before the war—for that matter during the war as well—we had our own book publishers in the South. Then from the end of the war until very recently, we had no serious commercial publishing originating here. What this has meant, what to a large extent this still means, is that we are provincial writers who must peddle our wares elsewhere among strangers, suspicious strangers, as it happens. Opinionated strangers as well. They have strong, firm opinions as to what constitutes the authentic tradition of southern literature. The problem is compounded by their suspicions that we are, in some way, trying to fool them, that even when we sound and seem (to their ears and perception) authentic, we might well be insincere. Insofar as we choose to write of and about the South, we have to sell ourselves and our vision to the publisher before we can reach any readers. Also, as suspicious provincials, we must establish other credentials, not the least of which is some kind of proof, preferably in the form and content of the text, that we are well aware of the latest literary fashions, habits, and conventions. For quite a long time, for at least a quarter of a century following the Civil War, this meant that most of our writers were condemned to be found not between the hard covers of published books but in the pages of newspapers and (sometimes) periodicals. Our tradition of quarterlies—the *Sewanee Review* as the prime and eldest example—grows out of this time. In a sense, the fate of many provincial writers was to be misunderstood. Mark Twain was, as you'll remember, a long time being accepted by the eastern *literati*—and he went into the publishing business himself.

Every southern writer has a deadly serious choice to make—to stay at home (if possible and as much as possible) like William Faulkner or to leave the South for other and greener pastures like, say, William Styron or Robert Penn Warren. Faulkner paid a heavy price for his elected provincialism—though, in fairness, it must be pointed out that his choices of a life elsewhere were extremely limited.

His fellow southerners—Allen Tate and John Crowe Ransom and others among the Fugitives and other Agrarians—opened up the possibility of teaching in the universities. Robert Penn Warren and Cleanth Brooks availed themselves of this possibility and taught at Yale. The next generation, mine, coming of age during and after World War II, arrived on the scene just as the colleges and universities routinely began to hire writers as teachers. By now, there are hundreds of institutions with writers on their faculty. And, by now, a thing that was certainly not the case when Brooks and Warren came along, the southern writer can often work as a teacher in a southern institution. In fact, some of the best creative-writing programs in the country are in the South—at Hollins University, UNC-Greensboro, Arkansas, Alabama, George Mason University, etc. Truth is, the chief patrons of contemporary literature in our time are the colleges and universities. At a time when very few American writers can earn even a modest living by writing, a large number of younger writers, many of them southerners, are indirectly earning a living as teachers, freed thereby, at least somewhat, from commercial restraints and trends and inhibitions.

It is a solution that ought to be better than it is.

There are a number of problems. For the writer, there is a new kind of academic publish-or-perish syndrome, an incentive to seek for maximum and prompt publication and for the highest visibility—grants and prizes and awards. Then there is the now-camouflaged but still armed hostility between the writers and the more strictly academic teachers who resent the invasion of the writers. Finally, there is the way in which many of the universities have allowed themselves to become bastions of the politically correct, holding out (it seems) not only against their own society but also against the drift and flow of the whole wide world. Southern universities, for a variety of reasons, some of them valid though none really compelling, have defensively grouped to prove themselves "worldlier than thou" by embracing alien doctrines. Thus the writer is supposed to prove himself to be fully dedicated to the advancement of unfamiliar goals. One of these is, like the poor victims of the Red Guards, to wear a dunce cap and to confess to a guilt beyond endurance for crimes, known and unknown, beyond forgetting or forgiving.

Any art emerging from such a context is in danger of being grotesquely crippled and is very unlikely to be part of any valid literary tradition.

The situation seems to me to be extremely unpleasant, but not beyond all remedy. It is too late to work much mischief on the writers of my generation. And the best of the younger writers—our new poets and fiction writers—are too gifted and too dedicated to turn away from the deep-rooted tradition that has already helped to shape and to form them and their art. The love of the land and of the language persist, perhaps more strongly so now that both are sorely threatened. The love of eccentric characters and the stories they find themselves in is so far undiminished. What this means is that our best new writers of all kinds, experimental as well as more conventional, love the individual human being and thus must likewise love the liberty that allows an individual to choose a way to walk in and to be responsible for that choice. Finally, and ideally, the code of manners persists in the writer's relationship with the reader, who must be invited (not seduced or tricked) into bringing to the poem or story the attention and commitment that permits it to come fully to life.

(1992)

Part Scam: *The Encyclopedia of Southern Culture*

Like a whole lot of other people, I have always loved lists and dictionaries and almanacs of all kinds and, of course, especially encyclopedias. The house I grew up in, the family I grew up with, had enough books among us to open a small public library or to start a major bonfire. And, among other things, there were several different kinds and forms of encyclopedias, including two versions of the *Encyclopedia Britannica,* the up-to-date edition, regularly replaced, and the wonderful 1911 edition, with its smooth and elegant soft-leather covers and its smooth and elegant prose—probably the *best-written* encyclopedia of all time. T. S. Eliot's famous and scornful reference in the early poem, "Animula"—"The pain of living and the drug of dreams/Curl up the small soul in the window seat/Behind the *Encyclopedia Britannica*"—while it may have hurt the feelings of many an encyclopedia freak, didn't change our bad taste and bad habits. We go right on reading, then, always hoping for something new and maybe improved (better); and, partly because there is a strong element of pure and simple scam in the whole reference-book business/racket these days, as there seems to be some part scam in most contemporary vocations, arts, and crafts, we are willing to settle for something that is at least honestly new. When it comes along, it can be a legitimate cause for celebration. It doesn't have to be genuinely original or innovative, just has to have a new spin on it, something that makes its arranged vision of reality a little bit different, slightly special.

The *Encyclopedia of Southern Culture* qualifies under those criteria. First the facts. It is a big fat book of some 1,656 pages, a two-hander measuring 8¾ by 11 by 3 inches and weighing a little more than eight pounds. On publication day, Gerald Turner, the chancellor of the University of Mississippi who, through his Center for the Study of Southern Culture, is vaguely responsible for this new encyclopedia, was quoted in the *Los Angeles Times* as putting the facts in proper scale and perspective: "If you carry this book around, you will not only grow in knowledge but in your physical fitness." This beat the sound-bite claim made by the co-editor William Ferris, who announced, "This encyclopedia is going to be a torch to light paths in the future." (Slow burning?) Its retail price, $49.95 until January, 1990, when it took a ten-dollar inflationary leap, was persuasively defended in the early advertising. "Only $5.98 per lb.," the ads read. "Same as catfish fillets." The *Encyclopedia* lists two editors, twenty-four consultants, and in excess of eight hundred contributing writers. It has more than three hundred photographs and illustrations (some pretty good ones) and fifteen maps. It has a brisk, brief, only mildly pontifical *imprimatur,* a foreword by Alex Haley, who is only slightly carried away into the rhetorical realm known, down-home, as "big mouthing": "Out of the historic cotton tillage sprang the involuntary field hollers, the shouts, and the moanin' low that have since produced such a cornucopia of music, played daily, on every continent, where I have been astounded at how much I heard of the evolved blues, jazz, and gospel—as well as bluegrass and country—all of them of direct southern origin." A mouthful of sentence, to be sure. But he likes it and he likes the book. "Never before," he writes, "has such a volume been produced by a team so committed to distilling and presenting our southern distinctiveness." It matters that Alex Haley supports this book, and it means something that the editors turned to him for their foreword. A generation ago, maybe even more recently (as many unvarnished facts in this volume make painfully clear), it likely would not have been seriously considered that the words of a black writer, any black writer, could be used to launch an *Encyclopedia of Southern Culture.* And, by the same token, it is hard to think of any prominent black writer of a generation ago who would have given name and support to such a project. In point of fact, the section of more than a hundred pages entitled "Black Life" is excellent, and the other twenty-three alphabetically arranged sections of the book, from "Agriculture" to "Women's Life," are unfailing in their recognition of and concentration upon the inextricable role of blacks, from the beginnings until now, in all aspects of southern life. That, in itself, would make this volume a worthy contribution to the constantly changing, redefined, and revisionary history of the region and the nation (world) of which it is a part.

Incidentally, in the section "Ethnic Life" and elsewhere, the sense of a much more cosmopolitan South, from the enduring Native Americans up through the Latin Americans and the boat people of Southeast Asia, emerges.

The rationale and defining concept of the *Encyclopedia* is *cultural.* Indeed, it is "a broad, inclusive" definition of culture that is used here to define the South itself. In their excellent introduction, editors Charles Reagan Wilson and William Ferris toy with several complex and subtle definitions of culture itself, before settling on the theories of Clifford Geertz, who called culture "an historically transmitted pattern of meanings embodied in symbols, a system of inherited conceptions expressed in symbolic forms" (get it?), to which they append the notions of T. S. Eliot as evidenced in *Notes Towards the Definition of Culture,* that culture includes "all the characteristic activities and interests of a people." Concluding: "Above all, the volume has been planned to carry out Eliot's belief that 'culture is not merely the sum of several activities, but a *way of life*'."

Each of the twenty-four basic sections ("major subject areas") offers, first, an overview essay produced by the primary consultant for the topic, followed by a series of alphabetically organized thematic essays, these in turn being followed by a sequence of short, alphabetically presented "topical-biographical" pieces. For the reader, this may seem to be a fairly complicated, even clumsy method of organization, but it is rendered more comprehensible by a good system of cross referencing and by a thorough index which, if not utterly free of inaccuracy (and what index, lately at least, is perfect?), is useful.

It takes time to learn to use any given reference work and the test of time and use to determine the value of it. Any reviewer who claims otherwise is either a better reviewer than I am or running a scam (*the reviewing scam*) of his/her own. But I have spent some time and energy checking against those areas and topics where I know a little already and sometimes (rarely) a lot. And I have "read around" in the huge book trying to get a sense of it and of its more obvious strengths and weaknesses. And there are some general and particular things that can be said. On the whole, there seems to have been a serious attempt to preserve and maintain a factual integrity. The facts may sometimes be, as they are here and there in some cases, distorted, carefully contrived to make a debator's point, or even suppressed, but they are, as far as I can tell, neither falsified nor denied. In this sense, then, during an age when playing fast and loose with facts is common enough to seem to be the norm, there is an old-fashioned honesty about the *Encyclopedia*. The general sections and their miscellaneous parts, thematic and topical-biographical, are uneven in quality, depending, simply enough, on the quality and ability of the individual consultants and writers. Thus, for instance, the "Literature" section, put together by M. Thomas Inge of Randolph-Macon College, with all its inevitable and inherent limitations, is excellent, mainly because of the first-rate people writing the pieces, people like Lewis P. Simpson, Fred Hobson, Mark Steadman, Thomas Daniel Young, Richard Calhoun, Robert W. Hills, and Charles East. Incidentally, editor and story-writer Charles East is responsible for one of the more brilliantly realized of the shorter pieces, this one on the late entertainer and comedian Brother Dave Gardner, in the "History and Manners" section, falling between "Fried Chicken" and "Gays." (There are many wonderfully odd, side-by-side linkages created by the alphabetical arrangement, as, for instance, in "Women's Life," the cheek-by-jowl juxtaposition of "Parks, Rosa/Civil Rights Activist" and "Parton, Dolly/Entertainer.") Professor Inge himself resurfaces in the "Media" section with a first-rate piece on "Comic Strips."

Other excellent pieces, outstanding by any and all standards, are the citations for "Barbecue," "Grits," and "Burma Shave Signs." Gordon Baxter's account of the "Pickup Truck" is wonderful; Bruce Kawin's entry "Faulkner, William and Film," Virginius Dabney's entry on the "Richmond *Times-Dispatch*," and Jordy Bell on "Atkinson, Ti-Grace" are accomplished and exemplary.

There are also plenty of less-than-shining examples of mature and critical intelligence at work. Some of my candidates for Minor Dumbo Awards: W. K. McNeil, in the piece on "Shine," the enduring trickster who, in black folklore, was reputed to be the sole survivor of the sinking of the *Titanic*— "In reality, of course, there were many survivors of the tragedy"; Emory Thomas, who solemnly informs us (in "Civil War") that "wartime is seldom conducive to contemplative pursuits especially when the war is going badly";

Stephen Wayne Foster, writing on "Gays," who tells us emphatically that "American concepts of masculinity are associated with the proletariat, and most concepts of effeminacy are associated with the middle class." Or, this beauty, a nugget from the overview on "Violence" by Consultant Raymond D. Gastil of New York City (is there a *joke* here, asking a bona fide New Yorker to discuss southern "violence"?): "The rise of the Ku Klux Klan and its repeated revival; an exaggerated interest in violent sports, such as football, cockfighting, and dogfighting [*dogfighting?* see any good *dog*fights lately?]; and the tendency of southerners to regard war as a game, as manifested in the historically greater interest of the South in the military, are all indicative of the region's violent tendencies." This also illustrates a potential danger, not always avoided or escaped by the *Encyclopedia,* of replacing one set of simplistic stereotypes with another.

My leading candidate for a National Dumbo Award is one Waldo Braden of Louisiana State University, who contributes this zinger to the slow evolution and accumulation of human knowledge: "Sometimes referred to as talking, chatting, visiting, jawing, small talk, or repartee, conversation involves the oral exchange of ideas, opinions and sentiments." Hey, thanks a bunch for sharing your thoughts with us, Waldo.

There are larger flaws and limitations in the purposes and mind-set of the *Encyclopedia.* Like so many contemporary southerners of good heart and good will, the editors and their whole crew are irrepressibly trendy, unquenchably cute, implacably worldlier-than-thou, and probably a lot more liberal than your mama. So? No harm done. Your basic southerner is sick and tired of being classified by others as a generic hick, a Brand-X rube. It's a no-win situation. The more you complain and assert your sophistication, the more you look like a kid dressing as a grownup.

Speaking of dressing up. On 24 July 1989 at Square Books, a local store on the famous courthouse square at Oxford, Mississippi, there was a publication and signing party for the *Encyclopedia.* To demonstrate just how sophisticated and trendy they have all become, the editors and more than fifty contributors and a crowd of aesthetes from Oxford showed up in costume to celebrate—the mayor of Oxford, Jane Rule Burdine, as Dolly Parton; a lawyer came as "Brown v. Board of Education"; University of Mississippi students came as Kudzu (*Pueraria Lobata*); novelist and storywriter Larry Brown came armed as "The Misfit" from Flannery O'Connor's story "A

Good Man Is Hard to Find"; and writer Barry Hannah announced that he was coming as Eudora Welty, but never appeared. Tell me we southerners aren't every bit as decadent as any Yankee alive!

A larger and more serious problem arises in part from the nonhistorical scheme of the *Encyclopedia* and in part not from ignorance but from the lack of imagination (and/or experience) of the editors and many of the contributors.

For example, there is repetitive emphasis on white guilt and white fear to explain, in part, both the improvement in race relations and the present climate of the same. The evidence for both feelings is, to say the least, sketchy. Outside of certain intellectual communities, where sources of personal guilt appear to be endless, there is in truth little or no indication of white guilt in the South or the nation at large. As for fear . . . if the southerner is half as violent and well-armed as he is so often described (including in the *Encyclopedia*), it is hard to imagine his fear of a minority whom he outnumbers ten to one. Guerrilla warfare is not a slam-dunking contest, and in war all men are as equal as their arms and power allow them to be. Virtue and a good cause have next to nothing to do with success or failure in combat, as any alert citizen must know well.

All of which is only to say that false guilt and false fear lead nowhere at all. Southern whites have elected to do the right (just as for many years they freely chose to do the wrong) for other, more complex reasons. It also needs to be said that nobody, including some who know better, keeps in mind the fact that for fifty years following Reconstruction federal power to work change was constitutionally limited. There is enough blame for all to share without systematically misrepresenting the truth.

The one enormous event that overwhelmed the South was the Civil War, which—never mind the economy and the social breakdown and the large civilian toll of death and disease—killed one out of four southern males between the ages of eighteen and sixty-five. In those terms, ratio of combat deaths to population, it is the worst war that we know of—worse, by far, than World War I or World War II for any nation. The horrible losses of the Soviet Union were approximately the same as the Union losses, that is, one in ten. Not even Cambodia, in our time, suffered losses of that proportion. The Civil War, and the rigors of Reconstruction that followed, are not in the least ignored in the *Encyclopedia*. But ground zero, the starting point of all comprehension, the simple fact that it was the worst war in modern history, is absent from discussion or imaginative understanding. And that deeply serious failure, as much of nerve as of intellect, leads to the ignoring of one of the true mysteries of our entire history, how, unlike almost any other war in history, the Civil War ended with the cessation of combat. The issues, insofar as they may have mattered by then, were settled if not fully defined. And somehow or other, the fathers of the brief, incredibly bloody Confederacy never looked back, at least to the raw reality of things, just as they looked forward to anything and everything except the most obvious—the restoration of a way of life. In a real sense, there could be no *Encyclopedia of Southern Culture* had not the surviving veterans of the war decided to let go and let be forever. Even the editorial innocence of this aspect of the *Encyclopedia* is a kind of tribute to the success of their choice. Still, the old-timers deserve better and deeper understanding than they have received or ever asked for. Strange, that after the tag end of a bloody and brutal century we still cannot imagine them fully. Until we do, no encyclopedia will do us much good.

(1989)

A Voice for the Voiceless: Review of *My Drowning* by Jim Grimsley

My Drowning is Jim Grimsley's third and finest novel so far. A gifted and award-winning playwright, he is writer-in-residence at Atlanta's 7 Stages Theatre, but he has been writing fiction all along, ever since he was a student at Chapel Hill. His first novel, *Winter Birds,* was copyrighted by the author in 1984 and first published in 1992 by a German publisher in German (*Wintervögel*). Two years later, the French brought it out, and, as *Les oiseaux de l'hiver,* the novel won the Prix Charles Brisset. Shortly thereafter, the book was published in English by Algonquin, receiving highly favorable reviews and nominations for a number of prizes, and it was chosen for the 1995 Sue Kaufman Prize for First Fiction awarded by the American Academy of Arts and Letters. *Winter Birds* was followed by *Dream Boy* (1995), described by critic Lisa Howorth (*Reckon,* Winter 1996) as "a sensitive but smart portrayal of homosexual love." *Dream Boy*'s rural setting and the fact that it concerns an adolescent love affair make it different from the typical gay fiction of our era. *Dream Boy* earned the ALA Gay-Lesbian-Bisexual Book Award.

Dark, harsh, bleak, yet shining with a delicate and sensitive (and unsentimental) poetry, Jim Grimsley's novels are not easily described; or, to put it more accurately, the story line can in fact be described in a few sentences, but the usual literary terms and definitions are not at all adequate and fail to do justice to the intense and complex experience of his fiction. The fault lies with our limited terms and with our stereotypical responses to the subject matter. Grimsley writes about southern rural life and poverty from the inside, from the point of view of complex, fully dimensional characters who, even as young children, possess an identity and inward and spiritual lives that are richer and deeper than the hard-edged facts of their social circumstances. Faulkner did this, too, of course, especially in his Snopes trilogy, but in a different way and with a different kind of music. Faulkner's art calls for a full symphonic orchestra. Closer perhaps to Grimsley's way is the work of the late William Goyen, who, as an actual composer, himself harvested ballads for and about his wonderful East Texas characters, mostly rural and desperately poor. But Goyen favored the special freedom of surrealism and was a master of the tropes of "magic realism" long before it had earned that official name. All of these southern writers, and more recently others like Lee Smith, Fred Chappell, Robert Morgan, even Maine's Carolyn Chute, faced the problem of finding a language that could do justice to the feelings, emotions, ideas, and inner life of characters who are (often but not always) nonverbal and uneducated in conventional terms. Grimsley, like Goyen, is much involved with myth and ritual and the subtle exploration of imaginative consciousness in all his work, but it is a very different kind of language—simple, luminous, breathtakingly clear, with which he clothes and invests his characters. Fred Chappell, who among other things is a leading poet and novelist of the modern rural South and is likewise a first-rate literary critic, has described it precisely in a book review: "There are few writers who sustain our attention through tone and voice. Jim Grimsley belongs in this elite group." Which is to say that a brief description of the story line of a Grimsley novel, out of the context of its special poetry, its subtle orchestration of tones and voices, tends to give a distinctly false impression of the work.

Winter Birds (an autobiographical novel in many details, as it happens, though that truth is not strictly relevant except as evidence of and for its unflinching authenticity) can be described as the story of eight-year-old Danny Crell, a hemophiliac and one of five children in a poverty-stricken country family, most sorely troubled by their father, the abusive, drunken, one-armed, long-suffering Bobjay, and somehow held together by their mother, Ellen. (Ellen in her childhood and youth is the central figure in *My Drowning*.) It is a brutal, violent story, clothed, though, in the raiment of Grimsley's narrative poetry and told in an interesting way. For this novel, he elected a rarely used point of view, the second-person singular, evidently representing the older Danny repeating and rehearsing the story of his life directly to himself: "You walk beneath the unalterable surface of clouds. Cool wind sweeps down from them, singing in the pines and scattering the cornstalks in the field." It may well have been this point of view, together with the dark subject matter, that delayed *Winter Birds* from finding a publisher. Certainly most American publishers take a very dim view of that point of view, that kind of narrative license, not realizing that soon enough whatever point of view an author takes and establishes for a story becomes simply that standard of this storytelling and quickly loses its quality of surprise and strangeness. Since the material of *Dream Boy* is somewhat unusual, the telling of the story is itself more conventional, mostly being presented in the traditional third-person limited point of view of the adolescent protagonist, Nathan. *My Drowning* is told in the first person and in both past and present tenses, narrated by the elderly Ellen Tote and chiefly concerned with her own childhood, though from time to time she steps forward to compare and contrast her contemporary life, characterized by a certain relative comfort and security, with the bitter times of her childhood.

Some of the power and intensity of Grimsley's work, then, derives from the contrast (if not direct conflict) of the ways and means of the telling with the material of the story. Other writers might well be tempted to emphasize the dark stories at the expense of the full complexity of the characters, making the characters more victims than anything else, but Grimsley seems to have decided from the outset that his characters must be dimensional, must cast long shadows, and that the material of the story speak for itself without captions or commentary. In the *Reckon* magazine profile, he is quoted, speaking directly to his attempt to portray his characters with a difference from the usual treatment of the poor: "A lot of people have written about poor people, but I don't think the *very poorest* people have been written about quite the way you really see them. The attitude in literature toward that class of people up until now has been that poor people were just like everybody else, only with fewer things. Nobody dealt with just how animalistic your life can become when you don't have *anything*." Certainly in *Winter Birds* and *My Drowning* the central characters, the family, spend most of their treasury of time and energy on the brutally simple matters of survival.

Nobody owns much of anything in either *Winter Birds* or *My Drown-*

ing, but the latter, set a full generation earlier than *Winter Birds,* in the heart of the Great Depression and World War II, is more deprived and "disadvantaged" by far. Ellen and her brothers and sisters—Otis, Carl Jr., Nora, Corrine, Madson, Delia, Hob, the crippled and dying Joe Robbie—are crowded and packed in the pathetic shacks they live in, always on the move because of the father's alcoholism and inability to work at anything for long. These are children for whom a biscuit, or half a biscuit, and some sweet coffee are a complete meal. They are hungry almost all the time. They carry no lunch to school and sit quietly and watch while the others eat at lunchtime. Whether they go to school, something they are eager to do, or not depends on the weather and the state of their shabby hand-me-down clothes.

All of this, and the steady cumulative details of Ellen's childhood as she tries to remember them, takes this reader, a child of the selfsame times, back to the scene and summons up a multitude of memories and ghosts. I can see again their raggedy counterparts and now, perhaps for the first time, through her words and feelings, at last understand the bitter mystery their blank faces seldom revealed: "When I look back there, turning over and over the memory of that hard winter in a house not fit for people, I amaze myself that my hatred does not burn me to a crisp. Even then I must have begun to understand. Other children had already begun to teach me about living. Other children lived differently than we did; they did not have to gather wood in a picked-over forest in shoes too tight, with socks for gloves." The details of this hardest kind of life are simply named and told as Ellen remembers them. There are grim and brutal events, but there are, as well, a few brief, shining moments of pleasure, even of joy, though these are few and far between. Because of the intense sensitivity, perceptions as delicate and subtle as any poet's, of these people, we, the readers, are fully aware of the great waste involved in their squandered lives. As a documentary of rural poverty, this novel is urgently authentic and as powerful and meaningful as, for example, James Agee's *Let Us Now Praise Famous Men* or Erskine Caldwell's *You Have Seen Their Faces.*

But *My Drowning* aims to be something more than accurate documentary. It is a book about memory, the nature and definition of memory, the whole process of remembering and of the inextricable blending together of dreams and memory. From first to last, there is a recurring image, a memory that may in truth be a dream—the image of her mother in the river (which

Ellen soon equates directly with the river flow of time) disappearing, then returning: "Kneeling in the river, submerged to her shoulders, she turns her face to the sky. The fat of her arms sways in the air, dips into the dark water. She takes a breath and closes her mouth. From me, from all of us, she slides away. . . . Mama rises out of the river gasping, throwing water from her hair. Her breath rises in trails of steam." Again and again, this memory, imperfect and enigmatic, always slightly changing, persists, finally to be "solved," both the event and the nature of the memory of it, in a revelation near the end of the story. Yet even so, the story that years later her dying older brother tells her may or may not be "true." As Ellen tells us: "Otis was the last to die before I was left alone in the family, and before he did he told me the story of the river, and when he told me the events echoed, as if I had heard it all before. On hearing the story, something akin to a memory unlocked within me, as if what Otis said were the truth and not simply the shadow of one more dream. So I nearly believed him, even if he was lying, and this may have been all he wanted."

This, the discovery of the meaning of the dream-memory of a drowning, becomes the "plot" of *My Drowning*. In between, there are the other memories, new stories and anecdotes of the family, and the constant questioning of the validity and value of memory. "I am remembering, I am looking back," she tells us early in the novel. "I am trying to see clearly, but I do not even know that what I am seeing is true." A little later she notes—"At times, as the memories pass through me, waves of water, I am astonished at how much I have kept. " There are dreams that are as palpable as memory and there are visions that are taken and accepted by Ellen as being as solidly true as the pain and pleasures of the senses. For Ellen, there is the ghost of a younger sister, Alma Laura, who dies in infancy, after three months and three days, for lack of medical attention. Alma Laura remains part of her life from then until after Ellen is married and pregnant: "Alma Laura grew, and I watched her progress when she was with me, and I never wondered how she could be here if she were really dead. . . . She grew as I grew, a little behind me. Sometimes, when she was not with me, I would see her walking in the distance, usually at the edge of woods or in some empty building near whatever house we lived in."

What follows from all of this is the sense that these people have deep and complex inner lives like Ellen's, that even the desperately poor in fact and in spirit also have a depth of being that can scarcely be imagined by others. This is a heavy burden for a slender, tightly trimmed, pared-down, evocative novel to carry. In his first three novels, Grimsley has found the voice and the tone to do the job gracefully, seemingly almost without effort. There are many other writers at this moment writing about rural America and, as well, about the world of memory, enough so that these things could even legitimately be called literary trends. But there is nobody I know of who writes like Grimsley, none among us who can speak so well for those who have been voiceless, if not ignored, amid the clamor of our culture. *Winter Birds* and *My Drowning* are said to be the first two parts of a trilogy. It is difficult to imagine where Jim Grimsley will take us next, but, on the strength of his achievement so far, it is a pleasure to wait in anticipation for his next novel. Meanwhile, we have in hand a remarkable and original work, one that achieves his primary goal of giving a voice to the voiceless, a new life to those whom life has most deeply wounded.

(1997)

Jesse Hill Ford's Play

The Conversion of Buster Drumwright: The Television and Stage Scripts (1964) was Jesse Hill Ford's second book, following after the novel *Mountains of Gilead* (1961). Since then, Ford has published three novels—*The Liberation of Lord Byron Jones* (1966), *The Feast of Saint Barnabas* (1969), and *The Raider* (1975)—with one collection of short stories, *Fishes, Birds and Sons of Man* (1967). Together with veteran screenwriter Stirling Silliphant, Ford is credited with the screenplay for the 1969 version of *The Liberation of Lord Byron Jones.* Reference books acknowledge Ford's years of work as "an anonymous screenwriter" for Hollywood, but no credits are listed, which seems surprising in view of the rather strict regulations of the Writers Guild of America, West (the old Screenwriters Guild). Most likely the absence of credits indicates that no project he worked on came to completion or, if so, contained very little of Ford's work in the final version of the script. This, in itself, is *not* surprising, for a rough estimate is that about four of five finished scripts are not produced as films. These leftover scripts are paid for, filed away, and more or less forgotten.

The files of Hollywood will one day prove to be a treasure trove for scholars, for large numbers of American writers, from three generations, ever since the advent of sound in motion pictures, have written scripts for the movies. Some, a lucky few, have made a good living at it quite aside from whether or not anything they have written has, in fact, been filmed. A few years ago, *Ploughshares* magazine was able to publish the unfilmed script by Richard Yates of William Styron's novel *Lie Down in Darkness*. All indications are that the files of producers and production companies are rich with synopses, treatments, and shooting scripts by some of our finest writers.

The book of *The Conversion of Buster Drumwright* is interesting and unusual in a number of ways. The preface by Ford offers an outline of the stages of the play—how it began as a play for television for the *CBS Television Workshop* (1959); how it was reconstructed and rewritten for the stage, mostly in Norway where Ford was a Fulbright Scholar in 1961; how the stage version was then produced by the Vanderbilt University Theater during the 1962–1963 session; how it was also produced (by the Vanderbilt cast and crew) in Ford's hometown of Humboldt, Tennessee. Ford's preface is followed by a critical foreword by Donald Davidson, who had been Ford's teacher at Vanderbilt (Ford also studied with Andrew Lytle at the University of Florida). While Davidson celebrates the publication of the play "in its two forms, illustrating by unusual good fortune the problems of composition in two media," he seems to prefer the original television version for its "perfect clarity and economy"; and indeed, the two-act stage version is expanded, adds more characters and details and builds to a significantly different ending. The handsome book, published by Vanderbilt University Press, also has some illustrations from both productions.

The Conversion of Buster Drumwright is based on a theme that has haunted the literature of this century (it haunted the Elizabethans as well): how, for some purpose or other, a character assumes a disguise or role and, in playing out that part, becomes more and more the new role, at any rate taking on ambiguously the mantle or uniform of what he pretends and professes to be. There are so many examples and variations on this theme, nationally (from Melville and Twain to the movie *Dave)* and internationally, that it might seem almost stereotypical, a paradigmatic story for our times. A memorable and relevant example is the Italian film *Generale Della Rovere,* where Vittorio De Sica, already established as a sleazy confidence man, is persuaded by the Nazis to play the part of General Della Rovere (who has been secretly killed by the Germans) and to go to prison in an attempt to discover who among the prisoners are members of the partisan underground resistance. In prison De Sica (mad or perhaps not) *becomes* the General and in the end dies as a heroic leader of the underground.

In *The Conversion of Buster Drumwright,* Ocie Hedgepath, who has been away in Texas for many years and is no longer recognized by the locals, contrives to act for the honor of his family and to revenge the murder of his sister and her infant child by pretending to be a preacher. As a preacher, he must manage to convert and baptize the murderer, Buster Drumwright, about as wicked a sociopath as Faulkner's Popeye or even Shakespeare's Iago. Working against time (Drumwright will be lawfully hanged in three days), Ocie must successfully preach the gospel to Drumwright in order to kill him. As Donald Davidson describes it: "Out of Ocie's impersonation came the series of quick-running scenes that lead to his interviews (at first violent and fruitless) with the condemned murderer and so finally to the triumphant climax during which . . . a bathtub is brought to the jail and filled with water for the baptism. Buster has been converted. But, in the astounding yet fully justified *peripateia,* Ocie has converted himself."

Generally speaking, television (and especially in the "wasteland" years that include 1959) does not lend itself to the complexities of spiritual ambiguity. Yet the television version, three acts and a total of thirteen scenes, succeeds admirably on the page as well as on the screen. (I watched it myself on a Sunday morning in 1959 and found it entirely credible and deeply moving.) Part of the reason for its success is technical. The accumulation of short fragmentary scenes, tightly focused and poetic, and the very quick ending, all work to let the reader/observer make the imaginative connections and project the future:

> BUSTER (anxiously): You . . . you still going to be there tomorrow, Preacher?
> OCIE (reaching through the bars to put his hand on Buster's arm): I'll be there.

Donald Davidson notes another strength that makes the play work, pointing out that "the Hedgepaths, Drumwrights, Stanhopes of Jesse Ford's play belong to Christendom—to the Christendom we recognize as American, as Southern, as honestly our own. . . . It draws from the deepest fountains of race memory—from the veritable *anima mundi* about which Yeats was so much concerned." All of which is to say that Davidson found the play to be, in a laudatory sense, traditional, part and parcel of a living as well as a literary tradition. Its focus and concentration (Davidson calls the stage version "a little faultily diffuse at some points") make the television version an *exemplum* of the literary ways and means of the Fugitive/Agrarian aesthetic.

The stage version is more specific in time, not merely a vague past—"They have electric lights, but not the electric chair or the electric guitar." Ford adds, as a part of his setting: "It is the golden age of fundamentalist religion, white spiritual music, and the vengeful Anglo-Saxon Jehovah." The implication from this precise distancing from the action to follow is that the story itself could not happen here and now, is a product not of a living tradition but of a dead and lost past. Ford says that what happened between the two versions was that he went to Norway and "absorbed the saga tales of Iceland, in which nothing figures more positively than an overweening hunger for blood vengeance." Adding: "The mood of these sagas fitted the feud-society atmosphere of the Southern hills exactly, it seemed to me." But it is possible to argue that the grafting of the pagan and pre-Christian tradition onto the essentially Christian theme of the play undercut the latter. Certainly it leads to a different ending. In the stage version, Ocie, having promised Buster Drumwright to be there at his execution tomorrow, goes outside the jail only to be stabbed to death by his own brother, Dan. This leads to some complicated, somewhat melodramatic action: "*(Dan flings down the knife and runs away as Rance starts to force his way past Fate into the jail. Mary rises from Ocie's side and falls on Rance's gun. Fate springs forward and disarms Rance.)*" Then the scene continues for several minutes with a good deal of talk about what has happened and the implications of all of it. The ending is powerful nevertheless, but it is not as moving as it was in the television version.

The stage version is somewhat more "talky," dependent more on dialogue to make its point and to focus attention in the absence of a camera and a frame. There are any number of minor changes and one major one. Here Ford introduces a new character, the singing, banjo-playing Ralph Swiggert.

Swiggert is a chorus figure who opens and closes the action of the play. (Banjo music is also used for time and space transitions.) Swiggert is the absent and estranged husband of the Hedgepath woman who was murdered by Buster Drumwright. This is a good and lively part, giving Ford a chance to add some humor to the original bleak version: "See the scriptures, see the book, my friends, and just remember that, whether you want to think about it or not, all our kin started in that book with this Jewish fellow, Adam, and his wife, Mistress Eve. You know what she done in cahoots with a snake."

But all this serves to diminish the story of Ocie and Buster. Our first impressions, and our last as well, are of Ralph Swiggert; it becomes a story that he narrates. I can imagine that the stage version, with a good cast and imaginative direction, could play very well, but it is a far cry from the catharsis created by the television version. And in that sense the two versions are separate and distinct.

Something happened between the two versions of the play just as, almost simultaneously, something happened between Ford's first novel, *Mountains of Gilead,* and his second, *The Liberation of Lord Byron Jones.* Both novels concern the imaginary town at the center of most of Ford's work—Somerton, Tennessee—but they are different technically and rhetorically. *Mountains of Gilead* is almost a textbook version of the "Agrarian" novel, almost as if composed to and by the criteria of *Understanding Fiction* and *The House of Fiction. The Liberation of Lord Byron Jones* is at once more adventurous, in both form and content, and more popular, accessible. When you see the movie, the novel seems to have been written to fit that form, an easy translation from page to screen. It was here that Ford seems to have parted company with his former teachers and, for better or worse, struck out on his own. Donald Davidson paused in his foreword to praise the short stories of Ford as signs of a productive future: "These may not be quite as central to our deepest concerns as *The Conversion of Buster Drumwright,* but surely they betoken much stronger work to come." In the book with the two versions of his play, presented in the sequence they were written, we can now see, *ex post facto,* where Ford was headed. As far as we know, there have not been any more plays, certainly none published or produced, but with *The Conversion of Buster Drumwright* Ford the novelist proved himself, at least in one version, also to be a gifted playwright with his own voice and vision. Perhaps, with time and the right subjects, he would have written other plays, but his one play about Ocie Hedgepath and Buster Drumwright has an honorable place in the contemporary dramatic tradition.

(1995)

William Price Fox's *Dixiana Moon*

William Price Fox's first novel appeared in 1981 with strong supporting statements by writers as respected and as various as Kurt Vonnegut, Richard Yates, Pauline Kael, and John D. MacDonald. And like each of his other works since the celebrated *Southern Fried* (1962), *Dixiana Moon* was moderately successful at the marketplace and yet mostly ignored by the reviewers and critics who have and exercise the power to make or break literary reputations. There is something of a mystery about Fox's reputation, for clearly his work has been appreciated by many readers over the years. And his fellow writers have long since recognized him as a vital and original storyteller. People such as Vonnegut, Yates, and MacDonald seldom write blurbs for anyone and have reputations for great and serious probity. That they should choose to speak out for Fox and his work is a matter of consequence. But the support of neither readers, writers, nor even the regional book reviewers in his native South—and these have been, by and large, generous in their appreciation of Fox's work—has not been able to give Fox the kind of national recognition that he seems justly to deserve. There are, perhaps, reasons behind, if not for, this injustice. And *Dixiana Moon,* a novel that shows Fox at his best, all his gifts in order, all his professional skills brought to bear on a pertinent and interesting (and, as always, highly amusing) story, is a good place to examine the discrepancy between his limited literary reputation and his considerable achievement.

It should be said at the outset, however, that this problem has not deterred Fox from continuing his own creative work. He continues to live in Columbia, South Carolina, teaching creative writing to students at the University of South Carolina. He has not lost touch with the other side of life in Columbia, that side made most familiar in his novels and stories, for he still holds frequent and energetic court at the Capitol Café on Main Street, where one can easily see many characters who appear to have emerged full-blown from the pages of a Fox novel.

The typical Fox story may push itself to the hyperbolic humorous boundaries of the credible, may end on the wild and woolly near-edges of the purely fabulous. But, unlike the fictions of many contemporary writers, it never begins there. Instead, it grows and then flowers out of the plain, gritty specificity of the familiar. The roots of his fables are real, and so it seems relevant that he has chosen to return to and remain at the place of his beginnings, to live close to his own roots. It is likewise significant that even when dealing with characters who are in many details distinctly different from himself, Fox tends to draw directly from the capital of his own experiences to invest imaginary figures with the breath of life.

For instance, Joe Mahaffey, the delightfully complex and indefatigable narrator of *Dixiana Moon*, is a salesman for a printing and packaging company. So, for a time, was William Price Fox. Mahaffey, in effect, runs away with a circus. So did Fox, once upon a time. But we are not dealing with anything so commonplace as a portrait and celebration of the artist as a young man or, for that matter, with a simple rejection of the hard-grabbing way of life in America in this last quarter of the century. True, Mahaffey gives up his career as a salesman to join the amazing mud-circus world of Buck Brody, but it is not an obvious and easy choice for him to make, and it is the cumulative experience of the entire story that allows him to make that choice. It is a natural choice, for love and for life, but we arrive at the wisdom of it at the same time that Joe does. It is not the typical situation of waiting for the protagonist to discover the obvious. We are not entitled to condescend to Joe Mahaffey (or, for that matter, to any of the others among the crew of major and minor characters), and we are not allowed to anticipate or outguess him. And therein lies one important difference between the fiction of Fox and that of many of his more prominent contemporaries. It lies in the fullness and richness of characterization. Again and again, his characters surprise us, and sometimes even themselves, by their capacity to be something more than the stereotypical sum of their parts.

Joe Mahaffey is a case in point. Happy and unhappy, he loves the performing craft of selling, and he does it well. He is a good salesman. One reason is that he has a real enthusiasm not merely for the business of selling a product but also for the product itself. He knows printing and packaging inside and out, and he knows and admires quality work even as he rejects the cheap and the shoddy and the phony. As a narrator in this first-person story, he is able to articulate, gracefully enough, both his enthusiasms and his ethical and aesthetic standards. A good con man himself, he is able to persuade us, more or less, to share them. Similarly and simultaneously, thanks to the lifetime experience of his own father, a dreamer and a schemer and always a loser, Joe is equipped to understand and, more important, to see through the scams of his southern buddy, Buck Brody, and also to recognize the rich self-delusions that serve to give life and breath to the con man's dreams. He knows well enough "how all they needed was a little time and a little money and a little break and it was going to be a brand new horse race." Yet, knowing and understanding, Joe freely chooses that way of life in the end.

What we are talking about here is unusual dimensionality of character, of characterization in the classic and dramatic sense—classic in that the author is equally involved, or equally disengaged if you prefer, with each and all of the characters, even with Joe as first-person narrator, who, after all, speaks only of and for himself and not for Fox; dramatic in that events occur and forces collide without other inference or commentary than that of the narrator, who, after all, is continually changing as he experiences the events of the story. This dramatic quality is almost purely Jamesian. Fox is often compared by other writers to Mark Twain, and justly so. There is much of the finest spirit of Twain in Fox's full range of humor and in his mastery of the living American vernacular and, as well, in the kind of story he tells. Here, for instance, the journeys and tribulations of Joe Mahaffey and Buck Brody deliberately evoke recollections of the archetypal Duke and Dauphin in *Huckleberry Finn*. But perhaps because the dazzling surfaces of his work divert us, we miss the truth that Fox is just as much in the moral tradition of Henry James, where both ambiguity and the power of resolution are derived, first, from a many-sided view of things and, secondly, from an insistence upon the free will of characters who must make moral decisions. That is to say, in the case of *Dixiana Moon,* no matter how much we, the readers, may *wish* for Joe Mahaffey to choose the life of the circus over the corporation and no matter how much he may favor the former over the latter, the choice, to have any meaning, must be a real one involving a weighing and sifting of good things and bad. Joe, a great maker of lists, is fully aware of that. And it must be a free choice; Joe must at least perceive himself to be judging, then acting freely. Now, add to this the fact that Joe Mahaffey is an "irrepressible optimist," that neither angst nor heebie-jeebies nor routine blues can keep him down or hold him back for long, and you can begin to see how far the world of Fox's fiction is from much recent American fiction. He writes comedy (though, like all good comedy, it hovers always on the edge of real disaster, even tragedy) at a time when comic fiction is rare. He creates dimensional characters at a time when the conventions of characterization are more ignored than honored. Intellectually, thus ideologically, he is at least a skeptic of the age's dominant, deterministic, Marxist-Freudian secular tradition or its offshoot—behaviorism. The kind of story Fox likes to write simply will not work if the characters are merely puppets manipulated by huge, invisible social and economic forces. These forces may or may not exist, like ghosts and other psychic phenomena, but his characters must at least preserve the freedom allowed by Boethius in *The Consolation of Philosophy*—that is, they must perceive themselves to be both free and responsible and try to act accordingly.

Finally, Fox's work is socially distinct from the prevailing contemporary mode (one is tempted to call it the Establishment) in American fiction. Fox accepts America, with all its ambiguities and contradictions intact, just as he accepts his characters and they accept their world, with an absolute minimum of judgmental posturing. Thus politics, political answers and solutions to problems, do not enter into his fiction very much except at a remove and by inference. At a time when much serious fiction in America—think of Roth, Heller, Mailer, Vonnegut, Malamud, Updike, etc.—is riddled with politics, Fox has chosen to deal with the subject only insofar as it may legitimately impinge upon the lives of his characters, which is to say not very much. Pop culture—the movies, songs, television shows, and commercials—is far more influential in their lives than the sound and fury of political action. Finally, at a time when national critics and reviewers have once again declared the southern literary renaissance and flowering to be over and done with, Fox is uncompromisingly southern, part of the southern literary tradition going back to Mark Twain and beyond him to Twain's roots, to the frontier and backwoods storytellers whose persistent haunting is the chief spirit of the southern tradition.

Among the moderns, he is closer to Erskine Caldwell and to some of Faulkner, especially Faulkner's comic novels (including *As I Lay Dying*), than to the more decorous Fugitive-Agrarian school. Among his contemporaries, he is at least kin to Calder Willingham and Harry Crews, though never so emphatically sardonic as the former and nowhere so trendy and fashionably surreal as the latter. And in *Dixiana Moon,* Fox offers a new twist to the southern novel, for Joe Mahaffey is not a southerner, nor is his off-again-on-again girl friend, Monica. Choosing each other at last, choosing the life of Buck Brody's mud circus, they also choose the South for a homeplace. So, in one sense, *Dixiana Moon* is a story of conversion—conversion from one way of life to another and from one place to a new one. For this to work within the strict demands Fox makes upon himself as craftsman, Mahaffey must be at once sensitive to and appreciative of place in general, the sense and feel of it. Which he is. And so, interestingly, some of the most sensitive renderings of the particular beauties and excitements of present-day Manhattan are to be found here in *Dixiana Moon.* Fox handles the city as well and as easily as and much more lovingly than many of the eastern urban writers for whom it is the chief locus of wonder and danger. Weighing the pros and cons, Joe perceives most of the faults of the South, old and new, and there is much about his life in New York that he loves without reservation: "But most of all I missed the action. Winter was half over now and in a few more weeks it would warm up and the balloonmen and the Italian-ice vendors would be out at Central Park, and Monica and I would be cruising through the zoo and heading over for the Tavern on the Green." What he chooses, though, and in so choosing follows the great national migration of the past two decades, is positive, not something preserved from the past but rather something else: "Something bigger and wilder and better, with more money and more fun and more everything of everything. And right there, steering the Olds down the Dixiana Highway, with the elephants blocking out the sun and the guitar sound and that great smell of cold beer, I knew exactly what I was going to do."

There is much more to single out for praise in William Price Fox's mature fictional art, as witnessed here in *Dixiana Moon*—the wonderfully clear and vivid and witty style, the economy and graceful pace of his story, the sensuously realized surfaces of places and things, his refusal to settle for easy labels and clichés, this refusal resulting in a continuing sequence of little surprises, his perfect-pitch ear for American speech of our time, his own irrepressible good humor and optimism, and, perhaps most of all, the pure fun of his invention. Very few others among our good, serious novelists—and we must certainly place Fox among the best and brightest; he has earned his way and right, with or without critical recognition—are as much *fun* to read as Fox is. If, as seems likely, he keeps on in the directions indicated by *Dixiana Moon*, the problem of critical recognition may prove to be irrelevant. Readers have already found him, and it seems only a matter of time before they will come together to offer the one kind of recognition that is irrefutable.

(1982)

Forest of the Night: A Declaration of Independence

In a remarkably open and interesting essay about his life and his work, written for *Contemporary Authors: Autobiography Series* (Vol. 11, 1990, pp. 171–87), Madison Jones said of this book, his second published novel: "*Forest of the Night* would turn out to be, I believe, the least successful of my novels. Yet I sometimes feel that it could have been my best." He goes on to say that the last third of the novel suffers from his own impatience, that its last part is, as a result, hurried and not fully realized. He is entitled to that judgment. He wrote the story, and he alone knew and knows now what he hoped to achieve with *Forest of the Night*. But by the same token, the sympathetic reader is entitled to deal with the experience at hand, what the book in fact is, not what it might have been. If that reader happens to be, as I am, a teacher of literature and a novelist himself, he may feel, as I do, that the author's judgment of the work is too severe and finally not strictly relevant to the reader's experience.

It is entirely in character and appropriate that Madison Jones should demand more from the story than he feels he created and presented. On the other hand, the engaged reader might well argue that the novel, public property as it has been since 1960, requires a quickly moving narrative line for its final act, some change and even relief from the tightly focused intensity of the first two-thirds. And a reader, this one, would have to report that there is no novel, even among the acknowledged masterpieces of the canon, that does not at some point reward the reader and his involved impatience with a more rapid working-out of the established premises and promises; otherwise, there would never be an end to any of them. And—and I suspect Madison Jones knows this well—if a serious and gifted writer were ever able to achieve in any one work the perfect model of what he has imagined, there would be no good reason to create another. What we learn from the experience of writing a novel is how we should have done it in the first place. If the novel is, in Jones's terms, "successful" (by which he clearly means not the success of sales or even of critical appreciation, but purely and simply aesthetic satisfaction), it is because the writer has managed, by craft and art, to camouflage overt and inherent flaws and to disguise the undeniable truth that this is only one way among many possible ways that a given story can be viewed and told. We aim always for the sense of inevitability with the neatness of a balanced equation, yet we always know that there is a kind of trickery or magic, smoke and mirrors, involved—the successful novel only *seems* inevitable. That is the most that we can ever hope for, though of course we begin and begin again and again, always hoping for something more.

All of which adds up to the desperate wisdom of the Wizard of Oz when Judy Garland and the others discover his duplicity: "Pay no attention to that man behind the curtain."

As for the other more mundane ways of measuring success, *Forest of the Night* seems not to have sold a great many copies, at least not enough to give Madison Jones the one thing most writers hope for, the gift of more time and freedom to get on with their work. It was not reviewed as widely or as well as his first novel, *The Innocent,* which had earned respectful attention, including a highly favorable notice in *Time* ("South in Ferment," 25 February 1957). *Forest of the Night* was by no means ignored, but it did not earn as much national space or as unmixed praise as his first novel had. *Kirkus* praised the immediacy and authenticity of the story while complaining about the "brutality" of it. *Library Journal,* perhaps more influential then than now, wasn't very helpful, inaccurately describing the book as "a portrayal of small town drudgery" and faulting the writing for "a style full of introspective platitudes," concluding in final judgment that it was "a waste of reading time." *Forest of the Night* earned a positive, if mixed, notice in the *Herald Tribune Book Review,* complaining that the book was "too dark."

This kind of thing, though it may hurt the writer's feelings, is chiefly important in another way. Publishers tend to take the initial reviews more seriously than larger and longer views. The chief concern of the publisher is the "shelf life" of the book at hand. In 1960, the shelf life of a novel, other than a best-seller, was about four months. Now it is more like four weeks. Madison Jones's relationships with publishers are typical enough to be emblematic of most of the serious—or, to use the more recent term, "literary"—writers of our generation. With the notable exception of a mere handful of American writers—John Updike is an example—most of our novelists have moved restlessly from publisher to publisher according to the critical and commercial success of their books. I count seven different publishers for the works of Madison Jones, four of them from among the major commercial publishing houses of the times—Harcourt, Viking, Crown, and Doubleday. The truth is, that is a fairly stable record for our era. My own record is probably more typical: sixteen different publishers, five of them large commercial houses. In his autobiographical essay for *Contemporary Authors,* Jones shows himself to have been cheerfully innocent at the outset about some of the problems and details of modern publishing. He earned only three rejections of *The Innocent* before Harcourt Brace accepted it, and those rejections troubled him more than they might have if he had known the publishing histories of many of his contemporaries.

More important to the writer, at least before mergers and conglomerates took over American commercial publishing, was serious critical attention conferred by literary critics of reputation and integrity. Their criticism could make (or break) careers. Their essay-reviews and critical pieces, if any, come on the scene too late, usually, to have any direct effect on sales and journalistic reviews. The major literary reviews and quarterlies appear months, sometimes years, after a given book has come and gone. With the support of his mentors and admirers, people like Donald Davidson, Allen Tate, Andrew Lytle (to whom *Forest of the Night* is dedicated), Walter Sullivan, and Monroe Spears, and friends like Flannery O'Connor, Madison Jones received a good deal of respectful critical praise. Two books in particular led to considerable encouraging attention: *An Exile* (1967), which became a film, *I Walk the Line,* with Gregory Peck; and *A Cry of Absence* (1971), which earned a prominent place on the *New York Times Book Review*'s best-seller list. Perhaps most important and helpful was "A New Classic" by Monroe Spears (*Sewanee Review* 80, no. 1, Winter 1972, pp. 168–72), in which Spears celebrated *A Cry of Absence* as "an authentic, pure, and deeply moving tragedy," and praised the novel as "a major work of art."

Partly because of the well-earned attention given to *A Cry of Absence*, the earlier and less conventionally successful *Forest of the Night* has subsequently received less critical attention than it might have. Ashley Brown's piece in the special edition of the *Chattahoochee Review* (17, no. 1, Fall 1996), "Experience in the West: Madison Jones's Immersion in History," is an outstanding and valuable exception, as is M. E. Bradford's earlier "Madison Jones" in *The History of Southern Literature*, edited by Louis D. Rubin, Jr. (1985). Bradford wrote of *Forest of the Night*: "There is no more powerful expose of the myth of the New Eden in our literature." Not long after the original publication, critic Arthur Mizener, in a chronicle review, "Some Kinds of Modern Novel," of eight recent historical novels for the *Sewanee Review* (69, no. 1, Winter 1961, pp. 154–64), praised *Forest of the Night* as the best of the lot, though he somewhat undercut the praise with extended comments on the limits and faults of the historical novel as a form. Ashley Brown's important piece places *Forest of the Night* in a southern literary context: "Lytle and his contemporaries almost inevitably wrote novels about the history that was accessible to them. . . . But the next generation, that included Eudora Welty and Peter Taylor, then Elizabeth Spencer, were seldom interested in the historical subject, and Flannery O'Connor and Walker Percy (a latecomer to fiction) shunned it on principle. This is largely true of Madison Jones; the exception among his books is *Forest of the Night*." (Bear in mind that Brown's essay appeared before *Nashville 1864* was published.)

The conventionally correct, and probably the most fruitful way to talk about *Forest of the Night* is to deal with it, both in general and in detail, within the context of all Jones's work so far. Certainly, as critics and reviewers early and late have noted, there are close connections in all his work, more intensely so than is the case with many of his contemporaries. In an essay published in *Southern Fiction Today: Renascence and Beyond* (1969), edited by George Core ("The New Faustus: The Southern Renascence and the Joycean Aesthetic," pp. 1–15), Walter Sullivan, dealing specifically with *An Exile,* writes: "The novel is clear, and the book like all of Jones's work is full of bucolic imagery, of sequences flagrantly calculated to show the evil of urbanization and the questionable nature of material progress." Thus Sullivan assumes, and it proves to be a safe and useful assumption, that there are both thematic and technical kinships in all of Jones's books. It is an observation made by an anonymous critic for the *Virginia Quarterly Review* (44, no. 1, Winter 1968, p. viii), likewise commenting on *An Exile* and its relation to the other stories: "Not many present-day writers are able to evoke an atmosphere of terror so overwhelming nor to conjure so artfully a sense of anxiety and dread." Others have noted the similarity, with variations, of his protagonists to each other. And there is some value in comparing and contrasting Jonathan Cannon of *Forest of the Night* with Duncan Welsh of *The Innocent*, Percy Youngblood of *A Buried Land*, Hank Tawes of *An Exile*, Hester Glenn of *A Cry of Absence*, Jud Rivers of *Passage Through Gehenna*, etc. Though they are each distinctly different and aptly representative of their particular times, they have in common, whether they realize it or not, the wound of Original Sin. Madison Jones has been unflinchingly explicit about this: "Adam ate of the tree of the knowledge of good and evil and was cast out forever, and we all share his condition. Evil is a prime fact in our existence: we may be forgiven for it but we cannot escape it" (*Contemporary Authors*). Speaking of Percy Youngblood in *A Buried Land,* Jones points out the pattern that links him to other protagonists: "Here my hero, in flight from a world he finds intolerable, like Duncan and Jonathan before him, commits himself to a different world where imagined redemption lies. But what awaits him is not redemption. No worldly rejection can separate us from the evils that are ours." The allusion is to the passage (on the reverse side of the theological coin) of St. Paul in the eighth chapter of Romans: "For I am persuaded, that neither death, nor life, nor angels, nor principalities, nor powers, nor things present, nor things to come, nor height, nor depth, nor any other creature shall be able to separate us from the love of God, which is Jesus Christ our Lord."

Jones tells us in *Forest of the Night* that he set out to write "a terrible ballad or legend," "a controlled nightmare," "a story about the making of a Harpe." It was originally to be a story of the Harpe brothers, savage and brutal outlaws of Tennessee and the Natchez Trace in frontier days. But the story of the Harpes, told directly, was limited by being too well known. So instead, though the Harpes do indeed appear in person and in character, he wrote of a young man of high hopes and Jeffersonian ideals and of admirable character who, bit by bit, slowly and surely, and in spite of all his better angels, becomes a kind of Harpe himself: who is, in fact, taken by others to be one of the Harpes. And in the feverish nightmare of the final part of the story, he comes to suspect that this is somehow true. Here is what Madison Jones had to say about the essential weakness of his central character in *Forest of the Night:* "My hero, Jonathan Cannon, is a young idealist with Rousseauesque ideas (ideas that entered importantly into the thinking of makers of our constitution) about the goodness of man in the state of nature, and evil as mere negation created by the dead hand of the past." Jonathan's initiation comes in the opening scene when he tries to comfort and help a terribly wounded and dying Indian who uses the last of his vital energy and strength to try to kill Jonathan. Jonathan has come west into the wilderness, coming from Virginia in the year 1802 in the hope of being a schoolmaster in Nashville or one of the settlements. As he tells Judith Gray, who will become the woman in his life: "Someday there'll be schools for everybody—free. That's what President Jefferson wants. . . . Did you ever think what a difference it would make if there were schools for everybody, rich and poor? I don't believe most people dream how much good it would do." Badly wounded by the dying Indian at the outset of his story, Jonathan imagines his father's voice explaining what has just happened: "He was blind with pain and in his blindness blamed you because you are a white man. You see how blindness inspired the act. Or, rather, delusion, nothing. It was an act without any real cause. . . . Because the blame lies with everybody and nobody. Whom would he have attacked? He could have done it only in blindness. And who can blame a blind man for not seeing? To understand is to excuse. Not to excuse him would be to keep the evil alive."

Evil turns out to be alive and well in Tennessee in 1802 and awakes in the heart and soul of Jonathan Cannon, whose enlightened views are tossed aside as he is inexorably reduced to a kind of brutal and loveless savagery. It is a dark story set in a dark world. It is, in Ashley Brown's words, "suffused with death." But even so, through it all there is an older man, Eli, friend to Jonathan, an exemplary man of courage, honor, and simple purity of character who sees what is worthwhile about Jonathan and who manages, several crucial times, to save him from others and from himself. Finally asked why and what for by Jonathan, Eli allows: "Like I owed it to you to learn you something." Jonathan answers: "You couldn't have taught me anything. . . . And it's too late now." To which Eli says, "Maybe it ain't . . . for you. It'll get to where you can live with it if you keep on living. But just don't never forget it." Not exactly a conventional happy ending, then, but also not without some solace. Life is at least possible, "if you keep on living."

Synopsis—and the best I have seen is in Ashley Brown's essay—does not begin to do justice to the power and subtlety of the story line, a well-made, virtuoso narrative rich and full with incident, urgent suspense, and complex, fully dimensional characters. Similarly, a more abstract approach, focusing tightly on the basic themes and ideas that are dramatized in and by the narrative, tends to be schematic at the expense of the experience. Like all art, the novel has to be taken, first of all, as a sensory affective experience. It has to be felt before it can be considered analytically. The problem for the writer (and the reader) is compounded when the work is historical and set back in time far enough to be at least somewhat alien to the reader's experience. The writer cannot allude to or easily summon up an alien and vanished world. It must be created by credible and authentic concrete details, by vivid sensory engagement. Here Madison Jones's acute sensitivity to nature, not the sentimental pastoral of the urban dilettante but the hardscrabble knowledge of a working farmer, joined with an awareness of the mystery and implacable indifference of nature to our comings and goings, all our doings, pays off handsomely. From beginning to end of this story, the vast wilderness, touched hardly at all by the lonely farms and the few rude settlements that pass for civilization, broods over the action of the story. It filters through the leaves of tall trees and pays out shapes and shares of light and shadow. Most of the story comes to us through the perceptions and consciousness of Jonathan. But it is not entirely a third-person, limited point of view. Rather it is omniscient, and the first consciousness that we encounter is that of a bear "standing in shaggy, brutish immobility," not so much a symbol of the wilderness as the creature of it:

> Then he stood upright. To a human eye the action might have suggested mockery; or else some secret power of metamorphosis in brute nature. The bear's posture revealed his age, the scars and slick, black patches of hide, the breast of an old warrior. Standing so, he seemed the type of the great passionate sire, begetting and murdering his kind throughout all the wilderness. Now his head, tilted a little upward, swung to left and right in deliberate inquiry. It stopped. He was all attention to something beyond the reach of human ears. With dignity he dropped onto four feet again. He angled across the road at a

casual, lumbering walk. Before an opening between two trunks he paused and looked back down the road.

Who sees the bear? Only the invisible narrator and the reader, not even Jonathan who is coming down the road breaking the silence. Much later in the story, he is clawed by a bear that might as well be the same one.

There are other abrupt switches of point of view, here and there, as needed; and at the tag end of the book, as Ell and Jonathan wait for some Indians to ferry them and their horses across a river, it is the Indians, like the bear of the beginning, who are the observers: "They waited close to the water's edge. As the boat slipped in toward the bank, the Indians stopped their poling. They stood upright, without motion now, and fixed upon the two white men the brooding gaze of the wilderness."

During a considerable part of the story Jonathan suffers from a nameless fever, and thus his perceptions are (long before "magic realism" came to North American attention) distorted and hallucinatory. At times he hears voices. So did the author, who writes in his autobiographical essay, "There are times in the woods when unexplained voices call to you." The triumph of *Forest of the Night* is that the author has managed to translate those voices for us into a living language and to create a compelling, vividly realized story that questions some of our most cherished and comfortable assumptions.

Madison Jones has continued writing fiction, a series of important and influential books, all of them aesthetically successful, several successful in more mundane terms. The question that inevitably arises among readers, if not often from veteran professional writers, is how has he done so much so well and yet not (yet) been appropriately recognized and rewarded. It is a question too complex to be easily answered. But a few things can be said. Like others among our finest literary writers, he has become the victim of new trends and the economics of commercial publishing. There has also been a critical change, a movement away from interest in and appreciation of the South and its writers. Once again, as in the years from 1865 at least until the turn of that century, southern writing is respectable in literary circles only insofar as it confirms presuppositions devoutly maintained by others. Since there is no way to deny the achievement of the earlier generation, the generation of Faulkner and the Fugitives and others, it is easier to write off the generations that have followed them. After *Forest of the Night* came the decade of the 1960s, which witnessed the transformation of everything, from high art to soda pop, into political statement. Which witnessed new threats to literature from all sides, from death by theory to the contagion of functional illiteracy. Which witnessed a radical change in American values and the rapidly spreading fungus, on a global level, of a vulgar popular culture that celebrates and hugely rewards rock stars, rap singers, and slam dunkers and honors celebrity for its own sake. Reviewing (southerner) Tom Wolfe's *Hooking Up* in the *New York Times Book Review* (5 November 2000, p. 6), Maureen Dowd points out the obvious—that his satire cannot keep up with American reality: "By the time we got to the Moliere bedroom farce of Clinton and Lewinsky, America had grown so wacky and gossipy and shameless and solipsistic and materialistic, satire was simply redundant." It is as if the very wilderness that Jones created in *Forest of the Night,* having vanished, has reappeared as inward and spiritual in an urban setting.

If so, then where is the place in all our culture for the serious and gifted writer who dedicates his life and art to the exploration of serious issues? There is, of course, no answer. Except for the fact that good work has been done and continues to be done and is waiting to be found.

(2000)

The Man Who Wrote the Movie: Faulkner and the Public Arts

To consider the achievements and the accomplishment of William Faulkner, giving special attention to his peripheral work in popular culture (and especially in film), to appreciate what he did and did not do, we need to pay attention to several things. Among them: a very broad, general view of the place of the public or popular arts in American cultural life during the twentieth century; then the place, the influence, both positive and negative, of the popular/public arts on the lives and works of our writers, particularly Faulkner's contemporaries; and finally, to concentrate on the subject of Faulkner and the public arts. Was his experience usual or unusual? What kind of work did he do when he worked in film, and (not to be ignored) what kinds of films were made from his own works, then and later?

Film as a commercial and popular art is coterminous with the life and times of the twentieth century. Superficially, much has changed since the speed-up pictures of the nickelodeon. We have technical improvements of many kinds, above all the arrival and introduction of sound to motion pictures—though we must qualify the impact of this extraordinary development by admitting that silent pictures were not completely silent (consider the regular use of orchestras and pianos during showings). And, as Alfred Hitchcock pointed out more than once in interviews, sound only allowed for what was already imagined in films anyway. In any case, the basic narrative materials, the strength and limitations of film, have changed very little since the beginning. The story, the screenplay, has to be told with the same basic means and materials as were available to Griffiths, Eisenstein, and the other pioneers. Films may look different, and new films have the advantage of the practice and the memory of earlier films. You can think of films as a kind of game played with the same shuffled deck of cards, but the truth is that films have not changed much in a century.

Meantime, the ways of storytelling in the novel have changed radically during the same period of time and are even now continually changing. One of the great pioneers and innovators who worked to change and expand the limits of the novel was William Faulkner.

Let me digress and jump ahead of myself for a moment and make the point that William Faulkner seems to me to have been one of the few writers who quickly realized the fixed limits of film narrative even as he was, from the beginning of his career until his death, extending and expanding the possibilities of prose fiction. In fact, it seems that his learned awareness of the film narrative helped to free him to develop new directions in fiction.

During our time, film was at its most popular and successful during the period of the Great Depression, beginning, roughly, in 1929 and lasting until World War II. More films of all kinds were being produced and released; more people were going to motion-picture theaters (more theaters also); and a great deal of money was being made and spent.

The subject of money calls for a couple of generalizations: first, films cost much more to make now than they did then (for many reasons); and second, the current handful of highly successful movies net huge sums in comparison with earlier times. But the value of money has changed during this period; that is, at last count, economists tell us that the American dollar was worth at least ten times more in the late 1930s than now. Moreover, the movie business was at the outset more or less limited to the U.S. Since World War II, film has been an international business and ever more increasingly so, which greatly enlarges the possibility of success and failure.

(By the way, *The Southerner*, with its script by William Faulkner, was an early example of the international picture, in its creative life, being directed by Jean Renoir.)

Many things have changed the movie business since World War II— television, the consequent video technology, the decline of the major studios, the diminished number of adults attending the theaters, etc. All of these things have added up to a significant change for American writers. More and more screenplays are being written by specialists with a record of experience and success. Where writers were once employed in large numbers by the major studios, so much so that there were whole buildings of writers at work on a wide and wild variety of projects, or, to use their word, properties, now there are only a few screenwriters, by comparison, at all stages of development. Nowadays, the chief employer of writers in America is the academy. Hundreds of American writers are teaching in colleges and universities throughout the country, where, as recently as World War II, there were only a few writers associated with educational institutions.

It is interesting that William Faulkner's career is exemplary of how serious writers in America earned a living in the twentieth century. At the beginning, he was able to make money as a short-story writer. Then he became a contract writer for the movies. At the end of his life, he was associated (for a brief period) with the University of Virginia. His career similarly proves that at no stage, early or late, was it possible for him to earn a living directly as a writer of books. If it had been possible, he might well have never spent any of his time and energy writing scripts for motion pictures. Certainly the writers of his generation, still in the shadow of the nineteenth century, began their careers with good reasons to believe that they could be writers of books who with a little luck could live, decently and modestly, on the earnings of their books. The novel was still viewed as a popular and public form, really in the same family as the motion picture. Of all the great masters of the first twentieth-century generation of American writers, William Faulkner is very unusual—indeed, he seems to have been the first among them in his recognition that there was no immediate commercial future for the kinds of books he had written and hoped and planned to write. In order to enjoy the luxury of writing novels, he would have to find ways of supporting himself and the habit of his art. Nobody else of that generation and era is on record as having come to precisely the same conclusion. If they were of like mind and had reached the same conclusion, they did not reveal it. They seem to have continued to hope to be discovered—or rediscovered, as in the case of Scott Fitzgerald—and to become popular/public novelists. There is no evidence or indication that William Faulkner ever allowed himself seriously to harbor such a hope.

There were two ways that the movie industry could help him. First, it was, then as now, the hope of everyone involved with a novel—publisher, agent, and author—that someone would option or purchase the rights to the novel and adapt it for the screen. This, of course, happened with several of the Faulkner "properties," though never with much success or accuracy until *Intruder in the Dust*. Horton Foote, a gifted southern dramatist, has written and spoken a number of times about his dramatizations of Faulkner stories. Foote is at once sympathetic and sensitive, yet you will quickly see that he assumes that the adaptor can and must exercise considerable liberty with the original material in order to, as he puts it, "do justice to the original." It is not often that filmmakers are much concerned about doing "justice" to the original. More often their principal concern is to exploit the material to create the most successful motion picture possible in their own terms. For the most part, they are not interested in preserving or representing the literary material unless the "property" has already achieved widespread popular fame in its own right.

It seems clear that William Faulkner understood the system and tried to work within the limits of it. Not only did he allow his work to be optioned and purchased, he also made an effort with a number of projects to create proposals and treatments that would make them more desirable "properties" for motion pictures. He may very well have not approved of what they did with his work, but he seems to have understood and to have accepted the rules of the game, not having any great expectations of what film might do with his work.

This rational attitude is more rare than you might imagine. It seems clear that Faulkner did not envision the prospect that a film, successful or not in its own terms, could either harm or enhance his original work. In one sense this is quite extraordinary, for the truth is that many novels are improved in their film versions. In no case have William Faulkner's words, either in general or in details, been improved by translation into film.

We also have the example of Faulkner's adaptations of the work of others—his contemporaries. With the tightly written and plotted *The Big Sleep* by Raymond Chandler, he followed the original closely, even managing, as it happens, to include some of the flaws of the novel. On the other hand, Faulkner's version of *To Have and Have Not* bears very little outward resemblance to the Hemingway novel; he could and would be as ruthless as need be in the craft of adaptation. But one needs to notice that, freely and loosely as *To Have and Have Not* is adapted, it is nevertheless astonishingly true to the essential inner spirit of that work and to Hemingway's work in general. Which, if nothing else, tells us that William Faulkner possessed an active artistic conscience even when he was working in a form like the movies. He may have been openly skeptical, realistic, even cynical about the business of moviemaking, but even so, he did not check his integrity or his artistic conscience at the door. Thus, whether they knew it or not, his superiors in the movie business got more than their money's worth from him.

One of the things that Faulkner understood at once and accommodated in his work for the movies was that the making of a film is always at once a corporate (commercial) and a hierarchical project. It is by definition art by committee and assembly line. Somebody's version—almost always the producer's—prevails. The writer's vision of the work and solution to its problems are vital, but only partial. Many other talents and crafts are involved; and although the quality of the script is crucial, the writer does not rank high in the hierarchy—even less so then, in the 1930s and 1940s, than now, because (among other reasons) with many writers, often two or more, collaborating on a single script (sometimes unbeknownst to each other), and all of them in those days more likely to be on a studio salary than on an individual contract, with even the simple matter of credit for one's contribution to a project also a matter of doubt, writers were, in fact, taken less seriously than now. Faulkner once advised his young friend Shelby Foote, who was considering a Hollywood contract, not to take the work too seriously but to take the people very seriously. Obviously, it was an entirely different process of creating than was the case with his fiction. There even his editors and publishers had very limited influence on the work. Had Faulkner not had films as a source of income, had he been wholly dependant on his publishers for his bread and butter, chances are good that their influence on his work would have been much stronger than it ever was and that the work itself might have been significantly different, certainly less adventurous and experimental. So one of the things that writing for the movies did for Faulkner was to free him to write his own work more or less as he pleased, keeping in mind the expectations of nobody else but an ideal, imaginary reader. Is it any wonder then that he rejoiced and reveled in the hard-earned liberty? After he began working in and for Hollywood, his novels became more complex in structure and texture, and more difficult for anybody but the author himself to adapt or change to fit the film medium.

If you chose to, you could describe the whole career of William Faulkner as a continuing attempt to revise and to redefine the nature of the novel. Some of his amazing freedom of prose on the page derives from his experience of writing entirely expendable work for a different sort of medium.

A good many critics have noticed that the chore of writing screenplays for a living—not only frustrating because of the writer's severely limited influence on the final product but itself relatively rigid in format and potential—taught Faulkner some lessons that were transferable. And this seems likely enough. Yet the positive and negative, the push and shove of contraries, are almost too subtle and complex to be talked about with authority except in the most speculative way. All that needs to be said is that from the beginning Faulkner seems to have viewed the craft of screenwriting as being distinctly different from the writing of fiction. It is that view, together with his acceptance of the implications of it, that separates him from many of his contemporaries who also had experience writing for films. There is plenty of evidence that he made distinctions among films and recognized good work when he saw it. There is also evidence that he did good work when he was able to, that he demonstrated the integrity of a good craftsman even when the task was unpleasant for him.

Here another parenthetical digression is in order. Even as Faulkner's pragmatic and honorable skepticism separated him from many of his fellow screenwriters, and especially from fellow novelists who wrote screenplays, the very fact that he was engaged in the making of popular/public culture tended to separate him from what might be styled as the intellectuals of his generation, not only those who reflexively considered writing for public forms to be a form of "selling out," by which I mean those who, for whatever reasons, could enjoy the luxury (illusion?) of aspiring to perfect integrity, but also those among his fellow southerners, particularly the Agrarian and Fugitive crew, for whom popular culture and its attendant technology were the enemies of humanism and high art. On the subject of integrity, we do well to study Faulkner's introduction to the Modern Library edition of *Sanctuary*, finding there a very precise, self-imposed, and even sacrificial definition of artistic integrity. As for high art, Faulkner never confused it with popular culture, but he was neither afraid nor contemptuous of the latter.

Later in life, he had serious doubts, even fears, concerning the larger context of American culture that centered on the popular arts. He foresaw and spoke out against the great dangers of an unbridled and irresponsible press, what we have come to call "the Media," and its threat not merely to individual privacy and freedom but also to the premise and promise of democratic government. He was one of the first of our prominent artists to speak out in warning against the destructive powers of the Media. Most other writers, owing at least some of their reputation and prominence to publicity, were less willing to challenge the Media and to risk that same reputation. Even though most of Faulkner's expressed fears for the future have come to pass, that situation—silence on the part of the most successful—remains to this day.

In his fiction and in many aspects of his life, Faulkner seems to have been singularly attuned to the rhythms of change. Much that he wrote or said—even when he was writing or talking about the past—has proved to be prophetic.

Something that he does not seem to have anticipated, ironically minor and almost irrelevant to his life and work in any case, was the changing place of film in the established hierarchy of the lively arts. During his lifetime, there was no compelling reason to imagine that film, like the modern novel a generation earlier, would become a serious subject for academic interest. In a deeper sense, Faulkner does not seem to have imagined the overwhelming and cumulative impact on viewers of almost a hundred years of film. Since (as I have argued) film is always similar, if not the same, an intricate playing out of the same dealt hand of cards, it is inevitably an allusive art that feeds upon itself, an art of constant repetition, elaborate variations composed on a few unchanging themes and subjects. We haven't the slightest idea what this experience has done to or for the psyche. A recent book about the film experience, Geoffrey O'Brien's *The Phantom Empire*, suggests some interesting possibilities: "A spectator can avoid certain movies but not The Movies. You have been part of a captive audience all your life. Love it or leave it. But even if 'they' permitted you to leave, there is no place to go. They own the airports. They own the telephones. They have seen to it that the pictures are everywhere."

Then there is the unanticipated market of video—of the worldwide rental or purchase of video versions of films, becoming, just as books had for a time, mass-market products. This fairly recent development has resulted in not merely the preservation of many of the films of the past, but, as well, in the simultaneity of the whole film backlist. This means, among other things, that films which were created for a brief, one-shot life in a greedy marketplace, films that were seen as expendable, are now risen from the dead for some form of afterlife. In that context, it is worth remembering that William Faulkner, a minor and part-time screenwriter, has several films on which he collaborated or to which he contributed that have become part of the list of film classics—certainly *The Southerner, The Big Sleep, To Have and Have Not, Air Force,* and others. Many full-time, life-time screenwriters cannot claim as much.

True, some of the value and attention accorded to Faulkner's films derives from the fact that he is a great master novelist and therefore everything he engaged in has special value and significance. But even so, these films have an interest and a value on their own. In that sense, Faulkner's dedication and integrity, devoted to what must have been a mostly onerous task, which in a way must have seemed foolish to his screenwriting contemporaries, paid off later in new and (for him) unimaginable ways. The best of his screenplays are well worthy of the artist who hired on as a salaried worker to do them.

(1990)

William Goyen's "Ghost and Flesh, Water and Dirt"

It is ironic that, for a number of reasons, William Goyen (1915–1983), one of the most original and innovative voices in twentieth-century fiction, especially the short story, should now need some words of introduction. Not that the man, poet, playwright (five produced plays), and editor (McGraw Hill), as well as fiction writer, and his work—six novels, five collections of stories, three other works—were or are unknown. Not by any means. In Europe, thanks in part to able and gifted translators, especially in France and Germany, his work has been highly honored and is widely studied. Here at home in America, aside from the many other writers who are on record as being his admiring readers, he early earned and has maintained the mixed blessings of a kind of cult status. In her perceptive introduction to Goyen's posthumous *Had I a Hundred Mouths: New & Selected Stories, 1947–1983*, Joyce Carol Oates celebrates the originality of his work ("A story by William Goyen is always immediately recognizable as a story by William Goyen"). And she focuses on the paradoxical conflicts out of which his singular method grew. How he is "the most mysterious of writers," she writes: "He is a poet, singer, musician as well as storyteller; he is a seer; a troubled visionary; a spiritual presence in a national literature largely deprived of the spiritual." On the one hand, he is lyrical and visionary. On the other, he is deceptively "artless": "So fluid and artless are the stories that they give the impression of being 'merely narratives of memory.'"

I like to think that William Goyen was a deep and altogether benign influence on me as a writer. As a reader, I first began reading him about the same time, 1946, that he began publishing stories in the *Southwest Review,* reading purely for the pleasure of it, he was for me a joyful discovery at just the time when I was discovering everything all at once. And over the long years, he has been a constant companion. The influence on my writing was always more a matter of exemplary inspiration than any kind of imitation. To the best of my knowledge and recollection, I have never written or even tried to write anything *like* William Goyen's work, though I surely envied him the options he exercised. Some writers open doors and windows for other writers. Others seem to help other writers just as much to find themselves by closing off certain possibilities. Goyen did what he did so well that it would have been folly to try to follow him closely. On the other hand, the full range and unique qualities of his voice challenge any writer to seek and find his own particular voice and variety.

I should add that besides helping me along in the never-ending quest to find my best voice and best subjects as a writer, besides affording me the richest pleasures as a reader, William Goyen was, briefly but strongly, a personal influence and example as well. He surprised me more than once by coming to readings I gave when he happened to be in the neighborhood. He filled in for me for a semester at Princeton when I had to be away, and as a teacher he was a great and good influence on some of my best and favorite students there, people like the young Madison Smartt Bell. Later, on turf that had once been my own, at Hollins College, he was more than helpful to young writers like Cathryn Hankla and Allen Wier.

Though rich in variety, his stories are all filled with his voice—the voice he created out of the common language of his East Texas tribe, and haunted by the selfsame music, a music he made out of the poetry of his place and his people. William Goyen was, after all, a composer who won awards for his music. And in any number of interviews, he has compared his stories to songs and invited the reader (and sometimes baffled critics) to think of his fiction as, among other things, music. In the preface to *The Collected Stories of William Goyen* (1975), he wrote: "I've cared about the buried song in somebody, and sought it passionately; or the music in what happened. And so I have thought of my stories as folk song, as ballad, or rhapsody." Each of his stories, dark or lighthearted, shares this kind of car-ing, and thus all are marked by an indelible identity. Everything he ever did, while always fresh and original, shares and demonstrates the qualities of his voice. There is nothing that Goyen allowed himself to publish that is in any way inferior, less than fascinating in ways and means, or insignificant in substance. I love his speakers, his people, ordinary East Texas folk riddled with extraordinary thoughts and feelings, speaking in a language that he first borrows directly from them, then returns enhanced by its essential poetry. My particular favorite has long been the title story of his first collection, "Ghost and Flesh, Water and Dirt." Part of my special interest and pleasure is derived from and heightened by the tape cassette recording I have (from American Audio Prose Library) of William Goyen reading this story, a tape I have often played for classes and workshops where students sat and listened closely with a rare, rapt attention, dazzled by his voice and the rhythm and music of it. I usually withhold the text until they have heard the story straight through, until they have *experienced* the story.

Not plotted in a conventional sense, "Ghost and Flesh, Water and Dirt" is a brief story covering most of the adult life of a woman, Margy, from a little Texas town, Charity (the imaginary version of Goyen's hometown Trinity). She is haunted by the ghost of her dead husband, Raymon Emmons, a railroad man who killed himself, and (as we learn) the ghost of their daughter Chitta, who was killed falling off a horse ("O I was broken of my sleep and of my rest disturbed"). At the urging insistence of her close friend, Fursta Evans, Margy goes off by train to California where, with World War II underway, she works "in an airplane factory," and where she meets a sailor, Nick Natowski, "a brown clean Pollock from Chicago, real wile, real Satanish," has a passionate love affair with him until he goes off to war and is lost at sea: "O what have I ever done in this world, I said, to send my soul to torment? Lost one to dirt and one to water, makes my life a life of mud." Goes back home to Texas and to a surprise: "Come back to this house, opened it up and aired it all out, and when I got back you know who was there in that house? That old faithful ghost of Raymon Emmons." A whole life, in fact several lives, in a few poetic pages, told to us in the resonant, credible voice of Margy. Who also, from first to last, considers the subject of telling life stories to each other: "Honey, why am I talkin' all this? Oh all our lives! So many things to tell." Abruptly, near the end, we discover that we are not eavesdropping on a dense first-person monologue but are being addressed directly as a particular person (ourselves a character in the story) in a particular place—"settin with you here in the Pass Time club, drinkin this beer and telling you all I've told." And Margy gratefully celebrates her life and offers us a closure, a kind of fairy-tale moral to the experience: "Us humans are part ghost and part flesh—part fire and part ash—but I think maybe the ghost part is the longest lastin, the fire blazes but the ashes last forever."

If Keats was right, where, in one of the letters, he said that poetry should surprise "by a fine excess," Goyen has written a folktale that moves into poetry. Goyen wears the skin and bones and knows the thoughts and feelings of Margy the way she says Nick Natowski was "tight as a glove in iz uniform." There is, in a complete engagement with character, humor but no cuteness, no hint or telltale stain of condescension (a very common flaw in contemporary short fiction). Nothing is wasted, no unnecessary gestures, yet it is in no way minimal. And in his mastery of the first-person narrative (it seems as easy as pie when Goyen does it, and it just isn't), he can build toward the kind of closure that the contemporary story and mind-set seldom allow.

Goyen loved the people he wrote about, and that is rare enough at any time; and he loved the form of the short story, how in a small room he could come to a great reckoning. Now he is a ghost himself, and we miss him and his way of doing things like nobody else, telling tales that nobody else can or does, speaking for people who seldom are listened to. But, like the ghost of Raymon Emmons—"All night long he uz talkin and talkin, his speech (whatever he uz sayin) uz like steam streamin outa the mouth of a kettle, streamin and streamin and streamin"—he speaks to us still and for as long as we can believe in the magic of words and books. "Ghost and Flesh, Water and Dirt," like the other twenty-five stories in *The Collected Stories of William Goyen*, does not need my endorsement, but I am honored and happy to recommend it to any reader (surely there are some somewhere) who is looking for something wonderful, original, and, yes, beautiful to experience. Think of this particular story as a gateway to his other work, an excellent introduction. After the experience and engagement and pleasure, his stories remain wonderful and strange. They are deeply simple and highly sophisticated, impeccably written line by line.

"Saw pore Raymon Emmons all last night, all last night seen im plain as day."

(2000)

New Market: The Cost and Waste of the War

You are cruising along the busy north-south route, Interstate 81 in Virginia, weaving among the big growling semis and the snowbirds coming or going. You are in the long valley running roughly between Winchester in the north and Lexington to the south, a beautiful patchwork of rich, rolling, fertile farmland between the aptly named Blue Ridge Mountains in the east and the dark hulking shapes of the Alleghenies to the west. (By custom from the days of the earliest settlers, you are going *up* the Valley if you are headed south and *down* if you are northbound.) Just north of Harrisonburg, you will flash past signs for Exit 264 for New Market, seeing a couple of steeples and a cluster of houses marking the town; and if anybody happens to be looking to the west of the highway, you can see a large, white two-story nineteenth-century farmhouse with its huddle of outbuildings, close by an orchard and a wide wheatfield, and, oddly inappropriate in the pastoral setting, a few high-wheeled antique cannons, some pointing north, the others south. House, field, and cannons mark the site of the Battle of New Market, which took place on May 15, 1864. It is a place that is well worth a stop and a good look around, wherever you may be going.

I have a friend, a writer, who possesses a kind of psychic divining rod, the same sort of intuitive sensitivity said to have been the gift of General George S. Patton. With or without signs and markers, she can tell a place that has been the scene of a battle, a killing ground, ancient or modern. I tend to believe that her gift (or curse, as the case may be) is a heightened form of the normal human reaction to the places where our history has left its mark. We find ourselves going, many thousands of us, to the sites of our great Civil War battles—to Gettysburg, Shiloh, Manassas, Fredericksburg, Antietam, etc.—subdued by the awesome quiet of these well-kept places, learning without quite believing the hard facts, the staggering numbers of the dead and wounded, the unimaginable noise and slaughter that swept over each place in its time like a firestorm. The New Market Battlefield Historical Park is special in a number of ways. It is manageably small, 280 acres, privately owned and maintained by Virginia Military Institute, and personal enough in the details of its story and in the artifacts that remain, carefully collected and elegantly displayed in the Hall of Valor Museum, and is able to have a powerfully direct impact on all but the most jaded or cynical sensibilities.

The connection with VMI is simple enough. The land was given to VMI by an alumnus, George Randall Collins, class of 1911. It was here that in 1864 the Corps of Cadets, average age seventeen, acted as reserves for the left of the lines of Confederate Major General John C. Breckenridge's outnumbered forces, who were stretched thin, roughly between the edges of Massanutton Mountain on the right to the two-hundred-foot cliffs overlooking the North Fork of the Shenandoah River. The cadets were ordered into combat for the first and only time during the war. True, the cadets had left the Institute from time to time to perform other, basically noncombatant duties—the drilling of recruits, guard duty, etc.; and some few of them had been in action before coming to VMI. But most of these boys had not until that rainy Sunday afternoon been placed in harm's way, under fire as a combat unit. Breckenridge had hoped not to use them at all, but the time came when he felt he had no choice. There was a dangerous gap in his line, and the cadets were all he had to fill it. "Put the boys in," he is reported to have said, "and may God forgive me for the order." In point of fact, some thirty-two cadets under Cadet Captain C. H. Minge had already been in action with the Confederate artillery, firing their two three-inch rifled cannons since early morning. But the bulk of the cadets, 226 of them, had been kept out of sight behind the lines. They had marched more than eighty miles from Lexington, beginning on the morning of May 11th, moving to the rhythm of a fife and drum. The first day, eighteen miles to Midway, was hot and dusty.

After that, it poured rain most of the time. They joined Breckenridge's forces on the evening of the second day at Staunton and were teased by the regulars. Musicians played "Rock-a-bye Baby" to greet them.

Now they were ordered to advance and, leaving their haversacks and coats behind, they came up and over a slight rise and into view and range of the Union forces on the high ground of Bushong's Hill. They moved with parade-ground precision, all wearing identical uniforms (rare that late in the war) and uniformly carrying long and almost antique Austrian muzzle-loading muskets. Their flag of white silk with the seal of Virginia at the center had not been seen by these Union forces before. For a moment, some of them thought that foreigners, possibly the French, had now joined the war against them.

You can walk the way they advanced, from the Hall of Valor Museum across a field of grass and clover, around the preserved farmhouse of Jacob and Sarah Bushong, and into the little orchard where Union artillery and rifle fire killed and wounded about one in four of the cadets (total casualties: 10 dead, 45 wounded). They were pinned down, hugging the earth behind the partial protection of a split-rail fence, then advanced again across a wheatfield and a muddy space now called the Field of Lost Shoes because so many cadets had their shoes pulled off by the deep mud, driving the Union forces off the high ground and capturing a cannon there. That was the end of it for the cadets, though the battle continued until dark and the Union forces retreated down the Valley. For better and worse, the war would continue for another year, and this battle was merely a small part of the big picture.

That smallness is part of the powerful impact of the New Market Battlefield Park. It is a short and leisurely walk of a few minutes now, all of it preserved and restored as it was and altogether of a size and scale to be fully imaginable. In the three levels of the Hall of Valor you can see things that belonged to young men with names, not numbers. You can see the grotesquely damaged rifle of Cadet Charles Henry Read, its barrel bent at a right angle from the shell burst that wounded him. You can see and read the final letter of Cadet J. B. Stanard to his family, written on the night of May 12th from Staunton, together with the telegram announcing his death. The sword carried by Cadet Benjamin Colonna is on display, as are the sketches by Cadet Moses Ezekiel, who lived to become a celebrated sculptor in Rome.

The names of the ten cadets who died there are part of a stained-glass window created for the Hall of Valor, and they are named and honored during an annual ceremony at VMI on May 15th. In the museum, there are photographs of a number of the cadets and of others like Eliza Clindenst Crim, a handsome woman of New Market who nursed the wounded of both sides.

Since 1988, there has also been the neighboring New Market Battlefield Military Museum (open from March 15 to December 1), the extraordinary personal collection of John M. Bracken, consisting of objects and memorabilia of American history from 1750 to the present and including materials from the Battle of New Market.

The experience of the battlefield and the museums is all on a small scale, deeply personal and undeniably real. We are haunted by the battlefields of our nation's short history, but nowhere does that haunting seem so profoundly simple as at New Market. The cost and waste of the Civil War, of all wars really, are clearly evident. And yet, perhaps a partial explanation of our continuing fascination with these places, the experience of the New Market Battlefield confirms another point of view as well, that of the war's survivors, as honored by the great Oliver Wendell Holmes in a Memorial Day speech of 1884: "The generation that carried on the war has been set aside by its experience. Through our great good fortune, in our youth our hearts were touched with fire. It was given to us to learn at the outset that life is a profound and passionate thing."

(1994)

The Death of Regional Writing

In 1980, a literary magazine at Wake Forest University sent out a letter—a letter with an interesting remark by Walker Percy—to a batch of southern writers and asked them to respond to it.

This is what Walker Percy said and what the editors of The Student *asked: "Walker Percy has said 'The day of Southern regional writing is all gone.' In view of the rapid assimilation of cultures within America, do you think regional writers still have a unique contribution to make? If so, how can such a contribution be made?"*

Nine writers sent back replies to this challenge: A. R. Ammons, Fred Chappell, Marion Montgomery, James Dickey, Staige Blackford, Andrew Lytle, Anne Tyler, George Garrett, and Robert Morgan.

Here is George Garrett's 1980 response to that query.

—J. C. M.

Mr. Percy is, in my opinion, a good man and a very intelligent and thoughtful man and a fine southern writer. I read everything he writes. I admire him and his works. I wish him well in everything.

But I think he is . . . well, uh, WRONG.

In one way, I *know* he's wrong, in the same way that another fine southern gentleman and writer, Robert Penn Warren, is wrong also, when (in "Under the Spell of Eudora Welty," *New York Times Book Review*, 2

March 1980) he praises the "special kind of conversational flow among Southern women," which, as he describes it, is narrative, anecdotal, etc.—"all the things that characterize 'a woman's talk.' . . ." He then goes on to say something, in this particular context, close to what Mr. Percy is saying: "Alas, the temper of our time has almost abolished that gift from the Southern female tongue. I now hear it in no one younger than fifty—and rarely that young—nor the imagination, sensibility, wit, humor, mimicry and pity that usually go with it." My answer to this is that *of course* there will never be another writer like Miss Welty. Every good and worthy writer—and we have had many good and worthy writers, men and women, in the South—is unique. Irreplaceable. But every good and worthy writer lives on in the words themselves, simultaneously and for as long as we have a language and a literature. Furthermore, every good and worthy writer has a direct and beneficial influence upon the good and worthy writers of the next generation.

There are many, not a few, young women in the South today who are writing in the grand tradition that Warren celebrates, yet also in their own voices.

Just so, judging only by the anthologies coming along and by the magazines and the news from the many and growing writing programs all through the South, there are many, not a few, very gifted young southern writers who have not heard—and probably wouldn't believe it if they heard it, even from Mr. Percy in person—that "the day of Southern regional writing is all gone." These young writers are already making their marks and will continue to do so. Their nostalgia may be every bit as real as that of their elders, but it is and will be different.

It is no wonder, and finally not important, that writers as distinguished and busy as, say, Mr. Percy or Mr. Warren don't know who these people are or what they may be up to. What is much more important, undeniably important, is that the young writers know very well who Mr. Percy and Mr. Warren are and what *they* are doing. And both these writers are a real, possibly profound influence on the young, though the young are not apt to settle for simply *imitating* them (or anybody else).

So my first reply to Mr. Percy's statement, allowing for the fact that what he means by "regional writing" may be either a very strict and specific definition or a very personal one, is that the present literary situation in the

South (and elsewhere, for southerners are as mobile as everyone else) proves him wrong.

But I would disagree with him even if there were not impressive numbers of young, clearly and unequivocally southern writers writing today. I would say that, in any case, there will be a distinctly southern literature to express and reflect the facts of a distinctly, and probably increasingly different, southern way of life.

A considerable, and very impressive, body of important thinkers believes and argues that throughout the entire world the most powerful force at work is the breakdown of large political and social units into small ones. The great nation states, even Russia and the United States, are threatened with radical internal change, both political and social, indeed even geographical. Danger, from each other, is holding the two big superpowers together, more or less. Meantime, there isn't a country or nation state in the world that is not dividing into separate and distinct parts of itself. In many cases, this division is accompanied by turbulence and bloodshed. Within the U.S., thanks to freedom and mobility, commendable changes are taking place swiftly and fairly quietly.

Large population movements. People are staying in the South, when they are able to. Many others are moving there, and not just for the climate and the weather. It is the life and the life-style that appeal to them. Just so, many people are cheerfully moving up here, to upper New England, where I am now living. The weather is savage; the life is quite wonderful. And not widely or deeply different from the South—because the same people, kinfolks and cousins really, settled here. Especially in Maine.

I am here because my wife's grandmother, who lived here until she was ninety-eight, died and we inherited this beautiful little house on the coast by a river. This area was always popular with southerners. Sidney Lanier used to vacation here. Direct descendants of Lanier live down the road. Mark Twain built and spent summers in a beautiful house on a bluff above the river about a half-mile upstream from my house. Also, Calder Willingham, a wonderful southern writer, lives over in New Hampshire, as does John Yount.

My children are southern by upbringing. Have lived all over the South. Have a rich and intricate network of kinfolk there. Yet, on their mother's side, they become the fifth generation of that family to live in this town, in this house.

Enough about me.

It's just that my situation is not untypical.

People move and live, in contemporary America, for many reasons. But there is a large element of *choice*. They choose to join a way of life. Like converts, then, they are apt to be more conservative and defensive of their acquired ways and habits of life than the native-born.

Today, the South is finally growing in population and in prosperity, while the great cities of the East rapidly decline in population and hover on the edges of bankruptcy. Indeed, without rich infusions of tax dollars from the South, the "Sunbelt," many of these cities would quickly go under.

New York is on its last legs, even as a so-called cultural center. Which has become its last leg. At the moment, the New York cultural elite is fighting a ruthless and savage rearguard action. Scorched earth is their policy. In literature, they deliberately and carefully ignore all but a few pet southern writers. They are pretending that young southern poets, novelists, story writers, etc., do not exist. They are wrong. And they know it.

In a fairly short time, it seems likely that different parts and cities in the South will (again) be publishing and cultural centers, able to sustain and support a creative culture.

What I am saying is that "the rapid assimilation of cultures in America" is more apparent than real. That, in fact, regions are becoming more distinct and, in many ways, more separate.

Given a period of peace and plenty, the U.S. would very soon resemble a modern version of the Confederate States of America.

Let me add something.

Precisely because I *am* a southerner, I believe that places are enchanted. Rich with spirits. All houses, sooner or later, are haunted.

So, if it's any consolation—and it *ought* to be, you know, no matter what happens, war, plague, flood, or fire—if we are all gone and you and I and Miss Welty and Mr. Warren and Mr. Walker Percy all vanish (equally) leaving no jot or tittle, no trace behind to prove we were ever here, and if we are replaced by survivors, strangers (most likely Chinese, if you trust statistics, but maybe distant and humble people like, for instance, pygmies, or Eskimos, or Bushmen, or even Abominable Snowmen), these people will feel the enchantment and the haunting much as we do and they will reflect and express this in a literature. For since they have language, they have and will have literature—oral or written or both, no matter. This literature will, inevitably and invariably, be southern. I have to believe that because I am a southerner.

I believe it would be the case even if everybody on earth were wasted and blown away. Martians (or somebody) would eventually land and live here and become southerners. Different, but the same, too.

I think—and I offer this thought for Mr. Percy—that the *only* imaginable place where regionalism is gone for good is Heaven. There are no regions in Heaven.

Otherwise, we, and all who come after, are stuck with them.

So the contribution will be much the same, however different in terms or degrees, as it has always been. For instance, a love of language (from rhetoric to lingo) for its own sake; a love of storytelling; a strong sense of blood kinship and family and thus of heritage, of history; a love of the land, of nature, then.

Now, we may change the forms, the ways and means, in the future. Who knows what form the storytelling of the future will take?

I don't know *how* the contribution can be made. Just that it *will be made.*

I am convinced that the South has contributions to make not just to the nation, but to the world. One of these contributions is cultural. One of these cultural contributions is literature.

Any suggestions? Well, I wish more southern readers—I wish there *were* more southern readers—would make an effort to know and to read and to support some of their own writers, the Unknown as well as the Known.

At the moment, the business of being "known" is conferred from elsewhere, from the dying cultural center in New York and not from our own region and people. Because we are polite, we follow the advice (might as well call it the Commandments) of others.

We are probably at the end of many superficial aspects of our southern way of life (and art). The essential things, the enchanting and haunting aspects, will not change.

I am bold enough to think that *that*, in itself, is a southern message. Very regional.

Of course, I'd be lying if I didn't admit that I think Mr. Percy was probably kidding around, in very southern fashion, very traditionally, trying to stir things up a little.

I guess he did.

(1980)

Soil of Hope: New and Other Voices in Southern Fiction for the Nineties

It is more a matter of accident and circumstance than anything else, but no matter how it came to pass, over the past year or so I have been busy putting together four separate anthologies of contemporary short fiction, not to mention all the usual amount of reviewing, editing, judging, and writing some criticism during the same period. I announce this chiefly in order to claim that I am up to my eyebrows in new southern fiction by new southern writers, some of them brand-new names to me and some of them not.

Do I detect any trends? That is always the first question that pops up. Trends have become the lifeblood of all kinds of literary journalism, which form of journalism is becoming more and more the heart of the matter in what passes for literary criticism these days. Answer: maybe so and maybe not. It is all too close and too confused for me to be able to arrive at any happy generalizations yet. Except for this one—that it seems pretty clear that the conventional and accepted descriptions of literary reality, in this specific case the outline and general characteristics of southern fiction as it continues to endure into the first decade of the twenty-first century, are mostly inadequate and often inaccurate. A whole lot more is going on right now than is dreamt of by the usual crew of critics and scholars, literary historians, and, yes, publishers.

This final category, the publishers, is an important one, for as the marketable chances of "serious" and "literary" fiction continue to dwindle and diminish, it is the publishers alone who are empowered to turn their particular picture of reality, no matter how distorted or illusory, into a self-fulfilling prophecy. As publishers of every kind can and have done ever since the military defeat of the Confederacy, they are able to make of southern literature whatever they please by publishing only those things that please them and conform to their preconceived views. Did you seriously imagine that *readers* have anything much to do with the process? Teachers, scholars, and critics can confirm this. Even when they are not serving as the shills and barkers for the sideshow of the literary establishment, even if they should sincerely make an effort to be both honest and thorough, still they can only deal with whatever the publishers give them.

I think it would be a swell idea for all the teachers and scholars and critics of southern letters to be required to put together at least a couple of anthologies of new southern fiction. Of poetry too.

On a level and pristine playing field, they (and you) would find that whereas the essential, traditional mainstream of southern literature continues—actually, it has been two streams all along, the straight guys (Agrarians, Fugitives, some of the good boys from Duke like Styron and Price, et al.) versus the off-the-wall-and-the-charts gang (Caldwell and Faulkner, Willingham and O'Connor, and, say, the wild and woolly guys from Duke like Mac Hyman and Fred Chappell), even so there are a lot of new and very gifted southern writers whose work is not so easily recognized and labeled. These people, coming from all available genders and races and even ages, are not, except in the closed minds of certain rigid editors and publishers, *outside* the southern tradition. But they have added a genuine sophistication arising from familiarity with world literature and, as well, from a self-awareness about their own tradition that allows them to distinguish between a cliché and a convention, a hawk and a handsaw.

Above all, the new southern writers are blithely and gracefully eclectic. They can be boldly, sometimes wildly experimental when they want to be or have to be. But they can also write very solid "straight" fiction if and when the spirit moves them to or the material they are using requires it. They can do it all, and they don't see any good reason to inhibit themselves.

Who are some of these people? Well, some of them are reasonably well known, people like Richard and Robert Bausch, Madison Smartt Bell, Kelly Cherry, Percival Everett, Al Young, and Allen Wier, for example. Others (they are many, but here are a few among them whose work keeps coming out, come what may) are less well known at this precise moment, but well deserve to be better known, people like Darcey Steinke, Tom Whalen, Dana Gibson, Dale Phillips, Anita Thompson, Cedric Tolley, Megan Gehman, Cathryn Hankla, Alyson Hagy, Judith Hawkes, Lolis Elie, and Randall Kenan.

The exemplary master of this powerful third force in southern fiction is R. H. W. Dillard of Hollins University. A scholar and critic himself, he is also a poet and the author of a good number of short stories and two very important and influential novels—*The Book of Changes* (1974) and *The First Man on the Sun* (1983). Dillard is also author of several prize-winning novellas, including "The Bog: A Naturalist's Notebook" and "The Road: A Story of Social Significance." These are master examples of the new southern fiction. The most recent work by him that I have seen is "That's What I Like (About the South)" (1992), a long, very funny story that serves, by savage demonstration, as a kind of manifesto for new southern writing, setting up as its seven-part structure the seven pontifical points made by (straight) southern editor Shannon Ravenel to define authentic southern literature. All seven points are deftly demolished once and for all in a story featuring characters who just won't sit still and be obedient to their self-proclaimed betters. Like the characters in the Dillard story, these writers are too many, too diverse, and too rich in energy to be kept away forever from the banquet table of the feast where writers and readers finally get to meet and to break bread together.

It has been exciting to discover that there is so much more to living southern literature than meets the eye. There is so much more variety than anyone has noticed or admitted. As the late John Ciardi once wrote (for *Contemporary Literary Scene II*, 1976): "In art, variety is always the soil of hope."

(1995)

The Ordways by William Humphrey

The Ordways belongs to the type of the chronicle, the remembered history of a family and of a place. But this record of memory becomes by suggestion and implication a type for something larger, the whole history and direction of the nation and, beyond that, of the land and its people, known and unknown, living and dead. Among other ventures and achievements in this form, William Humphrey's novel might be compared with John Cheever's two novels, *The Wapshot Chronicle* and *The Wapshot Scandal;* or it might be considered in analogy with Mary Lee Settle's *Beulah Quintet*. Historically, these in turn can be seen as deriving from the influence and example of the various works of, for example, Faulkner, T. S. Stribling, and Katherine Anne Porter. Yet with a difference, for the writers of the earlier generation were, like first-hand historians, recording and preserving a story before it could be lost in the shuffle and clamor of our times. They were in a sense bearing witness to our history. For writers of this generation, there is a different purpose and with it a different problem. They must approach the subject more as the historian who is richly blessed with secondary sources, always conscious that others have been there before, that the territory has been mapped and surveyed and to a degree settled. They come not as pioneers, then, but as settlers. They must preserve not only the history of the land and its tribes, but also the work of those who have gone before them. The surprising thing, however, is that this venture has appealed to so many of the younger writers, those who came to maturity in the years following World War II. For the times they have been living in and through have been characterized by a radically high value of the new for its own sake, by an impatience with and indifference to tradition, custom, and precedent as inadequate guides to the raw new experience of urbanization, the Cold War, the Space Age, and a multitude of undreamed-of problems and miscellaneous "breakthroughs." All of the arts, part and parcel of the world they come from, have placed high premium on and permitted great rewards for novelty. The traditional has, in general, been looked upon as suspect. Thus for an artist to choose to work deliberately within the terms and conditions of a tradition, particularly one that captured the imagination of contemporary masters, is to choose a career of danger and daring. Nevertheless, many of our finest writers have chosen precisely that direction. While others, perhaps the majority, remain deeply concerned with finding the ways and means of capturing the quality of contemporary life as it is (or seems to be), a considerable number have turned back to history, archaeologists digging for shards and fragments, looking for clues from the haunting past. One thinks of the fiction of Robert Penn Warren, of the fiction and the history of Shelby Foote, of William Styron's *Confessions of Nat Turner,* of Thomas Berger's brilliant re-creation of the myth of the Old West in *Little Big Man,* of Bernard Malamud's turn to history in *The Fixer.* Paradoxically, at just the time when all the world seems new and strange, if not very brave, a good many writers of our times have turned away from one function, that of prophet and seer, to another equally ancient and honorable one, that of custodian and retailer of the great old stories of the tribe.

It is in scope and size that *The Ordways* becomes a chronicle, an account of one family for several generations. The remarkable thing about this book is that this sense of scope and size is achieved by sleight of hand. It *appears* to be much larger than it is. Both *Wapshot* volumes and each of the books of the *Beulah Quintet* are, in fact, longer books. The effect of density, of almost epic scope, is gained by having the story told, in fact *written by,* a narrator, our contemporary, one of the Ordway clan. Seemingly unconcerned with characterizing himself, he nonetheless reveals himself without either arrogance or inhibition. He is not and does not conceive of himself as extraordinary. We can trust him. We can accept his judgments and need not quarrel with his values. He becomes a kind of chorus, then, his own voice, sane, intelligent, good humored and yet deeply concerned, recorded in a style that, if "literary," is neither stilted nor extravagant, his voice becoming a valid one, inviting the reader to join in. By imaginative involvement, the reader is drawn in, becomes a part of the chorus rather than a passive spectator. So much of the story is evocation that in large part it is the reader who invests the story with its weight and dimension. Moreover, the judicious use of this attractive narrator, sometimes narrating, sometimes commenting or proposing or explicating, permits a freedom within the context of the story to break the bonds of narrative without breaking the spell. The narrator can become historian as well. He writes essays, in fact, on a variety of subjects—North and South, the Civil War, the Westward Expansion—and combines these with a brilliant rendition of surfaces and with the age-old and untarnished device of epic lists and celebration.

Technically, the book is a masterwork, beginning with "graveyard working day" in Mabry, Texas, an annual custom that brings together all the living members of a family to repair and restore the graves of their ancestors, and in fact never quite leaving that day. Only a closer look reminds the reader that "graveyard working day" is the only present action of the entire novel, that all the rest comes from the past and comes directly out of that scene, indelibly set in the first part of the book, "In a Country Churchyard." The tone and terms of the whole story are set here. And here we are given what is perhaps the most powerful story of the whole chronicle, the story of how Thomas Ordway, blinded and terribly wounded at Shiloh, came, through incredible difficulties together with his wife and family, all the way from Tennessee to East Texas, bringing with him among other things the remains and gravestones of his ancestors. It is a story that *alludes to* without deferring to *As I Lay Dying*. Behind it are all the great epic journeys completed in spite of overwhelming odds and difficulties. This story is raw, brutal, primitive, an account of pride and the indomitable human spirit, and it comes within the context of a quietly discursive, almost casual chapter. Coming, as it does, at the outset, it dominates the rest of the story, casting a long shadow, becoming a memory for the reader against which to measure the events that follow. Though they skip and jump in time, gracefully to be sure, the remaining three sections are built around the story of the narrator's grandfather, Sam Ordway, and his efforts through a lifetime to recover his lost son, Ned, only son of his first wife, stolen away by a neighbor family who quite simply vanished one day. The long middle section of the book, "Sam Ordway's Revenge," moves from the epic to the picaresque, becoming a tall tale of the Old West, a chiefly comic and often hilarious account of Sam Ordway's difficulties and failure to find his son. We move from "frontier" to "backwoods." Mark Twain's ghost is summoned and smiles on this account. The final section, "Family Reunion," is just that. Ned, after being a symbol to one and all for years, suddenly reappears to lead the whole family, on the spur of the moment, on a long pilgrimage West to visit his remote sheep ranch. Ned ceases to be a symbol and becomes, however different, a character, a real and dimensional human being. And somehow the family is reunited in love and joy. Old scars do not disappear, but old wounds, even those most terrible ones of the westering pioneer, Thomas Ordway, become less awesome. Beginning in elegy, the story ends in joy, and it is at the ending that the narrator becomes a witness to events. Quite properly, then, at the very end, in the final sentence of the book, the whole story becomes *his* story and so ours as well: "But it was a long way from Clarksville, no matter by what means you traveled, and as I waved back to my Uncle Ned and watched him grow small, I knew in my heart that it would be a long time that I might even have to be my own man and could come out by myself before I saw him and his part of the world again, and so I was."

The Ordways is William Humphrey's finest and most ambitious novel so far. *Home from the Hill,* for all its power and success, was derivative, for he had not escaped the vocabulary and the technical devices of his literary influences. It would seem that at that point Humphrey had a choice: to find his own voice, he could turn his back on the ghosts of the past; or he could, a much more arduous task, come to know them better, in love and appreciation, finding his way, becoming his "own man" with all the aid and comfort they can offer. He chose the latter way, and here he proves it in a novel that in itself tells the story of how we all can come to terms with the past, not by denying or ignoring it, but by accepting it in love and honor.

(1966)

Cassandra Singing by David Madden

Outwardly, the elements of this novel seem to be familiar: the struggling of a family to endure within the confines of a dying small town, a place of dying hopes and a withering industry (coal mining); the struggle of the youngest of the McDaniels, Lone and Cassie, to become something, somebody. In the beginning, Lone lives for the thrill and speed of his motorcycle and lives in love and awe of Boyd Weaver. Cassie, confined to her bed, lives on memories and for the vicarious experiences shared with her by Lone. And she in turn shares with him the secrets of her imagination, part memory and part prophecy. They are lonesome, "alienated" youth, sharing their loneliness. And even that is fragile and threatened, for they are surrounded by a troubled family and haunted by ghosts. But if the ingredients of the story, as predicated at the outset, seem familiar, the compounding of them in the context of this novel works a kind of alchemy whereby familiar things become first fresh and renewed, then, at the last, altogether new and strange. An inexorable sequence of events—the homecoming and death of Uncle Virgil, the dynamiting of a coal tipple, for which Lone is jailed—leads Lone and Cassie to change places. Lone becomes the shut-in and the dreamer, renouncing his old way of life. "Saint Lone," he is called sarcastically. Cassie, in Lone's clothes, goes out into the world singing folk and gospel tunes on the radio and riding behind Boyd Weaver on his motorcycle. This condition changes, too, when a series of brutal revelations of naked truth leaves Lone and Cassie literally naked to each other and as alone together at the end as they were in the beginning. They are not so much changed by experience as *changing*.

There is a natural ease and grace, so simple as to be almost completely deceptive, in the author's method. His technique is that of a virtuoso. Outwardly, the story is a direct third-person narration told from Lone's point of view, shown dramatically in related scenes, dialogue, and through the alert senses of Lone. The surfaces of the story are clear, crisp, and evocative, as in "realistic" fiction. It is no surprise that the book has been bought by the movies. Madden can sketch a scene with elegant exactitude, as, for example, in this long-deferred view of the interior of the Gold Sun Café, much discussed earlier but seen by Lone (and the reader for the first time) after Lone's release from jail:

> The row of counter stools, almost all the plastic seats split, was empty, Behind the cigar and candy case, surrounded by rubber plants and a greenscummed aquarium, sat the Greek, as he had sat the first day Lone ever saw him, when Momma had come back to work for him for a few months, behind the cash register on a high stool, his feet jacked up, one hand stuffed in his filthy white jacket, the other resting lightly on the cracked marble shelf above his register drawer, a cigar butt dead in a corner of his clenched teeth. Like a man tending a still, he sat at the register waiting for the bead. He didn't move. Lone usually spoke, but the Greek never answered, though Momma used to report good things he said about Lone in the days before he began to run with Boyd. The three fans, hanging from the ceiling, moved slowly. Empty of people, the place seemed occupied by its various sources of light: the Pet Milk clock over the swinging doors to the kitchen, the advertising gadgets for beer and Royal Crown, the jukebox, the windows of the refrigerators, the high-mounted television, quietly snowing.

The landscape of eastern Kentucky becomes, through carefully limned and accumulating bits and pieces, a whole greater than the sum of its parts, harsh, hard, bleak, but strangely beautiful. The elements of time—what's playing at the movies, conventional brand names, how Cassie and Lone listened to *The Shadow* and *The Lone Ranger* once upon a time, how Dillinger once passed through Harmon—are created with precision, hand in glove with the sense of place.

Cassandra Singing may well be made into a fine film, but at least half of the quality of the book will be lost in the translation, which is curious when it would appear to be quite simple to translate and adapt. The essential quality that will have to be missing is the profound sense of the inner life of the characters. This inner life is consistently and precisely shown, too; indeed, it is dramatized, but not at all by conventional means where what is outward and visible serves as a sign of the inward and spiritual. In one sense, there is a constant conflict between the two levels, and they do not seem to relate. Boyd Weaver has the last word (it seems) when he beats and humiliates Lone: "But people that don't know us could look at us and not see no difference, though. Turn yourself inside out, Lone, so ever'body can see how pure you are! You need some way for ever'body to see the difference between me and you."

And this is true, part of the truth, the truth of a world in which the lives of all these people, though pathetic, are small and insignificant, their victories few and far between, their defeats continuous, their dignity deeply threatened. Nevertheless, each and all possess great dignity. And it is Lone, having endured the worst, who has the final word on the conflict and confusion of appearance and reality in the last scene when he strips Cassie, then strips himself:

> "Now look, damn it, I'm naked, too, see?"
> "Yeah, I see."
> "Well, so what?"
> "Nothin.'"
> "That's right. Nothin'."

But this is a moment of truth, which means everything. What they see is nothing, changes nothing. Yet at that instant everything changes. Change, which has been revealed as always the bright swift essence of their separate and equal lives, assumes command. These two can be and become at last not different from themselves and neither outer nor inner, but a wedding of both.

One of the things this book is "about" is transformation, how all living things are constantly changing shape and form, how living beings constantly change and exchange identity, through love and hate, without somehow losing what is unique and original. The title is singularly apt. For though this is basically Lone's story, it is also, properly, Cassandra's song. And the two become, gradually and finally , one and the same, marvelous in mystery. It is, then, a story without answers. Just as the everyday things, composed of convention, cliché, and nostalgia, are made new again, so there can be no *solution,* no ending to a story that celebrates the mystical union of flesh and spirit, partaking of the energy of life and time, which is change. It is afterward that the resonance of the whole story (like the noises of engines Lone could listen to and picture until the last sounds faded) reminds the reader that there was a transformer here behind the scenes, a magician whose sleight of hand has served one great purpose—the celebration of magic itself.

David Madden has proved himself to be a first-rate critic as well as a novelist and story writer. But he is a rare example of wholeness in that the critical discipline and act have not inhibited his power as creator. Instead, it seems to have liberated him, to have helped him find his own voice and way. Which direction he may go in the future remains to be seen. All that can be said is that, clearly, he can go anywhere. For the present, *Cassandra Singing* is full and sufficient cause for celebration, a triumph of the storyteller's art and craft.

(1970)

Crime and Punishment in Kansas: Truman Capote's *In Cold Blood*

1.

The book will be a classic.
—TRUMAN CAPOTE, *quoted in* Life

Maybe it will be. One thing for sure, it's bound to be a formidable success. This book makes its appearance with all the rockets, whistles, and fireboat fanfare usually reserved for the welcome of a brand-new ocean liner on its maiden voyage. Publicity, Promotion, Advertising, and the Sales Campaign are as massive and impressive as the Front Four of the Green Bay Packers. *In Cold Blood* has already been successfully and expensively serialized in the *New Yorker*. It is a Book-of-the-Month Club selection. Paperback rights and apparently movie rights are cut and dried and extravagant. It is already what they call a Big Package Deal. None of this, however, can in any way influence or affect the author's characteristic and disarmingly direct claim for his work, nor should it influence any critic's judgment of it. It would be easy to leap to the occasion and go off barking down the wrong trail, to ridicule the crude claims and clumsy commerce of the publishing world. That would be wrong and a waste of time. Publishers are not interested in "classics," except, of course, in the extremely profitable enterprise of publishing editions and reprints of long-since-accepted, tried-and-true works by decently dead authors. No, from the publishing point of view, *In Cold Blood* is a "major" book. As such, it is receiving the first-class major-book treatment. One cannot ignore this entirely, for it is not intended to be overlooked. One purpose, though not the most important by any means, of the major-book treatment is to overawe the reviewers and critics who are susceptible to demonstrations of affluence and, if possible, to spike the guns of those who can recognize real power when they see it. It is a waste of time both ways, however, for *In Cold Blood* is an excellent book and will no doubt be treated as such by even the most rebellious reviewers. All the to-do is irrelevant. Nor, for that matter, can Truman Capote's separate but equal career history as a "living legend," a type of celebrity, be permitted to add or detract from anything, except insofar as his notoriety and station may seem to be to the point, as, for example, as measurement of his veracity as a reporter or validity as a witness.

It has been a good twenty years since Truman Capote's first novel, *Other Voices, Other Rooms*, established him simultaneously and with wit and grace as a gifted writer, a successful one, and a colorful enough personality to merit the attentions of celebrity. The remarkable thing is that he has kept his gift demonstrably alive and kicking. Although he could not by any standards be called a prolific writer, he has continued to create, the steady and regular production of a good professional. From the first, his work has received and continues to receive considerable critical attention, most of it favorable. As a writer, he has continued to grow, change, and develop without the vice of obvious repetition, and at the same time he has managed to preserve and consolidate his place in the literary establishment. This is no mean feat in recent American literary history. (Whatever happened to Speed Lamkin anyway?) The distinction of his efforts is solidly attested to by his most recent book, *Selected Writings*. Excluding the poets, this is a rare thing, the kind of thing reserved for those writers whose reputation is firmly established in the literary sense and secure enough commercially to merit a publisher's interest in things literary.

All of which leads to a genuinely praiseworthy fact about *In Cold Blood*. The book is, flatly and without question, his biggest, boldest, most serious, most difficult, and best-written work—which is saying a great deal. In many ways, it is his most vital and interesting work, and certainly it is the most ambitious and risky. It is more, then, than a good book by a good writer. It is more than a demonstration of growth, power, and promise for the future. It is a frank bid for greatness. A great many of our serious writers would and indeed have settled for a good deal less than what Capote has already done and earned for himself—a long season of honorable and sustained creativity blessed with the fortunate comforts of recognition and an assured place in the literary hierarchy. Capote deserves great praise for doing this book. His action is exemplary.

Starting with a frankly brutal and sordid subject, one that could just as easily have languished in the pages of *True Detective* and *Police Action,* he has brought together his gifts and powers, already demonstrated separately, as a storyteller and as a reporter, to tell "A True Account of a Multiple Murder and Its Consequences." Using his gifts for a controlled and charged language and a beautiful style to advantage, he has arranged the telling, the sequence of related events, in such a way that the reader is compelled to share the whole urgent experience. Building around a conventional, four-part classical structure, he manages to keep suspense at a very high level throughout. The first three sections race along, breathlessly yet easily, moving back and forth between murderers and victims and, later, between the hunters and the hunted, without strain, always allowing for great freedom of time and space, for the metaphorically relevant digression, the superb use of the tricky flashback, permitting profoundly realized and dimensional characterization, and, not least, a cumulative, haunting evocation of place. In the final section, with the killers at last caught, devoted to their trial and punishment, we see the work of a virtuoso, for at this point the *original* suspense has been dissipated and the conclusion is obligatory. As Capote's artful arrangement of the story proves, he could easily have avoided this challenge had he wished to, for there is no such thing as inevitability in the structure of a story. It is the sign of a real storyteller that he makes his arrangement *seem* inevitable. Capote not only performs this magic trick, but he also manages to reach his own chosen and obligatory conclusion without a weakening of either intensity or interest. I can think of very few writers, living or dead, who could have done this.

These qualities and others in *In Cold Blood* may seem even more remarkable to readers who have followed Capote's earlier work. He has always been known as a distinguished stylist and as an imaginative storyteller, but he has not previously shown a great deal of interest in the possibilities of innovative arrangement. He has not been a technical experimenter. In the past, he has been conservative technically. And though he has created a rich gallery of interesting and memorable characters in his fiction, he has never until now displayed such ability to handle a large number of characters, all of whose lives and fortunes are intricately and subtly interrelated, and to treat them with depth and understanding. There are true moments of unveiling, of startling revelation. Before this, he had seemed content to offer a kind of fan dance, showing only glimpses, and then chiefly by the allusive method of signs, clues, hints, and symbols. Here the chief characters are stripped. If what is exposed is yet another veiled mystery, that is itself a profound revelation. It is exactly the kind of thing he seemed to be sidestepping in his other work. And, no getting around it, *In Cold Blood* is fundamentally a blood-and-guts story. Truman Capote's previous accomplishments have a great many virtues, and they have been acknowledged and praised, but nobody has ever accused him of being a blood-and-guts writer.

The fact is that he has been most frequently and conveniently labeled as a writer of romances, of the school of Poe and Hawthorne, a fabulist. There is a certain accuracy in this label. In *Radical Innocence,* Ihab Hassan sums up the general consensus this way: "The idea of romance, informed by the modern techniques of dream symbolism and analysis, suggests the general quality of Capote's work." Hardly a recommendation for a job of police reporting. Not a hint of the author's ability to deal honestly and powerfully with the brutal murder of a Kansas farm family. Certainly no indication that he could be trusted to report on such an event.

In Cold Blood is classic in the sense that it is an addition to the ancient and immemorial genre of the tale of crime and punishment that has fascinated writers and readers for as long as there have been any. In that sense, it stands as an important book. It is as "major" as any publisher or critic could ask. Whether or not it will end up as *a* classic, only time and the wheel of fortune will tell. However, by all rights it demands to be judged and must be judged by the highest standards. When this happens, the standards of "good writing" are vestigial, assumed but irrelevant.

2.

> *It's what I really think about America. Desperate, savage, violent America in collision with sane, safe, insular even smug America—people who have every chance against people who have none.*
> —TRUMAN CAPOTE, *quoted in* McCall's

No matter how different superficially *In Cold Blood* may seem to be from Capote's earlier work, both fiction and nonfiction, it is rooted in that work.

It exists as part of the context of all his work. Never mind for the moment that it is billed as an adventure in "a serious new literary form; the Nonfiction Novel." No one except the people directly concerned, those who are still alive, is competent to pass judgment on its final validity as *reportage*. That, too, is a false scent, a wrong trail. It must be seen always as a story, though always as a true one.

The marked difference between Capote's fiction and *In Cold Blood* ironically works to make the relationship between them more evident. In his three novels and his short stories, whether written in his "nocturnal" or "daylight" manner (as critics have seen fit to classify his work), Capote has indeed written a certain kind of romance or fable. For all their truth and decorative detail, both *Other Voices, Other Rooms* and *The Grass Harp* take place in a never-never land, a kind of no-man's land deliberately isolated from at least the world of "realistic" fiction, and even if the New York of *Breakfast at Tiffany's* is a real place, the central character, the marvelous Miss Holiday Golightly, is as extraordinary and magical as, say, Bellow's Henderson in *Henderson, the Rain King*. Moreover, she, unlike Henderson, is seen at one remove, filtered through the consciousness of a writer-narrator. One of the characteristics of the story that does not depend on apparent surface credibility or verisimilitude, whether it is fable pure and simple or romance, is that it has always been preeminently a *moral* tale, from Aesop until now. This is inevitable, since attention is by rhetorical consent and agreement diverted from what happened to what is being said. Classical and medieval rhetoricians, too often ignored at present, dealt with this kind of writing in all its possible forms in great detail. It was recognized as more directly *allegorical,* in the widest and deepest sense of that word, than work with what we might think of as realistic surface. On the simplest level, this merely means that though foxes, jackasses, and lions don't really talk to each other, what they have to say to each other in a fable and what they do may have truth and meaning. In a romance like *Other Voices, Other Rooms,* it means that nightmarish, grotesque, and surrealistic things may happen and be meaningful, that Joel Knox, Zoo, Randolph, Jesus Fever, Miss Wisteria, and all the others may suffer wounds, but the wounds are not real. Collin Fenwick, Dolly, Catherine, Judge Cool, and the others in *The Grass Harp* are more obviously involved in a social world. The world comes up against them where they sit, happy outcasts in a tree house, but again their triumphs and their suffering are seen at the little distance of romance. The effect is, by definition, allegorical and moral. Holly Golightly seems to be vaguely conscious of her own allegorical function when she defines it: "Good? Honest is more what I mean. Not low-type honest—I'd rob a grave, I'd steal two-bits off a dead man's eyes if I thought it would contribute to the day's enjoyment—but unto-thyself-type honest. Be anything but a coward, a pretender, an emotional crook, a whore: I'd rather have cancer than a dishonest heart." So, while apparently asserting a position beyond ordinary *morals*, she defines as honestly her own morality, her own clear sense of good and evil.

Even though each of these works is quite different, all have the outlines of a fairly clear, consistent, and conventional moral framework—conventional in the literary sense, which is to say unconventional only if measured against what are, again conventionally, thought to be the basic accepted standards of American middle-class morality. In each of the books, it is the outsiders and the outcasts who are, by virtue of their disengagement from worldly values, the examples of goodness. Those who seem to get along well in the "real" world—that is, the world of practical affairs—are exposed as either deceitful or self-deceived. It is they who work mischief and cause trouble, usually invoking the name of conventional morality; and in the end, thanks to the operation of a whimsical kind of poetic justice, they usually get what's coming to them. "Safe, sane, insular," long before that knockout punch "smug" comes along, these adjectives glisten like black hats on horse-opera bad guys to anyone who has ever read Truman Capote.

From the first, then, we shiver for the Clutters, fearing their fate, because they are such natural victims. You just know Mr. Clutter when he is first described: "Though he wore rimless glasses and was of but average height, standing just under five feet ten, Mr. Clutter cut a man's-man figure. His shoulders were broad, his hair had held its dark color, his square-jawed, confident face retained a healthy-hued youthfulness, and his teeth, unstained and strong enough to shatter walnuts, were still intact." There's more, but anybody familiar with the world of Truman Capote's fiction has already reacted with the stark simplicity of the movie audience of *Shane* when Jack Palance rode into town, clad head to toe in black and scaring even the dogs with his shadow. Each of the Clutters, in the terms of Capote's fiction, manages to include all the "bad" characteristics. In fiction, of course, neither the inverted morality nor the signs and symbols thereof are new. These are working conventions, bordering on pure cliché in modern fiction. Certainly in romance and even in more "realistic" fiction these conventions are accepted, perfectly (ironically) *respectable.* But here we are up against a real and different problem. The Clutters were real people, not symbols of anything, and their murder was a matter of brutal fact. At least at the outset, then, the effect is ambiguous. We find ourselves asking, no doubt as the author intended, is Capote still following the Old Law or will his work be a new dispensation? The larger audience reading Capote for the first time won't have that problem. Maybe that is just as well.

When we get to the killers, we begin to get answers. They come on as clearly labeled as the pilgrims in the prologue to *The Canterbury Tales.* Both are hurt because of accidents; both are tattooed, but there is a difference: Dick Hickock's tattoos are crude, cheap, conventional; Perry Smith's are "more elaborate—not the self-inflicted work of an amateur but epics of the art contrived by Honolulu and Yokohama masters." There is an explicit archetypal malevolence about Dick, with his head "halved like an apple, then put together a fraction off center," with his "left eye being truly serpentine, with a venomous, sickly-blue squint that although it was involuntarily acquired, seemed nevertheless to warn of bitter sediment at the bottom of his nature." Our first description of the remarkable Perry Smith is equally insightful. All Capote heroes have been cheerful narcissists, this in turn a symbol for richness of imagination and the interior life. Or as Capote carefully explains it:

> Time rarely weighed upon him, for he had many methods of passing it— among them, mirror gazing. Dick had once observed, "Every time you see a mirror you go into a trance, like. Like you was looking at some gorgeous piece of butt, I mean, my God, don't you ever get tired?" Far from it; his own face enthralled him. Each angle of it induced a different impression. It was a changeling's face, and mirror-guided experiments had taught him how to ring the changes, how to look now ominous, now impish, now soulful; a tilt of the head, a twist of the lips, and the corrupt gypsy became the gentle romantic.

Much, much later, Detective Nye, seeing him for the first time while Smith is being questioned, is struck by the "pert, impish features" that remind him of the suspect's pretty sister, "the nice Mrs. Johnson."

In short, Perry Smith is perfectly, patly, and in almost every detail a spooky embodiment of Capote's earlier fiction. He has all the right characteristics: a rich and childish imagination, his dreams including one marvelous recurring dream that is mystical in beauty and implication, his physical deformity, his sensitivity, even his background. What could be more perfect than to be the child of "a lean Cherokee girl (who) rode a wild horse, a 'bucking bronc,' and her loosened hair whipped back and forth, flew about like a flamenco dancer's"? Her name was Flo Buckskin, and her husband was a "homely-handsome Irish cowboy" named Tex John Smith.

It is probably the amazing fact that a real human being could accidentally have all the characteristics of his typical fictional protagonists that permitted Capote to give us through his study of Perry Smith a fascinating look at the curious workings of a murderer's psyche. By the same token, however, for or maybe because of all his natural sympathy and compassion for Perry Smith, Capote clearly sets him in sharp contrast to the other killer, Hickock. Hickock is intelligent but not nearly so interesting. The result is that he receives fairly short shrift in comparison to Smith, and much about him is given pejoratively: he likes to run over stray dogs; he pursues little girls; he asserts his dubious masculinity by making love in the presence of Perry, etc. All these things, by the way, must come to us through *Perry*, but in context are treated as facts. There is, of course, a narrative value to be derived from this contrast of the two. Since we never really know Hickock the way we do Smith and since we are never invited to squander much sympathy on him, he can serve beautifully as a conventional "heavy." It is necessary to engage as much of the reader's sympathy as possible for Perry, so there has to be a foil, a sacrificial victim served up to ease the reader's reluctant conscience and to appease, like patent medicine, the reader's taste for conventional morality. In the making of fiction, this method is honorable and traditional, and it works well here—so well that we are thoroughly engaged in the pathos of Perry Smith, and his final words from the gallows are deeply moving, come close to real tragic utterance, leave Perry at the end as a kind of inverted, midcentury Billy Budd. But when one realizes *how* this has been achieved, by the trick of fiction, that author and reader have conspired to make Hickock expendable, catharsis is dissipated by ambiguous feelings.

Again the problem is that we are dealing with a real murder and a real hanging. The author goes to great pains to emphasize the *reality* of the story. (And for an epigraph he has invoked Villon's "Ballade des pendus," which is for *all* the hanged.) That we do not get the same kind of involvement with Hickock as we do with Smith is a failure in this book. A wise failure, though, perhaps even a shrewd one. For the whole truth and nothing but the truth of this event, even if it were possible to articulate, would not likely be acceptable to the general audience. Better half a loaf—except that in one sense the trick of heaping the burden of evil on the head of Hickock is what is sometimes called cheating.

There are so many superbly realized things, large and small, in this book that one can be easily diverted and almost distracted from the other flaws. Almost, but not quite. The two chief and central actions of the book are the murder and the hanging. Although we are given plenty of the painful details of both actions, neither scene is presented as directly as other scenes. In each case, a little differently, Capote has chosen to shy away from the heart of these scenes, to "write around" them.

There is good narrative justification for holding back on the naked brutality of the murder scene until late. What happened is essential to the suspense of the story in Capote's arrangement, and so we do not really know and do not see the event happen until the killers have been caught and confess. Meanwhile, in the interim, something else happens. By then, we have been led into deep involvement with the killers. The account of the murder, though horrifying, is by then curiously remote and comes too late to damage the other rhetorical purpose. By putting the account of the murder exactly in the language of the confessions, gaining the virtues of documentation of course, Capote gains another more subtle effect. That language simply cannot compete with the author's. Possibly there is the horror of understatement by comparison, but the effect is to soften the event of the murder. It can be reasonably argued that Capote gives his reader a gracious plenty of detail from which to shape a completely *imagined* scene and that this, another time-honored device of fiction, is often much more powerful than a head-on and direct encounter with the scene. Nevertheless, there is a very real and nagging question as to whether or not the author wanted to give us that scene fully. Had he ever done so, early or late, he could probably never again have fully engaged the reader's sympathy for Perry Smith. And had he chosen to do so, he would have risked appealing to and arousing some very deep, atavistic human feelings that are more powerful than poetic. And had he done so, he might also have weakened the satirical effect of the fear and corruption that beset the little town. Still, it might have been more honest.

In a somewhat more subtle and complex way, Capote has managed to "write around" the hanging. The most shocking elements occur not at the hanging itself but in a nightmare of Perry's. But that is not precisely the problem. It is not a question of gruesome or explicit details. One of the most memorable hangings in fiction is Faulkner's disposal of Popeye in *Sanctuary* in a very few lines. In this case, it is a question of the right details, of something being missing. Within the exclusive context of the book, it is very hard to say what may be missing, just that as a scene this does not somehow measure up to many other less important scenes. The *Life* magazine article and interview, however, has come along with a kind of an answer. Capote was there. His own personal involvement and the scene he witnessed are described, and significant details are given that do not appear in the book. They are powerful and deeply moving things that had to be sacrificed, evidently, because of the author's decision to keep himself out of the story.

That decision was his and his alone to make, but it is a fair subject for consideration. In telling the story with a novelistic arrangement and the seeming objectivity of the novelist, Capote has had to exclude, except by implication, his own story, the entire story of his engagement and involvement. It is simply not in the book. But we know through the widespread publicity if by no other way that he was very much involved and not just reporting. He was witness to important parts of the story, and it is precisely his involvement and nobody else's that has shaped the whole story and its arrangement. What a story that might be! All that he has given us in the book, together with the true account of a highly sophisticated, civilized, sensitive, and successful man of letters who is suddenly fascinated by a newspaper story, captured and obsessed by the mystery to the extent of going to the scene of the crime. With a doggedness and persistence matching that of the police, he pursues his quarry (in this case the "story") to its bitter end. It would have an essentially nightmarish quality as bit by bit and piece by piece the abstract event became concrete and then real. With the odd logic of a dream, patterns began to emerge, patterns of fate, fortune, and behavior that had always intrigued him as a writer of fiction but which he could not have dreamed existed until, in this wild dream of discovery, there they were. Much as if he had been dreaming toward this for twenty years and waked to find his dream was real. Where you end the story depends on who is writing it. It could be tragic. It could be bitter and grotesque comedy if, for example, the author should find . . . himself! . . . and then vault to fame and honor, using six corpses for leverage. Perhaps, with a grand irony, you could have a story in which the author, starting from abstract fascination, digging up the facts, coming at last face to face in a dark mirror with the ineradicable horror at the heart of things, should then in the very act of writing and publishing his story purge himself of both the facts and the vision and come out untouched like a child, smelling like a rose.

I am not being facetious. A very large and important part of this story is at least concealed, if suppressed isn't a better word. Here I am not playing any innuendo game. What I mean is that while this deliberate suppression of self does give the narrative a fairly straight line and a great deal of strength, it also appears to be the cause of certain weaknesses. Some sign of final commitment is missing. Of course the author is already there, carefully arranging the order and sequence of events, moving his characters on and off stage, etc. If the truth about the "consequences" is really his concern, why doesn't he really appear? Curiously enough, the weakest parts of the book are precisely where the author had the most firsthand knowledge, the most direct encounter with the experience. *And he himself was very much part of the experience of many of the other characters.* His presence, his actions, his questions must have affected them, just as now the finished book is bound to have an effect on them too. If he has removed himself from the experience, we are entitled to ask what else he may have chosen to remove or suppress. A reporter need not necessarily deal with this question. A valid witness cannot ignore it and be really believed.

There is something missing, then, in this story that Capote says is what he really thinks about America. Of course, there is nothing new or shocking or even unfashionable in what he appears to think. We have been told by all kinds of people that unless we do something (nobody quite knows what) about all that's "desperate, savage, violent," we are going to suffer the consequences, and they will be very bad. Capote's tale, as it stands, reflects this profound concern with accuracy. Somehow, though, the Clutters were not representative abstractions, and neither were Dick and Perry. They did not live or die to prove any point or to illustrate what anyone may or may not think about "America." In spite of the local dismay and shock, the brutal and terrible death of the Clutters proves nothing about the nature of God or the universe one way or the other. The deaths of Dick Hickock and Perry Smith tell us nothing about justice. With enormous skill, skill and art beyond the means and reach of most of his rivals and contemporaries, Capote has managed to give some pattern and meaning to a brutal, stupid, pointless, senseless murder and some of its consequences. He has been able to arouse compassion and to evoke pity and terror. In all fairness, nobody is really treated like an abstraction. But somehow, in some almost indefinable way, the romancer has overcome the reporter, and the final effect is one of "nocturnal" romance. Which, of course, is a false rendering.

3.

There remains one more question: what about the "new" form? There is nothing whatever new about the use of the devices of fiction for nonfiction. A very long list could be made of such works, and it would include some very distinguished books, past and present. In recent times, one would not want to forget such classic examples as e. e. cummings's *The Enormous Room* or Hemingway's *The Green Hills of Africa, Death in the Afternoon,* and *A Moveable Feast,* each experiments, and so labeled, in the genre Capote is credited with inventing. Certainly you would have to include some of Wright Morris's experiments. And what would you do with the use of real events and characters in something like Robert Penn Warren's *Brother to Dragons*? The examples are multitudinous. And one would have to take note of all the books and the non-books done in the manner of Walter Lord's *A Night to Remember*. In what way does *In Cold Blood* really differ from these? There are some which can match it in distinction.

The claim of inventing a new form may be blamed on the publisher and dismissed as a device about on the level of the "new, improved ingredients" that show up with depressing regularity in advertisements for toothpaste, detergents, deodorants, and many other products.

The question of form, however, remains a challenge, unresolved and probably unanswerable. One would have to begin by saying that a very great number of writers, past and present, have in the form of fiction, in stories of crime and punishment, achieved as much as *In Cold Blood*. But this book is not fiction. Aside from the simple and statistical fact that many more people prefer to read "true" stories than fiction, the principal gain of calling the book a "Non-fiction Novel" would seem to be to call attention to the literary excellence of the reporting job. But what are we invited to compare this job with? *True Detective*? Newspaper and magazine stories? Conventional popular nonfiction?

In Cold Blood is a work of art, the work of an artist. There is much truth in it, though whether or not it is "true" is at least debatable. Whether or not it turns out to be a classic, it is an important and provocative book, one that is bound to generate the kind of deep interest, intense discussion, re-reading, and scrutiny that only a very few really excellent books deserve to enjoy.

(1966)

SHORT REVIEWS

Like a lot of other writers these days, I do a certain amount (when asked) of newspaper and magazine book-reviewing, working within the allowable boundaries of that brisk familiar form. One part of my own critical code is that, when space and attention are so rare and so competitive, I can't see any good reason to review a book that I really don't like.
 —G. G.

The Commonplace Book of William Byrd II of Westover, edited by Kevin Berland, Jan Kirsten Gilliam, and Kenneth A. Lockridge

It is not so surprising that our preeminent American diarist should have left behind a lively and at times fascinating commonplace book. For several centuries, from the late fifteenth and on into the eighteenth, a commonplace book was an almost indispensable part of the educated Englishman's literary equipment, first as a student, then later as a real or a would-be gentleman. In these notebooks, the author-owner, partly as an aid to memory and partly as a kind of self-referential anthology, copied down bits and pieces—from overheard jokes and snatches of conversation to maxims, epigrams, anecdotes, and serious historical, philosophical, religious, and scientific arguments and statements. A commonplace book could be said to serve as a kind of intellectual diary, always allowing, however, for the fact that all we can really know from other people's commonplace books is what they seem to have thought at a given time was worth noting. Like diaries, commonplace books are essentially private (therefore all the more entertaining in public) even as they are often rigged and structured for or against the possibility of an eventual audience.

William Byrd II is, among other things, one of the more interesting, indeed significant figures in the history of American letters. In his lifetime, the period of colonial America from the late seventeenth century up to the middle of the eighteenth century, he was well known as the successful planter of thousands of acres inherited from his grandfather (Thomas Stegge) and his father, and as the possessor of Westover, an elegant estate situated on the James River. He held important political offices in Virginia, is credited with founding Richmond and Petersburg, and represented the colony in London for some years. Truth is, until he arrived at the edge of middle age, Byrd spent more time there than in Virginia. Educated in England in a traditional classical program at Felsted Grammar School followed by some years studying law at Middle Temple, he was admitted to the bar in 1695, and he was also a fellow of the Royal Society and moved easily in the upper levels of London society. As he put it in the epitaph he designed for himself: "He was introduced to the acquaintance of many of the first persons of his age / For knowledge, wit, virtue, birth of high station." He collected portraits, the largest collection in the colonies, and, an inveterate reader, he accumulated close to four thousand volumes for his library, the second largest collection in America. Only Cotton Mather's library was larger. Byrd was at ease with six languages, ancient and modern.

But none of the above accomplishments, and others, would transform William Byrd II from colonial gentleman to man of letters; in fact, his literary works, and his consequent influence, had to wait until the middle of the twentieth century for scholarly attention and for publication. Beginning in the 1940s, the publication of Byrd's extensive diaries, originally written in shorthand and code, began and continued into the 1960s when the multivolume edition, *Prose Works of William Byrd of Westover: Narratives of Colonial Virginia* (1966), based on a wealth of manuscripts at Westover, appeared.

At roughly the same time, in 1964, the Virginia Historical Society acquired a manuscript notebook of Byrd's that turned out to be his only known commonplace book. Now, thanks to the Omohundro Institute of Early American History and Culture in Williamsburg, Virginia, and the coordinated labors of three scholars, we have a carefully edited text of this commonplace book together with a wealth of related scholarly materials designed to make the book at once more accessible and useful to general readers as well as to academics. As the editors write, "Byrd was not an academic scholar, and it would be disheartening to see his work ultimately relegated to the provinces of specialists. But scholarship is where, after almost three centuries, one begins." In addition to the text of the commonplace book, with 573 entries filling some 89 pages, the editors offer 96 pages of line-by-line commentary on Byrd's entries, together with a series of ten short essays on

Byrd in particular and the literary place and value of the commonplace book and such books in general. There is also a more extensive essay, "The Commonplace Book of a Colonial Gentleman in Crisis," by historian Kenneth A. Lockridge, senior scholar of the group and described by the others as "the first cause of this volume." Lockridge uses the commonplace book, seen from a postmodern, theoretical point of view, as material for a psychological portrait of Byrd, a tactic which, while interesting and ingenious, maybe even true, is highly speculative. The other two editors slightly distance themselves from Lockridge's conclusions, allowing that "each of us sees Byrd and his book a little differently, as will future scholars."

What the reader can see, and with pleasure, in the commonplace book is a man much of his age and yet in many ways a special spirit, a man of mixed, sometimes contradictory notions (like the rest of us). What comes across clearly, as in his diaries, is a man with a zest for life, with great integrity, and with few illusions. There are moments, as here in entry 464, when the observations fit our time as well as his own: "In our degenerate age People are ashamed of nothing but Innocence & being thought old."

(2001)

The Fabulous History of the Dismal Swamp Company: A Story of George Washington's Times by Charles Royster

The good news is that here is a narrative history of scope and of abundance, a fascinating story, first to last, arranged and presented by an award-winning historian (Francis Parkman Prize, Bancroft Prize, Lincoln Prize) and built solidly on a massive foundation of evidence. There are 172 pages of invaluable endnotes, supporting Professor Royster's narrative and argument and leading the interested reader in many new directions. Together with text and notes, there are twenty illustrations and five helpful maps.

Royster centers his story on the speculative Dismal Swamp Company, founded in colonial days and lasting into the early years of the nineteenth century, a company whose goal (more pipe dream than practical hope) was to clear and drain the Great Dismal Swamp along the borders of eastern Virginia and North Carolina and, sooner rather than later, to earn enormous profits from the land. With the history of the Dismal Swamp Company as his unifying subject, a symbol for the whole, Royster offers a large and complex view of the whole age, colonial and revolutionary, and of the motley crew of wheelers and dealers, schemers and dreamers, some of whom (Washington, Jefferson, and Patrick Henry, for example) time has turned into honored and monumental Founding Fathers.

There is a huge cast of fascinating characters, well known and little known, heroes and hard cases, winners and losers. We travel along the busy, dangerous routes of transatlantic trade to London and to the coasts of Africa and Antigua, to the Alleghenies and the West. We witness the accumulation of huge fortunes and the loss of same. And all the while, in both war and peace—at times, events like the French and Indian Wars and the Revolution seem at most temporary interruptions of the real business and concerns of the era—the elaborate shell game of acquiring land and property, not excluding the human property of slaves, felons, indentured servants, and common and skilled working men, continues unabated.

Overtly, Royster is nonjudgmental, mostly allowing the facts to speak for themselves, as here in a brief description of the slave ship *Hope:* "She needed manacles, fetters, and chains for three hundred men, women and children. Slave ships took gallons of vinegar to be poured over the lower deck for cleaning. The best trading cargo included colorful patterned cloth from India, silk taffeta, chintz, linen from Europe, felt hats, brass pans, gunpowder, gun-flints, tobacco pipes, bottled beer and malt liquor. . . . People could be enslaved for unpaid debts, for witchcraft, and for crimes such as murder, adultery, and theft. Others had been kidnaped." Just so, Royster does not highlight the most obvious parallels and connections with our own entrepreneurial end-of-the-millennium times. The overall effect is that the reader is set free to imagine a brutish world of Donald Trumps and Ted Turners and George Soroses disguised in powdered wigs, knee britches, and buckled shoes. These contemporary types become more a part of an established tradition than aberrant performers in a circus of greed. Contemporary relevancy speaks for itself. For example, the great crop from Virginia, so valuable it could serve as both capital and currency, was tobacco. Were the great tobacco merchants aware of and concerned about the dangers of the weed? "Charles Carter thought that people might quit smoking tobacco if fashion changed or if they learned 'of the great Proportion of poysonous Quality contained in this Narcotick Plant.'"

Some early readers have compared this book to the historical novel at its best, and, particularly in the examination of wonderfully realized characters, people like the ruthlessly self-made Samuel Gist, there is some truth in that claim. Yet, all in all, *The Fabulous History of the Dismal Swamp Company* is more a matter of telling than showing; the narrative is more expository than dramatic.

This is not a flaw. Narrative history, whether showing or telling or both, need not compete with the sensory affective experience of fiction. *The*

Fabulous History is not flawless, however. The complex structuring sometimes gets in the way of the story line and can be confusing. An alert editor might well have reduced the amount of redundancy. Too often, information is repeated. The book is too long to allow for that. And this reader, while delighting in the deft parallels implied between our own age and early America, could not help feeling that the men of those times, in order to survive, to get through any given day, were tougher, braver, and surely more admirable than (if not morally superior to) their contemporary counterparts.

All of which is to say that Charles Royster has written an exciting history that challenges our comfortable stereotypes and leaves us thinking about it long afterward. To ask for more would be ingratitude.

(1999)

A Consuming Fire: The Fall of the Confederacy in the Mind of the White Christian South by Eugene D. Genovese

This latest book by the distinguished and award-winning historian (best known for *Roll, Jordan, Roll,* which won him the Bancroft Prize) is at once slender—127 pages of text and argument, 40 pages of notes—and weighty. Slender because it is, in fact, a revised version of three lectures he gave at Mercer University, the Forty-First Annual Lamar Memorial Lectures. Weighty because the subjects, the ideas he is dealing with, are complex and subtle, sometimes and inevitably dense, especially to the contemporary reader who is locked into the secular assumptions of a predominantly secular society, all too often unwilling to credit the credibility and integrity of figures from the past who openly embraced other assumptions. What Sarah E. Gardner of the Lamar Lecture Committee says, that these are "challenging, provocative lectures," is clearly true.

What Genovese is up to here, based on the wealth of books, pamphlets, letters, and other primary materials that make his notes a treasure for students and scholars, is the examination of the arguments of white southern Christians, chiefly in and around "the War for Southern Independence," but also including the background of colonial and revolutionary times and, briefly in a fast-forward, some scrutiny of the positions of the clergy in our time, the time of the Civil Rights Movement and of the battle against apartheid in South Africa. What was the position of southern theologians, among others, about slavery? In the hands of a less able and less imaginative historian than Genovese, this could easily become almost farcical except for the terrible and bloody consequences of the intellectual quarrel between the abolitionists and southern Christians. But Genovese has the remarkable gift of being able to take seriously the words and thoughts of dead, and often forgotten, thinkers, taking them at face value, though never without retaining his own capacity to evaluate and to judge for himself. He opts for accuracy rather than easy-going opinion: "Pious, churchgoing, Bible-reading Christians had dreamed of a great Southern nation, and they fought for it with astonishing courage and tenacity during four horrible years of death and destruction." But at the same time, he is quite clear as to what that war was all about: "The Confederacy may have come into being as a bastion of constitutionalism, state rights, and traditional values, as its originators and many others since have claimed with considerable justification, but it also came into being as a slaveholding republic."

But it is the voices of others—many others and many worth listening to, people who were seriously listened to then and there—that he studies and examines. At the guaranteed risk of oversimplification (in this brief review), Genovese sees and shows, with a wealth of evidence, that the southern orthodox clergy and theologians, while defending slavery as an institution, with biblical authority, argued boldly and sometimes passionately for reform, most often against cruelty and mistreatment of slaves, against the separation of families of slaves, and against the various legal prohibitions involving literacy, teaching slaves to read. By and large, their purpose was, then, to preserve the institution of slavery and their own position as masters and, above all, to do their duty to God: "Southerners would have to prove worthy of His trust, specifically of the trust He had placed in them as Christian masters." That the cause of reform made little progress before the war is partly attributed to the practical inability of the southern divines to do more than talk, from the pulpit and in print, about it. When the war came to pass, they continued to speak out, basing their arguments on Scripture, classical and medieval history. "The ministers presented in general the message for Southerners: the God who was on their side was testing them, and the outcome of the War depended upon their passing His tests, including His test of their rectitude as slaveholders."

Things get more complicated. For example, "scientific racism," while popular in the North, was despised by the southern divines who "held their people to Christian principles in these and related matters, and they lost their battle only after secularization combined with the exigencies of segregationist politics to create a radically different moral atmosphere." Genovese defines these postwar changes as what happened when "the South adapted to the values and policies of a triumphant Yankeedom."

This brief book is alive with new thinking and rethinking. It will surely influence a lot of ongoing historical study and thinking. Here I have only been able to offer a few hints of its value and complexity. I urge interested readers to see for themselves. I also urge them not to skip past his acknowledgments in the preface, which will show clearly this tough-minded scholar's irrepressible good humor and wit: "So much for the amenities. What right my colleagues, to say nothing of my wife, had to find errors and faults, I cannot imagine. But find them they did, thereby subjecting me to acute embarrassment and the annoyance of having to make substantial changes. From their long experience in the academic world, they doubtless know what to expect: much resentment and little gratitude."

(1999)

"No Wonder People Got Crazy As They Grew Up": *Bastard Out of Carolina* by Dorothy Allison

"All the Boatwrights told stories, it was one of the things we were known for, and what one cousin swore was gospel, another swore was an unqualified lie," says Ruth Anne Boatwright, more often called Bone by her kinfolk and a few close friends. Bone is the narrator of the larger story of *Bastard Out of Carolina,* itself as richly various, with its stories and memories and dreams, as a well-made quilt. It is not surprising that this first novel is so abundantly anecdotal; Dorothy Allison has published stories in magazines and anthologies for some time, and her first book, *Trash* (1989), was a collection of stories that won two Lambda Literary Awards. What is surprising, however, is that the relentless narrative of this powerful novel in no way seems to be a patchwork of short stories somehow linked together. Everything, each part, belongs only to the novel. Indeed, the technical skill in both large things and details, so gracefully executed as to be always at the service of the story and its characters and, thus, almost invisible, is simply stunning, about as close to flawless as any reader could ask for and any writer, at any age or stage, could hope for and aspire to.

When I finished *Bastard Out of Carolina,* I wanted to blow a bugle to alert the reading public that something wonderful, a wonderful work of fiction by a major new talent, has arrived on the scene. It is one of those once-in-a-blue-moon occasions when the jacket copy seems inadequate and all the blurbs are examples of rhetorical understatement. Please reserve a seat of honor at the high table of the art of fiction for Dorothy Allison.

In a manner as authentic as any credible autobiography, Bone, the bastard of the title and the daughter of the beautifully realized Anney Boatwright, tells us the story of her life and her world up to the age of thirteen, when, as a result of a terrible trauma, she imagines her life as over and done with. (That she has gone on to tell this story to us later belies that grim conclusion.) Beginning in the deftly evoked 1950s, in and around Greenville, South Carolina, it is a story full of people, a host of characters, each distinct and memorable, each a recognizable physical presence. There is Reese, Bone's younger sister, and Granny the sharp-tongued Boatwright matriarch. There are cousins beyond counting, aunts and uncles by many marriages, Bone's n'er-do-well Boatwright uncles Earle and Beau and Nevil, and her aunts Ruth and Alma and, especially for Bone, Raylene, a proud, independent woman who once worked for a carnival and had another woman as her lover. And there is the menacing Glen Waddell, called Daddy Glen, who abuses and violates Bone in every possible way.

These people are (words not used in this book) white trash, rednecks, peckerwoods, crackers, members-in-doubtful-standing of the white working poor. Family, all the network and history of it, matters most. The men are proud, loving, violent, and spoiled. The strong Boatwright women keep them that way. They are complex people who manage to transcend their own disguises and society's stereotypes of them. Bone spends a lot of her youthful energy "looking for something special in me, something magical." On the other hand, she has plenty of evidence for what kind of future waits for her: "Growing up was like falling into a hole. The boys would quit school and sooner or later go to jail for something silly. I might not quit school, not while Mama had any say in the matter, but what difference would that make? . . . No wonder people got crazy as they grew up."

These people all work hard (at hopeless jobs), play hard, and are often poor enough to be ragged and hungry. The recited details of poverty are precise and exact. Bone is typical of the family in her love of gospel and country music. They swap stories continually, listen to the radio, watch a little TV, though not as much as you might think. The men drink and fight and find trouble in various shapes and forms. Bone reads a lot, unselfconsciously. Near the end, she has been able to sneak *The Group* out of the local library. All kinds of things, adventures and misadventures, happen to Bone and to her family. There are births and deaths, plenty of accidents, one horrible to consider, sicknesses and sorrows; and there is life and the humming energy of it on every page.

The literary territory that Dorothy Allison has set out to explore is a dangerous turf, a minefield strewn with booby traps, where the least false steps could lead to disaster. It is a great pleasure to see her succeed, blithe and graceful as Baryshnikov in performance. What dangers? Well, there is the whole southern thing. Terminal cuteness is the dread disease of too much new southern writing, especially first-person stories about eccentric families, a contagion compounded by the fact that too many people, reviewers as well as readers, are unable to distinguish the authentic from the spurious. The author, like her narrator, is often funny, never cute. But Ms. Allison has more serious threats to overcome, more important than purely literary matters. Anybody who wants to write truly and well about poor people has to contend with the temptation to turn characters into case studies. Again, too many readers and reviewers are relieved by that abstraction from the pain of felt experience. Similarly, sentimentality, with all its inherent denigration of intelligence and the human spirit, has become an acceptable mode in this sentimental age of ours. Allison can be deeply moving, yet never sentimental.

What saves her from all the possible pitfalls is the living language she has created for Bone. It is as exact and innovative as the language of *To Kill a Mockingbird* and *The Catcher in the Rye*. It stands well alongside the style of *Huckleberry Finn*. The special qualities of her style include a perfect pitch for speech and its natural rhythms; an unassertive, cumulative lyricism; an intensely imagined and presented sensory world, all five senses working together; and, above all, again and again, a language for the direct articulation of deep and complex nonverbal feelings.

Throughout the book, Bone dreams of being a gospel singer, but she lacks the voice for it. With the grace and magic of art, the author has transformed Bone's words and stories into something close to Bone's vision: "Their voices rose smoothly . . . rising into the close sweaty air, a song with no meter, no rhythm—but gospel, the purest gospel, a song of absolute hopeless grief."

(1992)

Eneas Africanus by Harry Stillwell Edwards

Less than two weeks after his tenth birthday, Harry Stillwell Edwards, a godson of Jefferson Davis, witnessed the first Federal forces entering his hometown, Macon, Georgia. Years later, in 1919, he wrote a short novel, *Eneas Africanus,* a comic novel concerning the trials and tribulations of an ex-slave trying to find his way home during the years of Reconstruction. It gives a picture of that period without a sign of anguish or rancor.

Edwards's first novel, *Sons and Fathers* (1896), won a ten-thousand-dollar award from the *Chicago Record.* His stories appeared in magazines like *Harpers* and *Century* and in several collections, the best known of which was *Two Runaways and Other Stories* (1889).

Even though it deals with the breakup of the Old South following the Civil War, *Eneas Africanus* is a comic novel, but the novel is concerned with another highly serious subject, what we have come to call "race relations." Since the mode is comic, the novel transcends the limitations of its subject matter to concentrate on the minor miracles of which comedy is created—the foibles, idiosyncracies, enduring characteristics of human beings. It is a tale that demonstrates, after all, charity in the ascendant.

To tell his story, Edwards seized on two conventions of the English novel—the mock heroic, based on the classics in burlesque, and the epistolary form. The epistolary technique, with letters written by individuals from a variety of social classes and from many parts of the South, gave Edwards the opportunity to display his gifts for capturing idiom and dialect. Moreover, this form, in which Eneas is seen through the eyes of others, allows the character to acquire the contours of legend before he finally appears in flesh and blood (though in a newspaper account) at the end of the story.

The value of the classical allusion to the original Aeneas is more complex. The idea of comparing an almost illiterate and irascible old man with the mythical founder of Roman glory is burlesque. But Edwards had more in mind than easy laughter. If this had been simply a story of wandering and homecoming, another classical figure, Ulysses, would have served as well. But the *Aeneid* is the story of the Trojan coming from defeat and devastation to found a new city—Rome. The *Aeneid* illustrated the virtue of *pietas*, which was, as its author Virgil saw it, the great inner strength of Rome. Eneas in Edwards's story, following the defeat of the Confederacy, wanders through seven states for eight years and over roughly 3,350 miles before he finds his way home. He arrives just in time for the wedding of the daughter of his former master, Major George E. Tommey, bearing the family's traditional silver bride's cup with which he had been entrusted eight years ago. The cup bears the motto *Semper Fidelis*, and loyalty is the virtue celebrated in *Eneas Africanus*, not the loyalty of ex-slave to former master, but the loyalty of man to man.

During his wanderings, Eneas has married and sired "a small colony of children." And Lady Chain, "a broken down old speckled mare" who has hauled Eneas's wagon, has also foaled a great racehorse named Chainlightning. What Edwards is celebrating is, then, the enduring fertility of the best of the old order in the world of the new.

None of these things would recommend the story if it were not packed with life and humor. Brevity is one of its virtues. It is really more of a short story than a novel, consisting of thirteen letters bracketed between two newspaper stories and covering, in actual time, the last two weeks of October 1872. It begins with Major Tommey's advertisement for the apparently long-lost bridal cup. Then letters begin to come in from all quarters revealing Eneas's quest for Tommeysville and revealing some of his fantastic adventures: he has raised crops and a family; preached the Gospel; made a lot of money with Chainlightning; told some fabulous lies; and, first to last, protected the silver cup and a sum of now-worthless Confederate money.

Like many of our finest humorists, Edwards's strength is in his moral vision, the shrewd, unswerving ethic of a naïve character, the pilgrim who, armed with no more than native wit, stumbles and pratfalls his way to Jerusalem. Americans have always enjoyed the paradoxical story of the wise innocent, so it is no wonder that, even though it has been mostly overlooked and forgotten by critics and scholars, *Eneas Africanus* has quietly sold more than a million copies over the years.

(1957)

A strange virus of consumerism has crept into the judgment of poetry: that work is thought best which shows a bottom line rich with spiritual profit, and for this reason boring propagandists like Nikki Giovanni and Allen Ginsberg are taken seriously by the misguided.
—FRED CHAPPELL, *"Every Poet in His Humor"*

A Way of Happening: Observations of Contemporary Poetry by Fred Chappell

Fred Chappell's *A Way of Happening* is a gathering of some seventeen critical pieces, together with an important personal essay about teaching writing ("First Night Come Round Again") and an essay-length introduction ("Thanks But No Thanks"), published between 1985 and 1997, all but three written expressly for and published by the *Georgia Review*. Chappell, author of seven novels, two collections of short stories, thirteen books of poems, and a book of essays, *Plow Naked*, not to mention his translations from classical drama and French Renaissance poetry, has earned a considerable and enviable reputation, and, as well, has received some significant awards, including the Bollingen Prize in Poetry, the Ingersoll Foundation's T. S. Eliot Award, and the Aiken/Taylor Award from the University of the South. For more than twenty years, Chappell has been writing book reviews and literary criticism of all kinds for a variety of newspapers, journals, and literary magazines. This new collection, focused strictly on contemporary poetry and consisting primarily of a sequence of chronicle reviews of more than eighty books, should justly call attention to Chappell's achievements as critic, one whom we most urgently need and ought to cherish.

Truth is, the reviewing and criticism of contemporary poetry are in a sorry state. There are some notable exceptions—one thinks of Henry Taylor, Richard Tillinghast, Ted Kooser, Brendan Galvin, Neal Bowers, R. S. Gwynn, and Anthony Hecht, for example, poets themselves of obvious integrity and sound judgment; but most of our reviewers and critics seem to be deeply and sincerely self-serving, eager players in a game dedicated chiefly to the care and maintenance of a particular, peculiar literary establishment, one they had much to do with creating in the first place and obviously have a vested interest in preserving at all costs. One result of their stance is that the establishment stars and celebrities, though deemed worthy of intensive criticism, are not, in fact, regularly subjected to the commonplace rigors of being widely reviewed. They don't need to be reviewed to be known and celebrated, to maintain place and status in the literary hierarchy. Most of our celebrity poets, all but a very few, are institutional (corporate) creatures, working for colleges and universities, by and large happy institutional campers. When, as here and now, image is almost everything and "reality" knocks only at the back door, what is poetry and how does it come into our lives? The celebrity writer is, on the one hand, strongly advised and sorely tempted to create a kind of brand name (voice) and, if it works well, to repeat it endlessly, mindlessly. Moreover, "successful" poets will not, as a rule, risk the capital of their modest celebrity by frequent tests and trials in the public arena. Another result, dependant on the above, is that new poets and, of course, the work of poets who are not, for one reason or another, members in good standing of the official literary establishment, are rarely reviewed at all. Thus the establishment remains largely unquestioned, unchallenged.

And then along comes Fred Chappell, fully aware of the limits of all literary criticism to do good or ill, as he wittily tells us in "Thanks But No Thanks" and in the brief, brilliant "Afterword" where he says that "my purposes in criticism have been to laud the ways I found beautiful and truthful and to censure, as gently as conscience allowed, the ways I found faulty and unfaithful." (How many poets have lately invoked beauty and truth as criteria of excellence? How many have even mentioned conscience?) Chappell does not need to assert, since he demonstrates and dramatizes these virtues in each of the essays, his sanity and decency, his hard-nosed humility, or a level of constant integrity rare enough to be breathtaking. *A Way of Happening* becomes what it is meant to be—a model for all of us.

To begin with, there is no separation of the well-known and little-known poets and their work, no segregation of sheep and goats. Poets like Alfred Corn, A. R. Ammons, Elizabeth Spires, Raymond Carver, Norman Dubie, William Matthews, Eleanor Ross Taylor, James Tate, Reed Whittimore, William Jay Smith, W. D. Snodgrass, T. R. Hummer, Carolyn Forché, James Applewhite, and others share space and equal, fair-minded attention with many others whose names and work are not so public. Chappell has long had a reputation for flinty integrity, extraordinary fair-mindedness. He will cheerfully (and fairly) kick ass when that is in order. Here he is on the honored and prizewinning efforts of James Tate: "Tate can write this stuff by the yard, and after one reads twenty or so yards, it all begins to sound the same, like the chaff of AM radio playing somewhere in the neighborhood" ("Every Poet in His Humor"). Or, in the same essay, a tough look at the art of Reed Whittemore: "Unfortunately, the book is more attractive as a physical object than as poetry. Almost all the poems here are intended as humorous, but few of them are because an apparent laziness in Whittemore's thought and expression invites sloppy banality." Friend or foe, no matter. All are equal. James Applewhite, for example, is a lifelong friend of Chappell, and Chappell has written and here writes admiringly of his work. Yet he is unwilling to suspend completely the critical enterprise: "For all his determination to confront the new, Applewhite still subscribes to the Agrarian fairy tale about antebellum culture. It forms the ground of his critical stance when he looks at the South about him now" ("An Idiom of Uncertainty: Southern Poetry Now"). Praise and criticism go hand in hand. And Chappell is secure enough in his demonstrable honesty to be fearless in his instruction: "I would be joyous to think I am wrong in my surmise, but I can't help gaining the impression that contemporary black poetry as represented in the *Fast Talk* collection doesn't really desire to communicate broadly, that it takes pleasure in ethnic exclusivity." What other matador would wave his cape before the multicultural bull?

It is more than worth the price of admission to come upon some of Chappell's discoveries. For example, he is not the first critic, by any means, to encounter and honor the work of Brendan Galvin, but his laudatory critique of the book-length *Saints in Their Ox-Hide Boat* ("Once Upon a Time: Narrative Poetry Returns?") is a genuine contribution to a particular problem for contemporary poetry: "If Alan Shapiro is accurate in predicting a return of narrative poetry, I would point to *Saints in Their Ox-Hide Boat* as the kind of narrative I would like to see produced."

In short, then, this remarkable book of criticism has a number of distinct values. Yes, it is a model of good criticism, good sense, and good writing when we need these most. Like the best criticism, it points and leads the reader directly to the books and themes discussed. And it is an exemplary reminder, here taken for granted by Chappell, that poetry matters, even now, that we need to be aware of it as best we can, in all of its successes and excesses.

(1998)

Gaining a Foothold in Old Jamestown with a Sovereign's Tightly Held Funds: *Big Chief Elizabeth* by Giles Milton

In *Big Chief Elizabeth: The Adventures and Fates of the First English Colonists in America,* Giles Milton has put together, from a wide variety of primary and secondary sources, a lively story, an entertaining account of English attempts to plant a colony in North America, beginning with John Cabot's first voyage of discovery in 1497 and ending as they finally began to succeed and to maintain a foothold more than a hundred years later, with the establishment of Jamestown in 1607.

The title of the book is somewhat misleading and perhaps may be confused with Alan Axelrod's gimmicky (though not entirely without merit) *Elizabeth I, CEO: Strategic Lessons from the Leader Who Built an Empire* (Prentice Hall), found in the business section of the bookstores these days.

It is true that the early (later called lost) colonists on Roanoke Island referred to their sovereign lady in the local Indian language as "Weroanza" (Great Chief) Elizabeth, and it is the truth that it was during the long reign of Elizabeth I that several serious attempts were made to create settlements on the vast lands named and claimed for her—Virginia. On the other hand, founding a colony in North America was never one of her primary concerns. She was, even so, positively and personally supportive, within her carefully guarded means, looking with favor, and as inexpensively as possible, on the efforts of various adventurers.

Among the first of these was the unlucky Sir Humphrey Gilbert; then, following his untimely death, she encouraged his half brother (and, for a decade at least, her special favorite), Sir Walter Ralegh.

Insofar as it is anyone's story, it is Ralegh's, and, indeed, an interesting and brief biography of Ralegh is threaded through the whole of this larger story. Ralegh outlived his sovereign mistress by fifteen years and lived long enough to learn of the success, created and enjoyed by others, of Jamestown, and probably also to meet the celebrated Pocahontas (Mrs. John Rolfe). Assuming the title of Lord and Governor of Virginia in the early days, Ralegh had high hopes for settling North America. It was not foolish, though it was perhaps premature, to hope that he and other original investors could earn rich rewards in the New World.

Ralegh also envisioned the possibility of English naval bases that could create serious mischief for the Spaniards who were busily and ruthlessly exploiting the Caribbean and South America, carrying home a wealth of booty. English sea dogs and privateers already shared in some of those rewards, but wanted much more. It was Ralegh's response to Spanish cruelty to the indigenous population that established the ideal of English policy, not always followed strictly in fact, of seeking to win the friendship of the Indians rather than trying to conquer and subdue them. Conquered and subdued they came to be, all in due time, but both in North America and in Guiana, to which Ralegh himself voyaged twice, whenever his policy of kindness was followed, it worked well.

If Ralegh is, in a real sense, the brightest star in Mr. Milton's narrative, there is also an all-star cast of fascinating characters, highbrow and lowbrow, large and small, who drive the story along, from the Bristol Merchants of the early sixteenth century, who tried and failed to market English woolens to the Indians, to Richard Hore, who set forth in April of 1536 with two small ships intending to capture a "savage" for profit: "He could then be paraded around the capitol and displayed—for a fee, of course—to curious Londoners." A total failure.

And there is Davy Ingrams, who, left behind on the shores of Mexico by Sir John Hawkins in 1567, decided not to wait around but to make his own way home: "Aware that English fishing vessels were regular visitors to Newfoundland—and ignorant of the fact that it lay more than three thousand miles away—he selected a band of his more adventurous colleagues and set off on what was to prove a very long march."

Davy made it safely back to Barking, Essex. Having lived to tell the tale, he didn't add much useful information about North America during his debriefing. Anybody tough enough to find his way on foot from Mexico to Newfoundland was probably indifferent, if not entirely insensitive, to a lot that he witnessed and experienced. He was, however, not indifferent to his upper-class interrogators, ably supplying them with some utterly improbable tales of red sheep and monstrous rabbits, buckets of silver and great lumps of gold.

Most of the book, except for the final section dealing with the more familiar story of Jamestown, concerns the attempts to create a viable colony near the Atlantic coast during the 1580s and '90s.

At one time and another, some very important Elizabethans were deeply involved and actively engaged in the enterprise, people like the great mathematician and scientist Thomas Harriott; John White, whose drawings are the first view most Englishmen had of the new land and its inhabitants; Ralph Lane, first Master of the colony; seamen like Sir Francis Drake, Simon Fernandez, Sir Richard Grenville, and Thomas Cavendish; and not to forget the pair of Indians, Manteo and Wanchese, who visited London and were presented at Court, or Wingina, the "Weroance" of Roanoke who caused the colony considerable grief.

The colonists themselves had all kinds of skills and trades and interests, except for the essential one of farming, about which they knew next to nothing. They suffered, and many died from strange diseases, starvation, terrible storms, and savage warfare with the Indians.

It was just as difficult, if not more so, for the Jamestown colony, which had, we learn, as great a share of troubles and, for a time, an implacable enemy in the imperial Powhatan. But if bad luck dogged the Elizabethans, good luck, as much as anything else, saved the Jacobeans. As for the former, "the lost colony," Milton in the epilogue speculates about their fates and persuasively argues that some, at least, must have endured, assimilating with the native population.

The author's text is graced with good maps, some fascinating illustrations, and a useful bibliography. Using narrative where it seems called for, Mr. Milton allows himself no more than reasonable flights of speculation and deftly manages to avoid the kinds of self-serving judgmental and moral stances that mar much contemporary historical writing. The book is exemplary of popular history at its best.

(2000)

The Sharp Teeth of Love by Doris Betts

Often in the short stories and novels of Doris Betts, beginning more than forty years ago with the twelve stories of *The Gentle Insurrection* (1954) and now including three short-story collections and five novels, disaster and real tragedy are no more than a half a step away from her characters. Things can and sometimes do go terribly wrong for them. This is also true of her latest novel, *The Sharp Teeth of Love.* Nevertheless, the novel is, in the strictest sense, a comedy. It spoils nothing to report that though the principal characters are tried and tested sorely, they eventually arrive at something which, of not exactly a Hollywood happy ending, is at once more plausible and hopeful.

In the world according to Doris Betts, deeply informed by her Christian faith and by a demonstrably allusive awareness of the Bible that she has been reading and thinking on since childhood, bad things happen to good people and vice versa; and even worse things could happen in the blink of an eye. But neither her characters nor, above all, their thoughtful creator lose a pervasive and, finally, unquenchable sense of humor. There is laughter at the heart of things.

The plot of *The Sharp Teeth of Love* is sufficiently complex, riddled with surprising twists and turns, and swiftly moving with, at times, the elements of an unabashed thriller to give it an extra boost of energy (it would make a good movie). But the overall story line is admirably simple and resonant. Madeline Lunatsky Stone, aptly called Luna, a lapsed Catholic and a talented young illustrator living in Chapel Hill, heads west in the spring of 1993 with her boyfriend, Steven Grier, a new Ph.D. in botany, who is moving to his first teaching job in Riverside, California. They are planning to be married in Reno—"If we get married in Reno where everybody else gets divorced it will be more binding." A wonderfully eccentric person in the first place, Luna is recovering from a serious breakdown. Steven is more beautiful than charming, more selfish and self-centered than anything else, and, outside the limits of his chosen field of study, as dumb and insensitive as a rock. In Reno, while Steven is briefly diverted by the pleasures of gambling, Luna (to the reader's great relief) has serious second thoughts and runs away into the High Sierra, leaving a note behind:

> Dear Steven,
> Let's don't get married after all.
> Good luck in California.

Already profoundly troubled by the recent fiery disaster in Waco (and by human suffering in general), Luna becomes obsessed by the story of the Donner Party, whose lives came to their terrible ending near where she camps in hiding. She is particularly concerned with the story of Tamsen Donner, whose ghost appears to her in visions that may or may not be "real," but are altogether palpable. (Readers familiar with Doris Betts's earlier work will not be surprised by this. There is a place for ghosts and visions in her world. One celebrated story, "Benson Watts Is Dead and in Virginia," is told in first person by a ghost.) Of Luna's relationship to Tamsen we are told: "Like Luna, Tamsen Donner had come to this place the long way around, had lived in North Carolina, too. Had taught school there at Elizabeth City on the Pasquotank River. From that land of fish and duck hunting and Dismal Swamp she had ended up here in the blizzards, and one man had eaten her time and her strength and her nursing care while another one—though he always denied it—had possibly eaten her flesh." Meanwhile two living, breathing people complicate and change Luna's life: Sam, an abused child prostitute desperately on the run from his "owners"; and Paul, a construction worker from Wisconsin, deafened by an industrial accident and wrestling with a strongly felt vocation for the Lutheran ministry. Pursued, and at times pursuers, these three have a full share of close encounters with the worst kind before love finally succeeds, if not at conquering all, then at least in saving some very worthwhile lives.

An admired teacher of creative writing—Doris Betts has been on the faculty at the University of North Carolina since 1966—she makes the conventional and difficult chores look easy. Her virtuosity is never overt or assertive. She writes a clean, clear, accessible prose, and she does not tease or trick her readers. She started her career as a highly praised story writer and has carried over from that form both economy and efficiency. No wasted motion. Scenes are quickly developed and disposed of, yet nothing feels hurried or perfunctory. She has been justly praised for her crisp, slightly off-center dialogue. Here, for example, is a quick but important exchange between Steven and Luna, a few words and a couple of gestures capturing their whole relationship:

> "The drinks are free," he said. "Go on, have one. Make you feel better."
> "Let me taste yours." It looked pale.
> He lofted his glass away in one hand while with the other pulling down his lever. "Order your own. They want you to stick around and gamble. My daddy would love it here."
> "Free drinks ought to give you some idea of the profit margin."

Large and small details—the way you play a slot machine, the intricacies of a full-scale search-and-rescue mission—are authoritative and authentic. "I take facts seriously," Betts said in an interview, "because they do turn symbolic."

Doris Betts is also an adventurous writer. Her characters are all, in the best sense, *characters,* unique individuals. Luna and Paul and Sam, as well as many of the minor characters, are complex enough to be acceptably inconsistent, even at times contradictory. She has a ventriloquist's gift at creating credible voices for them one and all. We find ourselves wanting to know more about them.

Doris Betts is a storyteller who strives for a tale that will carry a full cargo of meaning. As she put it in an interview years ago: "You spend all your life learning to write many-layered, so that the story is there and the echoes and shimmers are underneath it." *The Sharp Teeth of Love* is rich with "echoes and shimmers." Some readers may well find that this burden of meaning is a bit more than the story can easily carry, but anyone who cares about excellence in fiction will find a cause for celebration in the appearance of *The Sharp Teeth of Love*.

(1997)

The Big Ballad Jamboree by Donald Davidson

Set during the summer of 1949, in and around an imaginary place called Carolina City in the mountains of southwestern North Carolina, *The Big Ballad Jamboree* is a story about country music (a.k.a. hillbilly) and musicians, principally Danny McGregor, a guitar picker and singer with the Turkey Hollow Boys, a popular radio group, aiming toward the Grand Ole Opry someday; and Cissie Timberlake, Danny's childhood sweetheart in the old-fashioned sense of that word and ritual role. With a college education and energetic enthusiasm, Cissie is collecting versions of folk songs and ballads for her M.A. thesis. Their romance, moving through difficulties toward a comic and happy ending, is one among a number of well-plotted narrative threads that keep this story going and the pages turning. The whole story is told in the first person by Danny, who speaks in a flexible, credible, lively, colloquial style, accurate for the time and place, appropriate for a bright, only lightly educated young man who, like many others, is only a generation or so away from hard-scrabble subsistence farming, from the rigorous ideals, if not the inflexible habits, of hard-earned pride, self-reliant courage, of an uncomplicated sense of honor and an ineradicable sense of humor. Danny is a worthy literary descendant of Huck Finn.

There is also a wide variety of characters, ranging from Carlos B. Reddy, a fatuous congressman, through various academics, including the nincompoop, Dr. Hoodenpyl, to Ed Cooley, talkative barber, Buck Kennedy, balladeer and bootlegger, the shrewd Sheriff Looney, and Rufus Whitthorne, leader of the Turkey Hollow Boys. All these people, old and young, wise or foolish, share a history and a musical heritage that is still growing and changing in a world that is shown to be changing more suddenly and deeply than anyone can easily perceive.

The year 1949 is an important one, with the experience of World War II already fading to shadowy memory. The G.I. Bill is sending a whole generation of veterans to college and pointing them to a brighter future. The Cold War is not yet part of the consciousness of people in Carolina City. Television is just over the horizon; they can only guess how that may later come to change their lives. Meanwhile, however, all is not well. Industry is coming in, bringing jobs but also bringing its ills—greed, avid consumerism, pollution, depopulation of the rural countryside, disconnection from nature, and an increasing alienation of people from each other. Much of this impacts on Danny and the Turkey Hollow Boys, who have to court popularity by corny ways and means and who have to depend on advertising to earn their keep: "Big grown men acting like dummies and making funny noises just to advertise dressed chicken, wasn't it crazy?" Danny tells us. "Grand Ole Opry carried that kind of clap-trap, too, and you had to sing it as if you liked it. It was enough to make a hog blush."

In that sense, this first (and only) novel by Donald Davidson, written sometime in the 1950s but not published until now—indeed, not known to exist in a complete manuscript until it was found by the author's granddaughter—is an oddly apt parable. The problems just then becoming evident are still very much with us, only worse than all but the most pessimistic prophets imagined. Davidson, an honored poet and critic, distinguished teacher at Vanderbilt for years (among his pupils were Jesse Stuart, Robert Penn Warren, and Elizabeth Spencer), one of the original Fugitives and a leading Agrarian, along with John Crowe Ransom, Cleanth Brooks, Allen Tate, and others, was often taken to be a rigorous reactionary. People who knew the man and his work may be surprised by this book, for in spite of its serious themes and concerns, *The Big Ballad Jamboree* is a light-hearted and (in a musical sense) light-fingered book, balanced, fair-minded, accessible, and clearly intended for a popular audience. In an excellent afterword, Curtis W. Ellison and William Pratt tell what is known about the making of the book. Evidently, Davidson worked with an editor at McGraw Hill, but before the final manuscript could be submitted, the publisher eliminated its trade department. At about the same time, Davidson had a serious heart attack and afterward concentrated on other work. Davidson, who played the piano, was knowledgeable and enthusiastic about both folk music and the modern hillbilly music we now call country. That knowledge and enthusiasm give the novel unusual energy and authenticity; and this, in turn, moderates the bitter view of "progress" well expressed by Old Man Parsons, an unreconstructed mountain man: "I kin remember back to the time we didn't have no machines a-tall in Beaver Valley unless maybe it was a coffee grinder. I've seen the machines come, and I've seen the people go. And the better they make the machines, the worse they make the people."

Davidson clearly loved the land and the cycles and seasons of his homeplace, and that love shines through the descriptions of it. Environmentalists will feel a kinship with the author. Even the novel's strong streak of antifederalism (there's a child named States Rights) may be newly relevant to many readers. Meantime, we have a discovery and a surprise—a good novel coming to us thirty years late, but thanks to the skill and care of its author, still as fresh as a spring morning in the Smokies.

(1996)

White People: Stories by Allan Gurganus

It will not surprise anyone who has read Allan Gurganus's *Oldest Living Confederate Widow Tells All* that the author loves to tell stories, and not just that—he loves storytellers and the art and craft of storytelling, too. He takes and shares pleasure in imagining, then bringing forth, a rich variety of voices. In that novel and now in these stories, Gurganus tries out voices, tries on voices like somebody, half in jest and half in deadly serious concentration, trying on hats in front of a mirror. It's a wonderful kind of hat trick, at once childish and new and as strange and old as . . . well, storytelling. Remember Hector trying on his helmet for size, in the presence of his wife and child just before that great warrior goes out to face Achilles? What I mean to say is that Gurganus is a storyteller in the grand tradition, belongs there; and though he is clearly and fully familiar with the latest gestures of contemporary fiction—shifting tenses, changing points of view, turning time forward and backward, and the self-reflexiveness that seems to dare the reader to come forward and help to shape the story—still his stories are strongly traditional in their accessibility, in their amplitude. The whole thing about the influential but fading fashion of what has been called, crudely enough, "minimalism" is not a matter of fat or thin, long or short, but a kind of deft shadow play. Minimalism is always less than meets the eye. Worldlier than thou, the minimalist seems forever clever, hardly ever clumsy. It is very hard to be ample and accessible these days and to sound smart at the same time.

In the eleven stories gathered together in *White People,* Gurganus manages to do that gracefully and skillfully. The stories are of varying length; the shortest, "It Had Wings" (an old widow finds a handsome and youthful fallen angel in her backyard and sends him on his eternal way), is four pages; "Blessed Assurance" (an older man confesses a complicated guilt from his youth when he sold funeral insurance to poor and exploited blacks) is a sixty-page novella, dense and fully developed. Similarly, the stories are various in form and content. Settings vary: "Condolences to Every One of Us," though framed in a letter from a lady in Toledo, Ohio, concerns events during a revolution in a remote African country; the mildly Kafkaesque "Art History" is in Eastern Europe before the walls came tumbling down; the highly satirical "America Competes," another epistolary tale, has a scene or two in New Hampshire; the sadly erotic gay story, "Adult Art," is set in a heartland urban anywhere; most of the others are set in the author's homeplace—eastern North Carolina. Though they move freely in time, most are set quite precisely according to generation and decade, for Gurgangus has a serious interest in and a good eye and ear for the appropriate quotidian detail, the right phrase for the right time. One story, "Reassurance," is in the form of two letters, one an actual letter by Walt Whitman, the other a ghostly or dreamed or, anyway, imagined letter from a dead Union soldier, Frank H. Irwin of Company E, 93rd Pennsylvania, to his mother, both from the early summer of 1865.

All but one of the stories are dated, five from the 1970s and five from the 80s, the most recent—"Reassurance" and "Blessed Assurance"—dating from 1989, and are arranged more or less chronologically. The stories are various, too, in the places where they first appeared. "Minor Heroism: Something About My Father" was first published in the *New Yorker. Harper's* published four stories. Others came out first in literary magazines—the *New American Review,* the *Paris Review,* the *Quarterly, GRANTA*—a couple of chapbooks, and "Adult Art" was published in *Men on Men: Best New Gay Fiction.*

All this forms a strong first impression of diversity, and yet there is much that binds the stories of *White People* much more closely together than the anthology format suggests. For one thing, there are, carefully scattered, the closely autobiographical stories: "Minor Heroism: Something About My Father," "Nativity, Caucasian," "Breathing Room: Something About My Brother," "A Hog Loves Its Life: Something About My Grandfather." These constitute about half the book, involve the author's overt stand-in, Bryan, together with his father and mother, brother Bradley, grandparents, and others. They also involve some overlapping of events and information, becoming, thus, dependent on each other and, indeed, upon the sequence in which they appear. They become a continuing story we come back to, the backbone of all the rest. All of the stories, one way and another and pushing the limits of possibility, are first-person stories. They are, therefore, and even in the epistolary stories, spoken stories, composed in speech rhythms. They work well, maybe even best, when read out loud. In any case, it helps to listen to them as you read. So, though there are many voices and styles, well executed, there is also, behind all, an authorial style. It is made up of sentences that are graceful, often witty and funny, always well turned and not without the spice of continual surprise to save them from predictability. In construction, long or short, Gurganus takes his time, knowing that urgency in a story is a cumulative quality, that suspense begins, like the longest journey, one step at a time.

But, all said and done, the unity of this collection stands or falls, works or doesn't, on the basis of its subjects, its themes. Greater and lesser, they are recurring. The conflicts—art versus commerce, love against greed, open-mindedness against rooted bigotry, old versus new and young—are constants. And so is the primary image evoked by the title and sustained throughout, the place of white people in a changing world. Except for Ardelia, "our lifelong helper, cook, and company," and for the marvelously realized (and terribly important) Vesta Lotte Battle of "Blessed Assurance," all the characters in these stories are white people and suffer on account of it. The stories are linked by a color symbolism. Whiteness is associated with sickness, pain, blankness, rigidity. And in "Breathing Room," the sixth grader, Bryan, learns what this adds up to from his teacher, Miss Whipple: "If a group cannot bend, it fails to grow—it loses out to heartier and therefore worthier life forms." Clearly here and elsewhere, and sometimes with more than a little sentimentality, the author is making a statement. But he is too southern to be rude or insistent about it. When it comes to this statement, like any other, you can take it or leave it. Trust these tales, and through them you will come to know and enjoy the teller, who can tell his stories as well as anyone alive and kicking in our time.

(1991)

It's True South with a Sense of Humor:
The Sharpshooter Blues by Lewis Nordan

It isn't easy to be a southern novelist these days. It's tough enough to arrive on the literary scene a full generation after the triumph of the modern masters—Faulkner, the inimitable, Flannery O'Connor, Eudora Welty, the whole crew of Vanderbilt Agrarians, and all the others. Add to that burden the fact that the southern novel has gradually become a genre, every bit as formulaic as science fiction, the thriller, the historical romance, or the old-fashioned western. And finally, there is an increasingly skeptical, if not hostile, critical response that has not spared some of the literary stars of southern writing. The southern novel advances through a minefield of habitual gestures and conventions, edging closer and closer to the pure and simple status of irrepressible cliché.

So it is remarkable that some of the best writing of our time is still coming from the fertile South, and it is a pleasure to report that ranking among the best American writers in any genre and form is Mississippi native and now professor of English at the University of Pittsburgh, Lewis Nordan. Four earlier books—most recently *Wolf Whistle* (1993), a fictional version of the Emmett Till murder case—have earned him considerable attention, respect, and a string of prizes and awards. *The Sharpshooter Blues,* his finest work so far, stands an excellent chance of being the "breakthrough" book that will win him the larger crowd of readers he well deserves. Set in the same place where all of his fiction has so far happened, the imaginary Mississippi Delta town of Arrow Catcher, *The Sharpshooter Blues*, brief and fast-moving as it is, is strongly, tightly plotted, centering mainly on the complex consequences that result from an attempted robbery of William Tell's gas station and country store by two vicious strangers (who, by the way, are incongruously remembered as "the lovely children"). All the required and identifying characteristics of the genre are fully realized here—plenty of down-home sex and violence, deep and detailed evocation of place, a strong sense of family, celebration of undaunted eccentricity among its cast of memorable characters, and a powerfully pervasive sense of humor thriving side by side with genuine pathos and personal tragedy. It is at the outset that indefatigable sense of humor, the laughter at the heart of things, that, as much as anything else, marks the territory of Nordan's fiction as distinctly his own. I defy readers not to laugh out loud at several points in this story.

In a recent interview, Nordan has modestly asserted: "I know what I do well, and characterization of interesting people is part of that." *The Sharpshooter Blues* has a full measure of interesting characters, including, among many others, young Hydro Raney, a.k.a. Ramon Fernandez, a hydrocephalic raised at a fish camp on primeval Roebuck Lake; a Shakespeare-quoting undertaker known to one and all as the Prince of Darkness; ten-year-old Louis McNaughton, wise beyond his years, with an insatiable appetite for comic books (Nordan is marvelous with imaginative children); an Episcopal minister named Preacher Roe, who supervises public confessions at the William Tell store; Monsieur Dublieux, owner of the Arrow Theater, who pronounces his name W; Aunt Lily, an African American psychic and voodoo woman from the "Belgian Congo" part of town, whose magical crystal ball is as apt to show TV soap operas as past, present, or future realities; and many, many more. Jesus even makes a brief appearance in a bar as a man with pale hair, a British accent, and "an ironic smile" who announces that "It's always Happy Hour in Chez Jesus." The story, shifting from one point of view to another, advances through a sequence of adroitly constructed, tightly focused scenes. Nordan is a master builder of scenes that, like jokes, depend on perfect timing. There are also dreams and visions, hallucinations, and enough magic and supernatural activity for the book to be labeled as "magic realism," though the latter is more in the tradition of Eudora Welty than Gabriel García Márquez.

But what lifts Nordan above and beyond his chosen genre is the writing, sentence by sentence, line by line. The narrative voice is uniquely his own, a dazzling orchestration of the living American lingo, the deepest music of our language, from a high elegiac style, richly rhetorical, to an authentic reproduction of country colloquial that even Mark Twain might envy. Like the surface of "black and shimmering, wide, incredible Roebuck Lake," the glittering surface of the story contains, rather than conceals, a great depth of meaning, above all a sense of loving compassion that overrides "the sound of inexpressible grief and the fore-knowledge of lifelong pain that no one else could ever hope to understand or share." Here Lewis Nordan shares it all with us, his fortunate readers.

(1995)

Kate Vaiden by Reynolds Price

Surely his finest work so far, a wise and wonderful story told by an artist at the peak of his powers. Poet, story writer, and essayist of genuine distinction, Reynolds Price has earned his primary reputation as a novelist, beginning nearly a quarter-century ago with the brilliant achievement of his first novel, *A Long and Happy Life.*

Since then, he has been both productive and adventurous, largely ignoring the trends and fashions followed by others as he explored and developed his own considerable gifts. Never, from the outset, ignored, indeed championed by some of our most honored elders (for instance, Eudora Welty has been from the beginning an outspoken advocate of his artistic virtues), Price has likewise never been fully appreciated, certainly not nearly so much as he well deserves, by the arbiters of the literary establishment.

This is in part because he has never turned away from his upcountry southern heritage, the place he knows and loves best, the precisely evoked and realized region where his more-than-regional, altogether universal stories and fables thrive. And his fate is partly the result of his subtle, unassertive originality, a quality that manifests itself mostly in an impeccable style and an inimitable voice, not in self-reflexive self-advertisement.

With the story of Kate Vaiden (rhymes with "maiden"), told by herself, everything comes together with astonishing grace. The story is, as we learn toward the end, a manuscript of recollection written for her abandoned son,

Lee Vaiden, by Kate, now fifty-seven and able at last to make some sense of her life. It is a kind of confession, then, an apology without a hint of self-indulgence or self-pity, and it is mainly concerned with Kate's youth and adolescence, as she grew up in the 1930s and '40s, orphaned early by a terrible family tragedy (a mystery, really, that is not solved until the end of the story), survivor of two love affairs—one deeply passionate—which ended in loss and sorrow, and member of a larger family, including some friends as close as any blood kin.

The times and the places—chiefly North Carolina farm country and Norfolk in the war years—come truly to life, but the amazing virtuosity of the novel lies in the authenticity of Kate Vaiden's voice and spirit. She herself is no mean stylist, establishing and maintaining an appropriate colloquial style that is supple, energetic, and witty without once being merely clever or stumbling into cuteness. Price has not always fully avoided these pitfalls in the past, but here he never falters. The last least signs of any self-indulgence or self-condescension have been refined away. What's left is pure.

The result is that Kate, the teller, is so real that we very soon forget the presence of Price, the author, in the shadows. It seems to be genuinely her book, her story. Partly this comes from the prose style, but perhaps more impressive, it comes from the perfect realization of Kate as a fully dimensional character. At all levels, from acute sensory awareness of the known world to the darkest inner places where feelings move like inexorable tides, she is wholly alive, wholly herself and no other. I know of very few women characters in all contemporary fiction who are so fully and honorably realized, none at all by a male writer.

Kate is an admirable character, able to suffer and to rejoice, not even afraid to be happy when the times come and, above all, strong in her love for the life we must all, sooner or later, lose. As she puts it in a brief aside: "One small thing I'm proud of—not one time, in all I've done, have I ever asked mercy for being a girl. I've meant to be strong. Strength just comes in one brand—you stand up at sunrise and meet what they send you and keep your hair combed."

You will want to meet Kate Vaiden and get to know her. And in the end, if you feel as I do, you will want to stand up for Reynolds Price.

(1986)

The Collected Stories of Reynolds Price

Reynolds Price has been a significant figure on the American literary scene for more than thirty years. He has been recognized as one of our most gifted writers since his first published book, the novel *A Long and Happy Life* (1962), appeared and won the William Faulkner Foundation Award (this novel has been in print ever since then). Well before that, in 1954, while he was still an undergraduate at Duke, he earned the attention, interest, and practical support of visiting writers Elizabeth Bowen and Eudora Welty (whom Price has described in interviews as "the living writer I admire most" and to whom he dedicated *Permanent Errors*) for the story "Michael Egerton." A few years later, while Price was at Oxford on a Rhodes Scholarship, Stephen Spender published his story "A Chain of Love" in *Encounter*, which immediately captured the professional interest of the late Hiram Haydn, then an editor at Random House. Both of these stories are among the large gathering of stories, fifty of them and more than six hundred pages worth, in *The Collected Stories of Reynolds Price*, his twenty-fifth book in a dedicated and productive career in letters that has included poetry, nine novels, plays, essays, translation, memoirs, and three earlier collections of stories—*The Names and Faces of Heroes* (1963), *Permanent Errors* (1971), and *The Foreseeable Future* (1991). All of the stories of the earlier two collections are part of the *Collected Stories*. *The Foreseeable Future*, consisting of three long stories, is perhaps too recent to be included and would probably make the new collection unmanageably abundant. In a brief, evocative, and very useful note, "To The Reader," Price tells us that, except for slight editorial corrections, "the older stories stand as they first appeared in volumes," adding, "All of them stand in a new order—one which attempts an alternation of voices, echoes, lengths and concerns that would prove unlikely if I held to the order of the prior volumes or set the stories by date of completion." Thus the earlier stories are well scattered among the new and uncollected ones and remarkably, except for some old favorites and widely anthologized pieces ("The Warrior Princess Ozimba," "Waiting at Dachau," "The Names and Faces of Heroes" etc.), it is not easy for the reader to guess which stories came early and which are most recent. There is an unusual kind of uniformity demonstrated here, the uniformity of sustained, unflagging artistic excellence, all the more impressive since the author's arranged sequence and context stress variety of form and content.

There is no real model for Price's work. In interviews, Price has acknowledged the powerful influence of Eudora Welty, but in a special and complex manner—"I felt confirmed by her example in the validity of my own experience as a source of art." Price belongs to no school or movement. From first to last, Price's stories are technically straightforward in the telling and accessible, yet at the same time they manage to be subtle and adventurous in the complex experiences dealt with, the subjects explored. They are linked to each other (and to his other work) by somewhat similar ways and means of telling and, more deeply, by clusters of common concerns. Most of the stories are told by first-person narrators, each with a different, distinctive, and appropriate voice, yet each sharing some characteristics, chief among which is a delicate balance, an almost perfect blending together of spoken and written discourse. The sentences are solid and shapely, but always credible, convincing. There are brilliant, virtuoso stylistic moments, but they are fully earned and do not divert attention away from the story. Similes (a strict test of artistic self-indulgence) evolve naturally and infrequently, at once apt and surprising, as, for example, in "Endless Mountains": "It felt like I was the last live soul on a planet swept of the human race except for me, a lone man normal as milk in a bucket but lord of all"; or, "a shine like the memory of your best deed or dusk on the summer river, floating slow."

Setting is a vital force in Price's work. Mostly it is a North Carolina place, the farms and towns and cities he has lived in and around; but there are first-rate stories firmly set in England and Europe. Contemporary Israel is beautifully evoked in "Long Night" and "An Early Christmas." Most of the stories are set during the decades of Price's lifetime, but the range is, in fact, from the 1860s to the present, allowing for sudden allusions to an even deeper, more shadowy history as in this tourists' vision (in "Night and Silence") of Rome where "the Field of Mars still rocked in the dark to three millennia anyhow of soldiers' feet—wide-eyed delicate bird-voiced Etruscans, sun-kilned Roman legionnaires, the shaggy Goths (drunk on clear light) and us this past slow afternoon: polo-shirted, maps in hand." Price tends to be particular in time, not only in the setting of the stories but also in the exact time of telling. When the tale is told matters almost as much as who is the witness doing the telling. Here begins "The Company of the Dead": "Eighty-some years ago when I was a boy, Simp Dockett and I were in modest demand as reliable and inexpensive all-night 'setters.'"

All of these things add to the authenticity of the stories, an authority reinforced by clearly autobiographical elements. At least six stories have a character named "Reynolds" in them, and others play close to the edges of the public facts of Price's life. This in turn allows him to enjoy the freedom of unabashed nostalgia without sentimentality. He has established his reliability, and the reader will gladly follow wherever he goes. Sometimes, with undiminished credibility, he goes deeply into the precincts of dreams and dream visions (not surprising for a man who teaches Milton), and there are ghosts in any number of these stories; in "This Wait," a ghost is the believable narrator.

But as in all worthy texts, it is finally the spirit and not the letter of Price's stories that lifts them to achieve a grace beyond the art and craft of all but the finest few of his contemporaries. Nobody I know of writes so well about the joys and sorrows of the family. Nobody else can so deftly capture the lyric intensity of simple happiness. To do so, of course, he must come face to face with grief, loss, and pain. There are plenty of stories here that will break your heart, but there are precious few without the gift of laughter. Above all, Price writes his best work about the kinds of love—obsessional love and lasting love, love in the family, love between men and women, men and men, old and young, interracial love, all these treated with respect, without vulgarity or cynicism. In "To the Reader," Price writes: "From the start my stories were driven by heat—passion and mystery . . . and my general aim is the transfer of a spell of keen witness, perceived by the reader as warranted in character and act." The result of the aim is the accomplishment of this spellbinding collection, a book to be treasured for a long time to come.

(1993)

A Visitation of Spirits by Randall Kenan

This is a very daring first novel, courageous in its ambition, innovative in its execution, and, one is happy to be able to report, at once successful and exciting in its overall effect. It is also more than merely interesting for other than purely literary reasons.

Randall Kenan centers his story closely on two specific dates: April 30, 1984, and December 8, 1985. But as his story develops and those days play out their separate but related dramas, the story becomes much larger and deeper, touching on several generations of one black family, from slavery days until almost here and now, in and around Tims Creek, North Carolina, and being mainly concerned with the lives and times of two contemporary family members, cousins—James Malachai Green, schoolteacher and Baptist preacher, and the younger Horace Thomas Cross, a brilliant and gifted student for whom the future looks more than promising except for a terrible burden of guilt and confusion.

Using layers of richly allusive language—formal, demotic, biblical, confessional, and literary, the electric idiom of inner-city streets played off against the timeless lingo of the country tall tale, the rooted rural *fabliaux*, the full vocabulary of private prayer and public sermon—Kenan tells how Horace, profoundly troubled, indeed tortured by real or imaginary demons ("Whether or not the demon was a ghost of his mind, or a spirit of the nether world, this did happen"), recapitulates during one night his whole life, in a distorted vision or memory, in the very places and among the very people he has known and loved or hated. One of the epigraphs for the story, both appropriately and ironically, is taken from Dickens's *A Christmas Carol.*

The second plot line concerns one cold day in December when the young Reverend Jimmy takes his aging Aunt Ruth and his Uncle Zeke to Memorial Hospital in Fayetteville to visit Ruth's dying husband, Asa. It's a wonderfully funny and sad trip for all of them (and for the reader), ending with a sense of understanding that transforms everything and offsets something of the tragedy that has beset them all, especially the death of Jimmy's wife and the doom of young Horace. Ruth and Zeke have been childishly fighting each other, quarreling all day long with Jimmy acting as a desperate, hopelessly ineffectual peacemaker. Then, suddenly, standing together in a garage while Jimmy's Oldsmobile is being repaired, the two old people look out at a driving rainstorm:

"Raining hard, ain't it?"
"Oh, yeah. But I bet it'll turn into snow soon."
"Snow?"
"Yeah."
"You might be right."
They stood there. Silent. Jimmy expected quiet, soft conciliatory words. Then he realized he had already heard them, as pure and honest as the rain.

In both style and content, *A Visitation of Spirits* is breathtaking in its explicit virtuosity. Many first novels display a fine excess of verbal facility; it's something you look for in a brilliant beginner—and Kenan has his way with words, line by line. But he can do much more. He keeps a very complex time scheme going, moving steadily forward without clumsy confusion. He shifts his points of view—various kinds of third-person and first-person voices, occasionally relieved by a straightforward dialogue scene set on the page like a playscript. This latter device pays off when we learn how Horace spent a summer working for a local theatrical production, a "mish-mash of ill-conceived, ill-wrought, cliché-ridden drivel" called *Ride the Freedom Star.* Especially noteworthy, and worthy of praise, are Kenan's evocations of the sensuous affective surfaces of the "real" world. He engages all five senses fully and is particularly effective in waking the reader's sense of smell. Truth is,

Kenan tries pretty much everything, and he pretty much gets away with all of it, too.

One reason he succeeds is that the substance of the novel is even more remarkable. There are splendid set pieces on hog killing and chicken plucking and on the growing and harvesting of tobacco. But there are also pieces of equal weight and impact on contemporary music, high-school studies and sports, and on the comic books that Horace loves: "I remember wanting to be rich and white and respected like Bruce Wayne and invulnerable and handsome and noble like Clark Kent." This is New South fiction with a vengeance and with genuine panache. Kenan's most daring narrative choices are, first, to make Horace a credible and not unadmirable homosexual, amid a hostile environment for his preference; and, finally, to allow this young man to come to a violent ending which, in less careful and skilled hands, might seem to be a cop-out. It is, instead, at once tragic and mundane.

Some readers who have grown comfortably used to the hardening tropes and conventions of contemporary black fiction are in for some surprises here, too. Telling the truth as he knows it and feels it, Kenan joins the latest generation of new black writers, people like Percival Everett and Trey Ellis and Don Belton and Yolanda Barnes and many others, each of them different from the others, but all dedicated to a fresh and surprising vision of the real world. For example, here the hatred and fear of white people and of their injustices are mostly secondhand. For Horace and his generation, the days of segregation are more like myth than a memory, and the only overtly racist attitudes and remarks we encounter come from the older generation of blacks. Horace has more complex and subtle problems. Here he views himself and his four white buddies ("Musketeers, Caballeros, Brothers-in-Arms") at high school: "Consider that they might be condescending in their innocent way, accepting him merely as a reaction to the traditional racial bias of the area? That by showing their lack of prejudice and befriending a black as their peer, they could somehow show their superiority?"

It takes courage to call them as you see them. As I hope many readers will discover, Randall Kenan has talent and courage to spare.

(1989)

Nashville 1864: The Dying of the Light by Madison Jones

Even in the present season, a bleak one for American publishing and literature, for readers and writers, there come times and causes for celebration. One of these is here and now in 1997 with the return, after almost a decade of silence, of Madison Jones to the literary scene with his ninth novel—*Nashville 1864: The Dying of the Light.*

For many years, Jones enjoyed a well-earned reputation as one of the major figures of contemporary southern letters; indeed, his critical history and repute were recently highlighted and recapitulated by a special issue of the *Chattahoochee Review*. But clearly, as *Nashville 1864* demonstrates beyond doubt, Jones is not in the least content to be considered a regional icon. He is an active, energetic novelist and storyteller, daring to accept new challenges, to take new directions, an artist, then, whose career is alive and looking forward.

Civil War novels of all kinds are many, and most of them leave a lot to be desired. Still, there are a few that have accurately called up those times, that savage era, transforming history into present happening, enriching our knowledge and understanding. *Nashville 1864* belongs in the charmed winners' circle of that precious few.

The premise is that this is a manuscript by "my maternal grandfather Steven Moore, completed in 1900 in Moore's forty-eighth year." The short, resonant novel is told in the first person by Steven, who tells it from the point of view of the young Steven who was twelve years old at the time of the Battle of Nashville (December 15 and 16, 1864). The Moore family—Jason Moore, the father; Amantha, the mother; Steven and his two younger sisters, Kate and Liza; and the "slave help," "one family with two boys and a girl"— had a farm on Charlotte Pike a few miles west of the occupied city of Nashville. Dink, the youngest boy of the slave family, "was my age and my companion in most things."

Young Steven, at the time, is not much aware of the complex problems of slavery. At the outset, he sees the relationship as being "indeed, familylike." A number of things happen to change that comfortable innocence. And the older Steven, writing the story years later, allows himself a moment of "digressing into the realm of polemics," aptly presenting the mixed views of his maturity, acknowledging and condemning the faults of the "Peculiar Institution," but still defending his homeplace and his people against charges of "abuses much advertised, and much exaggerated in the North." Many a working novelist, less courageous and honest than Jones, would have dodged the issue or at least given an acceptable late-twentieth-century point of view to his storyteller.

With efficient skill Jones is able to give every one of these central characters their just due and dimension so that we are, as they were, always aware of the fragile, vulnerable community they comprise. With Jason off at the war, serving first under General Johnston, then under the aggressive and unlucky Hood; with official and punitive harrassment from the occupying Yankees and with real danger from predatory stragglers and deserters, the family struggles to survive. Finally the two boys, Dink and Steven, have to go out together urgently searching for Jason. Thus they find themselves in the deadly middle of the Battle of Nashville, which, from their tense, fragmentary, and inexperienced point of view, becomes painfully real to the reader. What happens to them and their quest is the rest of the story.

Madison Jones, a part-time, full-fledged farmer himself, handles the details of southern rural life with knowing authority. Few of our novelists can summon up weather (the heat and cold, the wet and dry) or define the contours of terrain as adroitly as Jones. Like his characters, Jones loves the landscape of home.

But the greatest strength of *Nashville 1864* lies in the language—"tone perfect for those times," writes Tennessee novelist Madison Smartt Bell. It is marked by clarity and simplicity, a perfect melding of the words of the mature Steven with the thoughts and feelings of himself as a child on the edge of manhood.

Historically (if not politically) correct, *Nashville 1864* stands as a rare example of valid and viable historical fiction and joins the ranks of the best and brightest books about the Civil War.

(1997)

The Thanatos Syndrome by Walker Percy

There is a delightful mystery at the core of the art and craft of Walker Percy, something on the order of the mysterious practices of a first-class chef. The ingredients are familiar yet somehow always surprising, always new. He writes novels like nobody else's, creating a world not quite like any you have ever visited. Place—in this case the parish of Feliciana, Louisiana—is not so much described or evoked as very precisely assumed. You can bark your shins on the sticks and stones there. The people are familiar, from both life and art, and yet oddly eccentric, as if seen only in the distorting mirrors of a carnival fun house.

The story line has all the machinery of good old-fashioned plot fiction and the rushing stimulation of many trendy concerns (in this case, among other things, AIDS, child abuse, pornography, crime in the cities and on the streets, and computer technology). Yet taken all together, we have something very different, something very close to fable, the purely fabulous.

With *The Thanatos Syndrome* we are in the territory of Dr. Tom More, a student of both the brain and the soul. On parole from a stretch in prison, Dr. Tom tries to pick up his life and practice again. One of the first things he notices is that his old patients have gone and changed on him, not necessarily for the better—"Maybe they, my patients, are not crazy, but something's going on here. What I need is objective evidence, more cases."

He notices changes of personality toward "a curious flatness of tone";

changes in sexuality ("less missionary positioning"); changes in language "reminiscent of the early fragmentary telepathic sentences of a 3-year-old"; context loss and *idiot-savant,* computerlike response.

Together with his cousin, epidemiologist Dr. Lucy Lipscomb, he achieves a surprising breakthrough. It is a high-tech parallel to one of the most celebrated solutions in the annals of epidemiology—the tracing by John Snow of the sources of polluted water causing the cholera epidemic in London in 1849, and has much of the excitement of the original. They discover that one modern nightmare is true: somebody is putting drugs in the water supply. It's supposed to eliminate crime, disease, and antisocial behavior, and to improve our minds. It does, but it also frees up the monsters in ourselves. The rest of the story primarily concerns the efforts of Dr. Tom and a small crew of good guys to stop the harm that's being done and to return us to our place as the normal, imperfect creatures that we are. This time the good guys win one, bumbling and muddling through in a nice mixture of high seriousness and high-spirited slapstick.

The characters in this modern fable are our contemporaries, after all, but they seem to have been transmuted into players from some medieval mystery or morality play. Fanciful? This novel has serious, memorable scenes involving a good priest who won't come down from a tower and a bridge-playing physician named Van Dorn who becomes the pupil of a gorilla ("a morose female named Eve") in a cage. Van Dorn, sent to prison for various and sundry nefarious crimes, ends up in the best modern manner: "As resilient as ever, however, he was soon running the prison library, giving bridge lessons, and writing a book. *My Life and Love with Eve* was an immediate and sensational best seller, serialized with photos in Penthouse and eventually made into a six hour mini-series for stereo-V, the Playboy channel. It made such a hit with the Louisiana governor that he pardoned Van Dorn, who has since been busy on the talk show circuit and making appearances on the Donahue show, often with Dr. Ruth."

And in Father Smith, a wonderfully realized and dedicated old priest, Percy creates one of the finest priests in all our fiction. Father Smith is the one person entitled to some last words about the story and our times. Here are some of them: "More people have been killed in this country by tenderhearted souls than by cruel barbarians in all other centuries put together."

It is a Christian book, a Catholic book, to be sure, but it will challenge and delight everyone who reads it.

To read Walker Percy is to fall under his spell. It was Keats who said that "poetry should surprise by a fine excess." If that is a good definition, and I think it is, Percy has been writing novels that are poetry. *The Thanatos Syndrome* is surely one of his finest.

(1987)

Celebration by Mary Lee Settle

Whenever Mary Lee Settle's novels have acquired critical and public attention, as they have at several different times, on various occasions during a long and productive career (nine novels and three nonfiction books), the thing that has surprised and delighted her "discoverers" most has been her almost uncanny art of characterization, a virtuoso's capacity to create fully dimensional, wholly credible people of all ages and backgrounds, of every gender, race, creed, and sexual preference.

It is as if nobody had told her that we are supposed to be so limited in imagination that we are prohibited from any true understanding of one another. It is no surprise, then, to her longtime, regular readers to find the likes of Anne Tyler, Ann Beattie, Walker Percy, and E. L. Doctorow, among others, celebrating precisely this rare accomplishment in her new book, her best so far, *Celebration*.

And in this case, it is earned praise worthy of the title, for what other American writer could have imagined, created, and brought together such a gallery of fascinating people? There are: Father Pius Deng, a seven-foot Dinka Jesuit from the Sudan; Noel, Lord Atherton, a gentle and superbly intelligent English homosexual; Ewen McLeod, a geologist who is writing a book on the Great African Rift and is every inch a Scotsman; Teresa Leonard Cerutti, a young American anthropologist and widow who is recovering from a close encounter with cancer. These all tell their own stories.

And there are so many others, lesser figures in the scheme and structure of the book, but real enough to be well remembered. Even the least walk-ons—Dr. Dangle, the unimaginative psychiatrist; Fred Funkhauser from the CIA; Dean Withers of the college where Teresa taught; O. Stuart Starr, a deputy sheriff with dreams of glory; and many more—live fully enough to cast real shadows. Even wholly imaginary characters—Teresa's dream companion, the black monk, or Pius Deng's mythical force for disorder, Abou Baba Moosa—are believable.

The story line is, as they often say, "deceptively simple." In this case, that cliché serves as an accurate generalization. Teresa comes to London in 1969, alone, to collect herself. Her fate is to meet Ewen in the Reading Room of the British Museum. These two have many things in common, including the fact that each is recovering from a deadly serious illness. Gradually, almost in spite of themselves, they fall in love, and essentially *Celebration* becomes a love story, ending appropriately with their wedding. In between, there are deaths and entrances, many large and small events.

Adding weight and shadows to the central love story are those separately elaborated stories (each, also, a story of love and death) of Ewen's best friend, Pius Deng, in Africa, and of Teresa's best friend from early childhood, Noel, in Hong Kong, all of whom meet each other on the occasion of the Moon Landing and later at the celebration of the wedding. All of whom share, separately in vivid and adroit flashbacks, the complex story of their lives. All of whom have been "to the less naive side of the river Styx." They know about death and, indeed, their knowledge and wisdom are sorely tested here and now as one of their number is murdered just before the wedding. There are all kinds of events, but the essence of the book lies in its characters. Their stories are the story.

There is much more to Settle's art than brilliant characterization. Nobody I know of can create a better sense of time and place. Her other novels have ranged, easily, between the here-and-now and the seventeenth century, with all points in between.

There are breathtaking excursions deep into the heart of Malakastan, of Hong Kong, of Africa, fully developed stories growing naturally out of these places, places Settle knows by heart. Then there is the matter of style. Sentence by sentence, line by line, Settle is surely one of the finest, most supple and subtle stylists in our language. Among working novelists, only

John Updike is a real competitor, and his pyrotechnics tend to call attention to himself and get in the way. Settle's language goes beyond polish to purest clarity.

But finally, and most important, her people and places and words matter. She writes about things that matter. This novel is a love story, several love stories (including the impeccable rendering of the love of Noel for the Chinese boy, Wei Li) celebrating the triumph of life and love over death by survivors who have seen death.

There is tragedy here, but the story ends in joy, an earned joy for these few good people who have found each other in the global storm. Joy, too, for the reader who follows in their footsteps. And joy for this reviewer in being able to recommend *Celebration* as a magical experience.

(1986)

Wolfe in Wolfe's Clothing: *O Lost: A Story of the Buried Life* by Thomas Wolfe and *To Loot My Life Clean: The Thomas Wolfe–Maxwell Perkins Correspondence,* edited by Matthew J. Bruccoli and Park Bucker

What we have here are two good books published by the increasingly adventurous University of South Carolina Press in celebration of the centenary of Thomas Wolfe (1900–1938). *O Lost* is the original version of what became *Look Homeward, Angel* (1929), the text being carefully established and edited by Arlyn and Matthew J. Bruccoli from a pencil draft in seventeen ledgers, a typescript carbon copy (with a few missing pages), and five clusters of the ribbon copy. The editors tell us that "the setting copy of *Look Homeward, Angel* is unlocated and presumed lost." The job of composing an accurate text—a labor of love by the editors, who have foregone any earnings and royalties in favor of the Wolfe Estate—was more complicated than it might have been, since neither Wolfe nor his famous editor, Maxwell Perkins, nor his typist, Abe Smith, troubled themselves very much with small details. Most of the line editing and proofreading and correction for Scribner's was accomplished by poet-editor John Hall Wheelock. A few months after publication of *Angel,* Wolfe received a letter from Louis N. Feipel, whose hobby was proofreading published books, who sent Wolfe a list of hundreds of errors and inconsistencies. According to the editors, none of these errors and inconsistencies in *Angel* was ever emended. The scholarship is solid, and the strategy of the editors direct. "The rationale for this edition is to establish the text of *O Lost* that should have been published in 1929 by Charles Scribner's Sons after necessary editing, house styling and proofing."

To Loot My Life Clean: The Thomas Wolfe–Maxwell Perkins Correspondence, published simultaneously with *O Lost,* is what it announces itself to be and something more. It offers some 251 letters exchanged between Wolfe and Perkins, John Hall Wheelock, Charles Scribner III, and others at Scribner's, roughly two thirds of which have never been published. The letters are presented chronologically from the March 1928 "Note for the Publisher's Reader," written before Wolfe first made contact with Perkins, to Perkins's final telegram to Fred Wolfe on the occasion of Tom's death—"Deeply sorry . . ." In addition to useful notes, there are five appendices—"Undatable Letters," "Unmailed Wolfe Letters," "Maxwell Perkins' Biographical Observations on Thomas Wolfe," "Errors and Inconsistencies in the Published Text of *Look Homeward, Angel,*" and "Scribner's Alteration Lists for *Of Time and the River.*" Taken together, these two books, among other things, definitively dispel the popular myth that, somehow or other, Wolfe was an invention of Maxwell Perkins. As Bruccoli and Bucker put it, "According to the popular version of this story, Wolfe was an undisciplined writer whose exuberant, overwritten prose could only be published through a collaboration with his editor. Perkins is portrayed as a controlling editor-father to Wolfe, the child-writer, from whom words flowed unhindered and unexamined. . . . The letters published here document Wolfe's artistic and professional problems and demonstrate how Perkins, as both editor and friend, aided Wolfe in solving them. They set the record straight."

Perkins, who worked with a variety of well-known writers—Hemingway and Fitzgerald, Caroline Gordon, Nancy Hale, and Marjorie Kinnan Rawlings among them—seems to have concerned himself chiefly with questions of structure and point of view. Thus, the fundamental differences between *O Lost* and *Angel* are structural and depend on limiting the point of view, as much as possible, to the consciousness of the protagonist, Eugene Gant. *O Lost* was clearly intended by Wolfe to be a much more inclusive and omniscient narrative. Certainly the book, though composed of much of the same autobiographical materials as *Angel* and *Of Time and the River,* is a different novel and one well worth the expense and effort of resurrection. Whether or not it is, as the editors assert, a "better" novel than *Look Homeward, Angel* is a judgment call: it all depends. What is certain, though, is that, as a first novel by a new and unknown writer, it would not likely have been published by Scribner's (or anyone else) except in some kind of cut and rearranged form. Not that *O Lost* was, by any serious standards, too long or too experimental. Once *Look Homeward, Angel* had been published and had achieved considerable commercial and critical success, length and size were less of a problem, as witness the next novel, *Of Time and the River.* In combination, *O Lost* and *To Loot My Life Clean* serve to answer some longstanding questions, even as they raise others. After them, Wolfe has to be taken as demonstrably a more assured craftsman, possessed of a larger and more complex vision than he has usually been considered to have had. Perkins was uniformly helpful and sympathetic, especially in the making of *Of Time and the River,* but Wolfe was always his own man. "Real life" was somewhat more complicated, however. Driven by a fierce hunger for fame (something more than "celebrity"), Wolfe was often difficult and disingenuous, often, in Perkins's word, "turbulent." Like Hemingway and Fitzgerald, his presence on the Scribner's back list ultimately earned the publisher a fortune. Wolfe, however, had serious money problems: Scribner's was considerate, but niggardly. With full appreciation of the venture of the University of South Carolina Press, one must wonder if the present-day Scribner's were not the appropriate publisher of these books. We are also left wondering why it took so long for all this to matter—that is, why Wolfe's literary reputation suffered after his untimely death and in spite of his undeniable achievement. The Perkins myth, overturned by these books, is part of it. So is politics. The 1930s version of political correctness was, if anything, even more obnoxiously obstreperous than the current one.

    Finally, there is the aesthetic factor. Though Wolfe was much admired by readers and many other writers, he was an original, a romantic, not easily understood or honored by modernist and postmodernist critics. Nevertheless, his works have remained in print and his influence on three generations of American writers seems undiminished.

(2001)

Peter Taylor: A Writer's Life by Hubert H. McAlexander

Literary biographers face daunting challenges. Maybe the most troublesome is that, allowing the notable exceptions (Hemingway on safari, Fitzgerald splashing around in the Plaza fountain, etc.), writers are not in serious competition with captains of industry or action heroes. They are private people engaged in solitary performance. Outwardly and visibly, they sit quietly at desks. Inwardly and spiritually, they are busy casting spells designed to turn their lives (even themselves) into words on a page. The best of them somehow become their work. Sometimes the work endures, and it is the work that matters most. The rest is mostly irrelevant. Hard as it is in our time—an age that celebrates public life ("image") above all, an age grievously infected by the culture of celebrity—for the writer to make the old magic work, it may be harder for the literary biographer to make good sense and lively copy out of the counterlife of an artist.

Hubert H. McAlexander has done pretty well by Peter Taylor (1917–1994). Taylor, important, original, and influential, especially in the art of the short story, arrived on the scene brilliantly with his first book, *A Long Fourth and Other Stories* (1948), and, overcoming the ups and downs of fickle fashion, retained a well-earned place in the literary pantheon, creating an important body of work—fourteen worthy books. McAlexander, an English professor and editor of two earlier books concerning his subject, *Conversations with Peter Taylor* (1987) and *Critical Essays on Peter Taylor* (1993), gives a fascinating account of the facts of Taylor's life and a sense of his artistic accomplishment, and the richly intricate story of his family background. What a colorful crew were his ancestors, his kith and kin: Tennessee governors and senators, men of substance and character as well as wealth and privilege. McAlexander has chosen not to clutter his story with much literary criticism. If that is a weakness, this biography has other and significant strengths. With primary access to the letters and papers of Taylor (and others), the author uses them well, quoting extensively and thus allowing the reader to enjoy the pleasures of the prose of a writer who couldn't turn out a bad sentence at gunpoint. McAlexander's writing is appropriately clear and workmanlike and does not try to compete with that of his subject.

If there is only rudimentary literary criticism, there is plenty of literary history and lively gossip here. Taylor was a charming and courteous man, a gregarious social animal. His deep, long-lasting literary friendships with Allen Tate and John Crowe Ransom, with Eudora Welty, Randall Jarrell, Robert Lowell, Jean Stafford, and many others offer us some rare verbal snapshots of these people, taken by a sensitive and wholly credible witness.

The early pages dealing with family and Tennessee background are a real contribution. McAlexander is able to define the world out of which Taylor's fiction bloomed. Closely following the details of Taylor's career—stories accepted and rejected by magazines, grants and fellowships and awards and prizes won or lost, good reviews and bad, the hard labor of teaching at a variety of institutions, sometimes happily and sometimes not—McAlexander produces an exemplary documentary of the changing literary situation in America in the second half of the twentieth century.

Peter Taylor was a hardworking writer, courageously so in his last years when he suffered terribly from ill health. Off duty, he liked to party down, and some of McAlexander's best attention and most engaged writing are devoted to his subject's social life. There are a whole lot of parties here. Taylor also enjoyed gardening, and together with his wife, the poet Eleanor Taylor, who survives him, he bought and rehabilitated and sold (profitably) an astonishing number of houses. Peter Taylor had a lot of fun. He was a witty and sometimes outrageously funny man, a world-class southern gentleman with an irrepressible streak of rowdy hillbilly. People who knew him well will miss some of that paradoxical quality in this biography.

Are there other weaknesses? Nothing serious. A sprinkling of minor factual errors and, perhaps more serious, self-imposed limits on the scope of the study. Even though McAlexander interviewed a large number of former students and colleagues and friends, he has missed any number of others whose testimony could have made for a fuller, more fully dimensional portrait. The book seems a little hurried. What we have, then, is a readable first biography of one of our finest writers, and we can be grateful for it. Other books, biographical and critical, are said to be in the works. Meanwhile, *Peter Taylor: A Writer's Life* is a helpful aid to the understanding and appreciation of a major American writer.

(2001)

Bow to the Bull's-Eye: *To the White Sea* by James Dickey

The story line of *To the White Sea* is as straight and sure and simple as the flight of an arrow, bow to bull's-eye. Sergeant Muldrow, a gunner in the crew of a B-29 Superfortress, a small-sized man of enormous willpower and physical strength, flies out on a bombing mission, Tinian Island to Tokyo, on the night of March 8, 1945. Over the target, his plane is shot down by enemy anti-aircraft fire, but he manages to escape and bails out into the night sky, coming down near the harbor. Muldrow finds a hiding place and waits there for an expected firebombing of the city, hoping to be able to escape to the countryside amid the chaos and confusion of the raid. History tells us that he did not have to wait long. On the night of March 9–10, General Curtis LeMay sent more than three hundred B-29s, carrying 1,650 tons of a new kind of incendiary bomb featuring jellied gasoline (napalm), to Tokyo, where more damage and casualties were inflicted than in any other air raid, including the atomic bomb attacks on Hiroshima and Nagasaki.

We experience this event from Muldrow's point of view as he works his way through fire and smoke and frightened crowds to escape the city. His difficult predicament is intensified by his certainty that if he is captured he will be castrated and beheaded. Once clear of the city, Muldrow heads north on Honshu, trying to survive and to make his way to the island of Hokkaido. The bulk of this quickly moving story becomes, then, the account of Muldrow's adventures and misadventures, told entirely in his own voice, as he incredibly makes it all the way to Hokkaido and meets with a surprising fate there. Because, from beginning to end, we are locked into Muldrow's consciousness, sharing his thoughts and perceptions, his memories and, above all in a Dickey fiction or poem, the intensely sensuous physicality of his being, much of the sustaining power of this survival story depends on the reader's involved interest in the gradually revealed character of Muldrow. We know him first by the language he uses to speak to us, which, except for the very rare possibilities for direct dialogue, is colloquial, simple, but charged with energy and poetry. It is not exactly the language of the poet James Dickey, but at times it moves very close to the language and concerns of any number of Dickey's well-known poems, especially "The Firebombing," "Falling," "Encounter in the Cage Country," "For the Last Wolverine," and others among the earlier collections. In a sense, Muldrow is a mouthpiece for a great many themes and deep concerns that have engaged Dickey's attention throughout his literary career. Similarly, Muldrow thinks and speaks in images and patterns like a poet. It is in this sense that the publisher has carefully chosen to call the novel, in jacket copy, "a transcendent meditation on one man facing desperate odds."

But Muldrow has a life of his own. He is a singular and surprising character, not a shadow of James Dickey nor very much like anyone else you may have encountered in life or art. Inevitably there are vague echoes here of *Robinson Crusoe,* of Hemingway's Nick Adams (especially in "Big Two-Hearted River"), and of *Pincher Martin* by William Golding; but Muldrow is about as close to being a genuine original as you can find. Raised by his father (who is now dead) in near isolation in the remote Brooks Range of Alaska, now without kith or kin or much more than casual interest in others, he is passionately in love with the icy purity of cold, with color and the absence of color; and he is wholly caught up in the continual natural equation of predator and prey, a kind of intricate dance in which he can easily imagine and identify with both sides: "I knew in the white outfit I used to wear, that if I closed my eyes I would be as out of the world as the snowshoe hare—the snowshoe hare on one side or the lynx on the other." He is likewise of two minds, one focused on details, ruthlessly rational, the other a kind of dreaming, something ironically close to the way of Zen: "The way I do things is to concentrate real hard on the first part of a problem that leads to another part, and then bear down on the next one, the same way, when I get to it.

Sometimes you find yourself in a situation where it's better not to think, but just to let go of everything and ride—there's a split second when you tell your brain to go out of you and something else in yourself takes over. You don't have to worry anymore; it'll all work out." Muldrow is capable of admiring, even honoring others for skill, courage, and common decency, but he loves no living human being. He is stoical, utterly unsentimental, perfectly ruthless (he has to kill any number of people to survive); and yet he is not cruel and hates cruelty in others.

The book is of two minds, also; in part a credible and detailed survival story, in part dreamlike, timeless, and implausible. This latter quality proves to be perfectly appropriate when we arrive at the surprise ending. Before that, it adds a vaguely mystical dimension to the action.

Admirers of Dickey's poetry and of his two earlier novels will likely find in *To the White Sea* an example of his work at its finest. Others, unconverted, may trip over various minor flaws, including a little too much careless repetition and a certain flattened sameness acquired from the strict limitations of a single point of view. In any case, the arrival of the book is a literary event; and, according to the advance publicity, we will probably see this story, like *Deliverance,* translated into a film version.

(1993)

As fire is kindled by fire, so is a poet's mind kindled by contact with a brother poet.
    —JOHN KEBLE, *Lectures on Poetry, XVI*

A Letter from Earth

James Dickey: The World as a Lie, by Henry Hart
Crux: The Letters of James Dickey, edited by Matthew J. Bruccoli and Judith S. Baughman
The James Dickey Reader, edited by Henry Hart

Dear Jimbo,
    I am sending this c/o the Dead Poets Society. I hope it reaches you all right. Sure, it's doubtful, I know. But, then again, why not? About the afterlife . . . well, let's not get into a big argument about all that. I remember we used to argue sometimes about whether there was anyone else, besides ourselves, out there in the universe. You said we were all alone here, and I said that statistically there were probably hundreds of James Dickeys out there writing poems at any given moment. I was only kidding. I do, however, believe in the afterlife. Even if I did not, I would strongly argue that all that wealth of energy (and you had enormous energy to waste and burn until your very last sad days!) can't just disappear. It seeks and probably finds a homeplace in this lonesome universe. And, to use somewhat less cosmic terms, your poems, the best of them—and they are many—are still very much alive and, I venture, will continue to be as long as our beleaguered language lasts. Critics and reviewers can and do and will give you a full share

of ups and downs. They can praise you or blame you. But it is way beyond their power and authority to strike or destroy a word of your life work.

Lord, it's been years since I've been in touch with you. Ever since I bailed out of the University of South Carolina to go and live in our house in Maine (and to finish up a book or two), we seldom, if ever, wrote and only called briefly and on business. Met here and there a few times. I remember you introduced me—and a funny and generous introduction it was—when I came back to South Carolina to give a reading for the Thomas Cooper Society. We saluted each other at one or two meetings of the Fellowship of Southern Writers. And I had a chance to chat with you briefly at the Scott Fitzgerald Festival at USC in September 1996. You were pretty much confined to a wheelchair (a neat-looking blonde babe was pushing you around, of course), sucking on an oxygen tank (it failed once during lunch), and you looked frail and weary; but I honestly did not guess how close you were to dying. Sorry we didn't have a chance to talk more and maybe to swap a couple or three stories.

The purpose and occasion of this letter is to bring you up to date on a number of things. Mainly it is, or can be so called, a review of Henry Hart's biography of you. But there are other things, too, that deserve to be mentioned. Chris's book (*The Summer of Deliverance,* by Christopher Dickey) came out in 1998, got a lot of attention, and made its mark. It seems to have shocked some people with its picture of you in the years after *Deliverance* (1970), as self-destruction and disintegration followed hard on the heels of success. It was a good book, well written and well reported. He told a moving story from his point of view. His portrait of you, warts and all, anticipates and muffles at least some of the aftershocks that will inevitably follow Hart's more objective and thorough biography. Chris's book may help people to understand your story and better appreciate what Hart has done.

Things have been pretty busy since your death (January 19, 1997). The primary texts have been put together in *James Dickey: The Selected Poems* (Wesleyan, 1998), edited by Robert Kirschten; and in *The James Dickey Reader,* edited by biographer Henry Hart (and dedicated to your literary executor, Matthew J. Bruccoli), including representative selections of your poetry, fiction, essays, and criticism. Also published in 1999 was *James Dickey,* the nineteenth volume of the Documentary Series of the *Dictionary of Literary Biography,* edited by Judith S. Baughman. Matthew J. Bruccoli and Miss Baughman are the editors of *Crux: The Letters of James Dickey.* Using roughly 20 percent of the available letters, the book adheres to the twofold logic of Bruccoli's assembly: "The double rationale for selection was first to document the growth of a major writer . . . then, second to document the ways he fulfilled his genius and advanced his career. Jim was unabashedly a careerist."

Bruccoli is putting it nicely. What comes across in these letters is the portrait of a hard-driving literary hustler and con man, perfectly willing to say or to do almost anything to advance himself and to promote and enhance his public image. The evidence is right there, even in this mildly sanitized version, Jim, that you were willing to bootlick and ass-kiss any other poets, critics and reviewers, agents and editors, whenever deemed necessary, to embrace your enemies and betray old friends, in the constant search for jobs, fellowships, prizes, awards, and better deals with better publishers! Book reviewers made a good deal, maybe too much, out of this. In the *New York Times* ("One Poet's Prosaic Correspondence," 10 December 1999), Michiko Kakutani opines that "a distressingly large portion is devoted to poetic politics: to snide putdowns of other poets, insider talk about prizes and fellowships, and catty remarks about rival cliques and claques." Similarly, poet and editor J. D. McClatchy (*New York Times Book Review,* 19 December 1999) assumes, in the trendy contemporary manner, a stance of high morality: "But most of the book is consumed by Dickey's literary resentments and intrigues, betrayals and backbiting. It's a sad and off-putting spectacle."

But negative reviews to the contrary, the letters in *Crux,* together with other letters quoted in Hart's biography, don't expose you as a carnival pitchman. Instead, they illustrate a shameful and ongoing period in our cultural history when even our poets, some of the best of them, were infected with the insidious virus of celebrity, aspiring to be elevated to that new American nobility of celebrity rock-and-rollers, slam-dunkers, breakdancers, and gangsta-rappers, a time when poets of several generations began to behave like packs of feral dogs, growling and snarling at each other or submissively wagging their tails in savage, unrelenting competition for crumbs and thin bones on the cultural garbage heap. You played the same game, from first to last, and you were better at it than most of the poets of your own generation. (You were a better poet than most of them, too.) You did not invent the game, but you certainly mastered it One of the funniest scams you ran had to do with John Hall Wheelock's *Poets of Today* series (Scribner's), which published three first books bound together in a single volume. That is how your first book, *Into the Stone*, was published. But before that, you spent time flattering and honoring Wheelock while simultaneously badmouthing the series in letters to several young poets, cleverly discouraging the competition.

It's a pleasure to watch how easily you could handle those guys. What a bunch of jerks!

Once, you and I had a serious talk about careerism and hustling. You said that, by dint of dedication and hard labor, we were sometimes given the glorious gift of maybe half a dozen poems (or stories or novels) that were touched with greatness. You said it was our bounden duty to be faithful to those gifts; that we must not allow what we had been given to disappear; that to be faithful we must be willing to take any risk, to do anything, not for the sake of ourselves and our large or small careers, but for the sake of what we had been given.

Looking at the younger poets coming along behind you, the young and the restless, I think you might be troubled by the way things have gone. Even in our deepest cynical moments of disillusion, I don't think we could (or would) have imagined a generation of poets who would squander their modest gifts, devoting themselves not to the discipline of contemplation or to creative art, but rather to crude manipulations and to shameless, ruthless self-aggrandizement. Names? You and I know who they are. Let interested readers examine the index and read the letters of *Crux*. Let them read Henry Hart's excellent biography, *James Dickey: The World as a Lie*.

Hart's biography is a long one, 811 pages, and it is going to bother a lot of people. (It may even trouble you, Jim, though I doubt it.) Has bothered some people already, well before publication. Your old buddy (and mine), Bill Starr of Columbia's *The State*, reacted with shock and surprise ("Brutal Biography May Jolt Devotees of Dickey's Work," 15 February 2000). Bill doesn't criticize or quarrel with Hart's biography. But he is deeply troubled by the revealed content of your life: "Hart's biography, subtitled 'The World As a Lie,' charts Dickey's banal self-absorption and pathetic self-destruction in minute detail, which gradually becomes so revolting as to make reading a painful act."

Well, maybe so . . . and maybe not.

I do think, though, that you would be pleased by what Hart has accomplished. He has interviewed large numbers of people who knew you from childhood to the end. He has followed the intricate paper trails, pursued every conceivable lead. The biggest problem facing him was that you almost never told the factual truth about anything. Hart had to sweep aside an enormous amount of misinformation and disinformation, mostly planted by you, like a veritable minefield. All writers create, to a greater or lesser extreme, a dream autobiography, based on exaggeration, deepest wishes, or pure fantasy. It comes with the age and the territory, Jim, this great American con game of inventing or reinventing ourselves. After reading Hart's biography, I have to say that nobody in the literary world could ever match you in this liar's craft. You understood this from your brief (and incompetent) days in the advertising business, how easy it is for image to overwhelm and replace reality. How image-makers (poets in the art world, media in "real life") are the high and low priests of this secular religion. You turned your life, as Hart proves, into a good, if highly improbable story. The jock stuff, the combat stories, the hunting with bow and blowgun, the guitar playing, all of it proves to be either outright fabrication or at least radically different from what you claimed. And nobody cared. You were interviewed innumerable times and each time with a different story. It would have taken fifteen minutes, a phone call or two, to check. No literary journalist did so. Nobody cared. It was a story. More fun than most. Even Hart may have been reluctant to present the mundane facts lest he, and the reader, lose sight of the poetry. But in all this, poetry as well as factual accounting, Hart has done a fine job and a daring one.

Daring? In order to set the record straight and to balance against this his obvious admiration for your poetry, he had to write a long and detailed story, for which he will probably be faulted by many reviewers. His problem was not unlike that of Joseph Blotner and his initial biography of William Faulkner. He had to start from scratch and establish all the facts. He has done so. Hart is accurate, judicious, and thorough. Later versions of your life (and they will come along soon enough) will have to depend on this one. The great curses of biography in our age—psychobabble and judgmentalism—are amazingly absent. Disillusioned or not, Hart is fair, and his good judgment is not clouded. He maintains a clear, unobtrusive, and appropriate style; and he has managed some significant criticism, skillfully dealing with your work in its complex relationship with both your fictive and factual lives. He writes well about the poetry, especially the often ignored, intensely difficult, self-indulgent later poems. He follows the conception and gestation of the novels, which you thought about and toyed with most of your adult life. He places your literary criticism firmly in the context of the times. And, most surprising to me, he is able to say some interesting things about the coffee-table books you made money on during the last years of your life. He treats them seriously and demonstrates the validity of the proposition that everything by a major writer, large or small, slight or deadly serious, finally matters.

Are there any flaws? Of course. There are tales I heard (and told) differently. There are things I would interpret differently. And there are minor quibbles. For instance, I wish Hart, who is justly interested in sales and money, had distinguished between hardcover and paperback sales or had related your advances and earnings to those of your peers. You made a good deal of money, Jim, but not as much as some other writers I know. You blew most of it away. We could use a more comprehensive examination of your finances.

A final test. Even though I knew you pretty well for a while, I learned a lot about you that I didn't know then or later. Some things genuinely surprised me. Some things have given me a lot to think about. On the whole, Jim, my guess is that you would be pleased with a job well done and with the prospect that, in part because of this, you and your work will be the subjects of serious interest this year and, likely, for many years to come.

Best wishes from the first days of the new millennium.

Sincerely,
George

(2002)

INTRODUCTIONS

There are two kinds of introductions here: spoken introductions of writers and their work that were made at specific public events and occasions, and written introductions intended for published reprint editions. These forms are, of course, slightly different from each other in style and tone of voice (among other things), but in both cases my chief aims were to be at once celebratory and as brief as possible.
—G. G.

Introducing Wendell Berry

1994 Aiken Taylor Award, Sewanee

In a passage in Wendell Berry's novel *The Memory of Old Jack* (1974), the central character is thinking about the basic themes of his life: "He knows that as one of the inescapable themes of his life: the departure from him, from the beginning, of men and women he has loved, of days and years, of lightness and swiftness and strength. The other theme is faithfulness to what has remained. What has always remained is the earth, promising the return of what has been taken from it. What has remained is the good darkness out of which all things come, even the light, and to which they all go back again." These two themes (among some others) lace together the poems, essays, and fiction of Wendell Berry.

Wendell Erdman Berry was born in Kentucky on August 5, 1934. He earned his B.A. and M.A. at the University of Kentucky and studied at Stanford as a Wallace Stegner Writing Fellow. Although, for a variety of good reasons, he cannot be called an academic, he has in fact taught at Georgetown, New York University, Stanford, Cincinnati, Centre College, Bucknell, and the University of Kentucky. And, at last count, he has received eight honorary degrees. But mainly Wendell Berry has been a multitalented and prolific writer and a working farmer. Since February 7, 1965, when Wendell and Tanya Berry put their names on the deed, he has made his home and farmed the land at Lanes Landing Farm, Port Royal, Kentucky. (Port Royal is the original for which Port William is the fictional version.)

It is hard to keep up with Wendell Berry's literary work. The checklists and the reference materials are almost always out of date and incomplete by the time they appear in print. The best count I can come up with at this point, beginning with the publication of the novel *Nathan Coulter* (1960), is four novels, three books of short stories, twenty-three collections of poems, including chapbooks, and fourteen books of essays and nonfiction. He has earned an impressive, enviable list of honors and awards, large and small, including, recently, the T. S. Eliot Award given by the Ingersoll Foundation, of which (by the way) he is one of only four American writers to receive that award. He is a founding member of the Fellowship of Southern Writers.

What you can see at a glance is that Wendell Berry, though first and foremost a poet, is also that rare being, a full-fledged man of letters. And the truth is, he is something more than all that—a master. Touch the work of a master anywhere and in any form, and you'll find it alive and kin to all his other work. In all his work, Wendell Berry has been intensely critical, a prophet really, crying out against the rapacious, self-centered, self-destructive elements and habits of our sorry times. But he is also a hopeful and happy warrior. As he wrote in "Some Thoughts on Citizenship and Conscience in Honor of Don Pratt" (published in the ravaged year of 1969):

> And so, difficult and troubling as the times are, I must not neglect to say that even now I experience hours when I am deeply happy and content, and hours when I feel the possibility of greater happiness and contentment than I have yet known. These times come to me when I am in the woods, or at work on my little farm. They come bearing the knowledge that the events of man are not the great events; that the rising of the sun and the falling of the rain are more stupendous than all the work of the scientists or prophets; that man is more blessed and graced by his days than he can ever hope to know; that the wild flowers silently bloom in the woods, exquisitely shaped and scented and colored, whether any man sees and praises them or not. A music attends the things of the earth. To sense that music is to be near the possibility of health and joy.

Wendell Berry is in every sense an important and a serious writer. But to say that does him a serious injustice, for it fails to mention his persistent good humor and his irrepressible wit. Without illusions, he sees the comic spirit wherever it can be found and rightfully belongs—including within himself.

Here are some lines by Wendell Berry that say it all exactly:

> I wish I was easy in my
>   mind, but I ain't.
> If it wasn't for anger,
> lust, and pride, I'd be
>   a saint.

Ladies and gentlemen, Wendell Berry. . . .

(1994)

Introducing Reynolds Price

An International Celebration of Southern Literature, 1996 Olympic Arts Festival, June 6–9, Agnes Scott College, Decatur, Georgia

It is not true that Reynolds Price needs no introduction, but it is fair to say that of all the dignitaries assembled here, he needs one least. And, more to the point, he deserves much more than any brief and formulaic introduction can promise or perform.

It is my pleasure to give that inadequate brief and formulaic introduction this evening.

Edward Reynolds Price was born in February 1933 in Macon, North Carolina. He attended public schools and then, from 1951 to 1955, he studied at Duke, after which he was a Rhodes Scholar who earned his B.Lit. at Merton College, Oxford. He returned to the States and brought out his first novel, *A Long and Happy Life*, in 1962. And he joined the faculty at Duke where, except for visiting other schools (Chapel Hill, Greensboro, Washington and Lee, Kansas, etc.), he has been ever since and where he now holds the James B. Duke Chair in English.

Since he produced *A Long and Happy Life* and introduced us to the unforgettable Rosacoke Mustian, he has been a remarkably productive professional writer, publishing some twenty-eight books, including novels, short stories, essays, criticism, poems, memoir, plays, and translations, most recently *Three Gospels: The Good News According to Mark and John,* and, bringing it all together in his own version: "An Honest Account of a Memorable Life."

This is an age of specialization and focused exploitation. Very few of our writers have possessed such a lavish variety of gifts and the daring and bravado to follow wherever they may lead. Price's work in all forms has received serious and mostly favorable attention; though he is good enough to have evoked critical savagery from some quarters. He has earned a share of prizes and awards; and over the years, as a teacher and by example, he has been a strong, good influence on many younger writers, acting as a mentor to new talents just as Eudora Welty and Stephen Spender, among others, helped him on his way. His influence has grown and expanded and now touches on all of us who care.

In May 1984, during an eclipse of the sun, he checked into a hospital and began a battle with cancer that has involved operations and painful therapy and yet has somehow become the source of a truly extraordinary period, more than a decade of dazzling productivity. Sixteen of his finest books have come to us during this time, for which we have to be grateful to his undaunted spirit.

But there is something more, simpler and deeper. Those of us in my generation, his generation, those of us who have inevitably made the acquaintance of that dark angel who aims to have the last word, our last words, can take comfort and heart from Reynolds Price's courage and integrity, believing that what we are doing, our art and craft, is worth the candle. We would be ashamed not to go on working.

Like Jacob, the son of Laughter, he has met that dark angel alone on the riverbank and wrestled through the long night. Though sorely wounded, like Jacob, he did not yield in the end and earned an angelic blessing and the shining signature of honor for his name.

Ladies and gentlemen, Reynolds Price....

(1996)

Foreword to *The Liberation of Lord Byron Jones* by Jesse Hill Ford

The Liberation of Lord Byron Jones is an important novel for a number of good reasons. When the book, Ford's fourth published book and his second novel, appeared in 1965, it received considerable critical attention, most of it highly favorable, some of it extraordinary. Ralph McGill called the novel "magnificent." Some reviewers allowed that they were troubled and confused by the multiple viewpoint, the shifting points of view divided and shared among a large cast rather than a single character. Some others, particularly in the South, were troubled by what they took to be the presented image of the contemporary South and by what they inferred to be the attitudes, the social and political positions of the author. But the novel was widely greeted with mostly favorable reviews in the United States, and it likewise received overwhelmingly positive notice in Great Britain, Europe, and even Japan. Not a major best-seller in hardcover, it was nevertheless a highly successful book commercially, a rare joining together of the ways and means of "serious" fiction—what these days would be identified as a "literary novel"—with the accessibility and conventions (then and now) of the "popular" mode.

These days, *The Liberation of Lord Byron Jones* would be called Jesse Hill Ford's "breakthrough" book. Certainly it made him something of a literary celebrity. Later, the story, the book, and its author received even more attention when the film based on the novel, written by Ford together with screenwriter Stirling Silliphant, appeared in theaters in 1969. Ford had already earned an enviable reputation as a serious literary artist. In his foreword to the published text of Ford's play, *The Conversion of Buster Drumwright* (1964), Ford's former Vanderbilt mentor, Donald Davidson, had cited the late Stark Young's definition of "a work of art that is pure," that is, the ideal of a work of art "free of considerations outside itself and untouched by the intrusions of another world of aims." Davidson went on to call *The Conversion of Buster Drumwright* "a remarkable example of the operation of this high principle, so generally neglected in our confused period of tendentiousness, dull absurdity and prurient sensationalism." Of the limited vision of many of Ford's better-known peers, Davidson wrote: "Their connections are with libraries, publishers, agents, and cocktail-party-givers, rather than with the people of a living society, and certainly not celestial."

The story of *The Liberation of Lord Byron Jones* is a complex accounting of the network of consequences arising from the fact that a decent and finally heroic black undertaker, L. B. Jones, a man of honor whose young wife, Emma, has an affair with a white policeman, demands equal justice under the law—a legal divorce from Emma. This uncompromising demand is the trigger for violence, mayhem, murder, and great tribulation for those central characters left alive and outwardly untouched. Like most writers dealing with credible, "realistic" fiction, Ford made use of whatever was at hand. He had written about the imaginary West Tennessee town of Somerton (loosely modeled on Humboldt, Tennessee) in a number of short stories and in his first novel, *Mountains of Gilead* (1961). In fact, Lord Byron Jones and his Lord Byron Jones Funeral Parlour for Colored have a part in *Mountains of Gilead*. Somerton and its history and family networks continued to play a crucial part in the later fiction of Jesse Hill Ford, notably in *The Raider* (1975), a historical story concerning the Civil War. In an author's note for *The Raider*, Ford insists on the factual basis and rooted reality of his story: "*The Raider* is the story passed down to me through my father, my mother, and my grandparents; it is the story of my people and of the land as it was in the old Southwest, that territory which we know today as the South." Of course, whenever a fiction writer shapes and transforms "real" raw material, there is always a small audience of readers more or less familiar with the original models, an audience that may understandably be confused by differences and discrepancies from the factual reality as they perceive it. Writing in the *Georgia Review* ("What Are You Doing There? What Are You Doing Here?:

A View of the Jesse Hill Ford Case," vol. 26, no. 2 [Summer 1972]: 121–44), novelist Jack Matthews pointed out: "When Jesse published *The Liberation of Lord Byron Jones* in 1965, a lot of people in Humboldt saw the book as an unmistakable version of an actual local murder case of ten years before, in which a Negro undertaker named Claybrook was shot and killed." This kind of reaction and perception might be entirely irrelevant, except that for some time afterward Ford continued to live and to write in Humboldt.

The popularity and success of Ford's novel allowed some readers who were uneasy both with the charged subject matter and its treatment to ignore the validity and the integrity of Ford's vision and, at worst, to misread his story. *The Liberation of Lord Byron Jones* was close to the times and the events that it deals with, so close indeed that it was easy for many readers at that time, myself among them, to misinterpret, to distort many elements of the story according to personal experience and the precise angle and point of view of the individual beholder. This kind of distortion often arises with a work of fiction that touches directly and deeply on things that matter; the artist takes the enormous risk that this version of events, the artist's vision of them, is not in itself a distortion and, finally, inauthentic, *untrue*. Though the story line in the novel ends with a full and satisfactory closure, the larger events of the same time are even now far from finished. In the final chapter, we learn of the death of President Kennedy in Dallas and the predictably mixed reaction to the news by the people of Somerton, Sligo County, Tennessee, and, too, of the personal inner feelings of Oman Hedgepath, the lawyer who is as near to being the central character and consciousness of this novel as its method of multiple viewpoints will allow. In a rare moment, naked of his characteristic defenses of irony, Oman tells us of "the dull pain I felt, the emptiness and sorrow and loss that filled me and sickened me," and relates those complex feelings to the story.

Not even a prophet could have fully imagined the sequence of brutal public events still to come in the years that followed close behind the publication of *The Liberation of Lord Byron Jones*. Nobody would have predicted (the prophesy would have been as outrageous as it was unbearable) that the racial conflict, and other attendant issues at the heart of the novel, would remain as serious and unsettled now as then.

The Liberation of Lord Byron Jones is in no way prophetic, and yet the passage of time has proved it to be true, a true bill of particulars. Quite aside from its significant aesthetic virtues, it has a double historical value. It is an authentic picture of the early 1960s, of events, attitudes, the clashes between old and new, the beginning of much that followed directly and much that is far from finished even now. Because of its clear authenticity and its relevance to recent history, the novel can also be taken, not unjustly, as a documentary background of how we have come to be where we are.

It is clear now that Ford was creating a tragedy in the classic model. One thinks, for example, of *Antigone*, where Creon's worldly wisdom and sense of justice clash head on with Antigone's abstract and uncompromising dedication to higher powers and principles. Neither is wholly right or wrong. Judged by the tragic results, both bear a burden of responsibility and guilt. Just so, judged against Steve Mundine's idealism or L. B. Jones's stubborn sense of honor and justice, Oman Hedgepath, defender not of the faith but of the status quo, seems compromised, unworthy. But he, too, is as wounded as he is wounding and, abstractions aside, has as good a case to make as anyone else in the story. All the principal characters make choices, some of them bad choices; but, much as in the working out of Greek tragedy, the end of things in pity and sorrow and loss seems to be inevitable, fated by the whole creaky mechanism of our society, a machine with history but without gods, things destined to be whatever they will be and become because of the conditions of character, the qualities of soul.

Ford's artistic method and choices emphasize all this. These characters, not puppets or stereotypes, are allowed to speak and to feel for themselves, to present themselves in third and in first person. Each viewpoint, no matter how firm in the mind of the character, is tentative, fragmentary. We are invited to join the chorus, to bear witness to the whole of it in a way no single character can. Each of the characters is given a slightly different idiom and style. By the end, at the funeral ritual of L. B. Jones, we can easily recognize their voices.

Of all Ford's novels, this one makes the most deliberate and intense use of sensory detail as filtered through the limited sensuous perception of the various characters. See how much odors and textures, the touch of things, matter here. The effect of the high level of sensory perception proportionately renders the characters vulnerable, alive, far from types or symbols of this and that. Sometimes, as in the case of the highly sensitive brute Mosby, it is a paradoxical characteristic, giving him a shadow, as it were. In all cases, the sensuous intensity, created and dealt out as a gift by the author, adds to the pleasures and the pains as they are experienced by the characters and thus by the reader.

Time has proved *The Liberation of Lord Byron Jones* to be a more mature, a sadder and wiser book than we knew at the time. Maybe even Ford couldn't have known it. He set out, as every novelist does, with the first fatal step on the long march, to imagine a tale and to tell it in the best way he possibly could. Like every worthy artist, he learned his way and earned his luck as he went along. Now it is, once again, in our hands, and we are lucky to have it.

(1993)

Introduction to *So Red the Rose* by Stark Young

Shortly following its official publication date of July 24, 1934, *So Red the Rose* established itself as a best-seller. It rose quickly to the number-two spot on the fiction lists, close behind *Anthony Adverse* (which, until *Gone With the Wind* came along a few years later, was the all-time best-selling American novel), and went through twenty printings in the year that followed. Stark Young's novel was widely and prominently and very favorably reviewed. Even the reviews with some serious reservations were genuinely respectful, only cautiously negative. The young Mary McCarthy, for example, reviewing the book for the *Nation*, gave it a mixed notice, summing up that it was "long, luscious, and finally cloying." Paramount moved promptly to buy the movie rights for $15,000, which was an excellent price for those Depression years; and with a screenplay partly written by Maxwell Anderson, directed by King Vidor, and starring Randolph Scott and Margaret Sullavan (and introducing Robert Cummings), the eighty-two-minute film was released in 1935. All the terms of an extraordinary success for the time were fulfilled.

Judging by Stark Young's letters (elegantly selected and annotated in two volumes by John Pilkington—*Stark Young: A Life in the Arts, Letters 1900–1962*, Louisiana State University Press, 1975), both the author and his editor, the celebrated Maxwell Perkins of Scribner's, were more than a little surprised by the commercial success of the book. Young had been publishing his work—plays, drama criticism, travel books, and three earlier novels, as well as fiction and nonfiction in a wide variety of both popular and literary magazines, beginning in 1906 with his first book, a collection of poems, *The Blind Man at the Window*. Young was an editor and contributing writer, writing book reviews, drama criticism, and other pieces, for the *New Republic* and *Theatre Arts* magazine. He had, likewise, been the drama critic for the *New York Times* in 1924–1925 and, during the 1920s, he had directed plays for the Theatre Guild. By that time of his life (he was born in Como, Mississippi, in 1881), Young was in no way naive about the American literary scene, and, indeed, for some months prior to the publication of *So Red the Rose* he had been dutifully and carefully working in a variety of conventional ways to drum up support from friends and colleagues to help the book along its way. Had the book followed its anticipated "mid-list" course, as had his three previously published novels—*Heaven Trees* (1926), *The Torches Flare* (1928), and *River House* (1929), all his preparation would have been well spent, necessary, and might have paid off modestly in sales and attention. As it was, the astonishing success of *So Red the Rose* made all that personal effort irrelevant. It is clear that neither Stark Young nor Scribner's, represented by the skilled and experienced Perkins, had any idea that this book would be such a major critical and commercial success. There was little precedent for it, though there had been significant fiction dealing with the Civil War both earlier and more recently. Young's distinguished friend, Ellen Glasgow, had brought out *The Battle-Ground* in 1902; and Mary Johnston, herself the author of an enormously successful historical romance, *To Have and to Hold* (1900), had published two gritty and hard-edged sequential Civil War novels—*The Long Roll* (1911) and *Cease Firing* (1912). (Essays about both Glasgow and Johnston's novels appear in *Classics of Civil War Fiction*, edited by David Madden and Peggy Bach, University Press of Mississippi, 1991.) There had been novels like James Boyd's *Marching On* (1927), Evelyn Scott's *The Wave* (1929), William Faulkner's *Sartoris* (1929), and T. S. Stribling's *The Forge* (1931), not to mention Stephen Vincent Benet's best-selling poetic "epic," *John Brown's Body* (1928), or one of Stark Young's favorite lyric poems, Allen Tate's "Ode to the Confederate Dead," which was in *Mr. Pope and Other Poems* (1928). And in 1930 that influential and provocative gathering of the Agrarians, *I'll Take My Stand,* had appeared, containing as its final essay Stark Young's "Not in Memoriam, But in Defense." In short, the subject of the South and the Civil War, its causes and long-term consequences, was, by the middle of the 1930s, a kind of literary genre, legitimate, not without interest, but without clues, signs, or portents that it might soon be a source of large profits for publishers and Hollywood. At the moment of its publication, the success of *So Red the Rose* was almost unimaginable. Just over the literary horizon was *Gone With the Wind*, even more extraordinary in its impact, surely prepared for by *So Red the Rose*. Would the New York editor Harold Latham have bothered with Margaret Mitchell's huge and confused mass of typescript if *So Red the Rose* had not already made some publishing history?

The literary world of the early 1930s, dominated as it was by the big cities of the Northeast and by an intellectual community that was often outspokenly unsympathetic to the ways and means of the South, seemed unlikely to accept passively and without question a southerner's view of the past that challenged a host of fashionable political and social assumptions. We know now what was only suspected then—that much of the intellectual American Left was organized and collusive in its patronage and its systems of punishments and rewards to writers and artists of all kinds whose work was measured chiefly by and against the shifting standards of political party lines. Even working at the *New Republic*, Stark Young managed to hold his own and to get along with his colleagues, including Malcolm Cowley, on the staff there. The only serious quarrel, one that popped up in print in the magazine, concerned Young's objections to coverage of the notorious Scottsboro Case written by Mary Heaton Vorse, author of *Strike: A Novel of Gastonia* and member-in-good-standing of the writers of the Left. Though pressed, Young stood his ground and, in spite of various interoffice machinations, managed to keep his job at the *New Republic*. At exactly this time, 1933, he was busy writing *So Red the Rose*, and, knowing the rules of the road, he had every reason to anticipate an ambush of his book by some of the more political-minded literary critics. The risks were real, though the early success of the book seems to have surprised his potential critics as much as it did the author. At any rate, except for some more-or-less predictable pieces like Mary McCarthy's in the *Nation*, *So Red the Rose* was spared the kind of sociopolitical mugging that was not uncommon in those years.

Even today, it is difficult fully to understand the how and why, the essential mystery of *So Red the Rose*'s triumph in the marketplace. Its considerable literary and artistic virtues, splendidly delineated by Donald Davidson in his introduction to the Modern Standard Authors' edition of *So Red the*

Rose (Scribner's, 1953), are solid and significant. Technically, Davidson points out and praises the constantly shifting points of view, depending on a large and complicated cast of characters and linked by the omniscient point of view of an adroitly neutral narrator, like one of the family, really, who happens to know a little more than everyone else. He takes note of Young's remarkable ability to keep the large cast of characters continually in action, not only the Bedfords and McGehees but also "their kin, friends, visitors, slaves—the whole complex of plantation life and, by implication, of Southern life in general." He deals with Young's bold use of "real" characters— Sherman, Grant, Jefferson Davis—in cameo appearances that ring true. He argues persuasively that the dramatic form of exposition by which Young leads us directly into scenes and situations without elaborate explanation, allowing the reader to arrive at inferences and judgments on his own, a device Davidson labels "uncertainty of orientation," works perfectly to give this story drama and concentration and a restraint defined as "a non-committal kind of implication." In general terms, Davidson especially praises Young's "unique position" in the literary scene, the ways in which "he stood apart, independent of the cliques, doctrinaire movements, and bizarre literary fashions that rioted through the New York scene and flooded the hinterland."

In addition to praising the art and craft of the novel, Davidson is especially concerned with its complex implications, its central meaning to readers here and now for whom, justly, the Civil War is merely a historical context. Davidson does not see *So Red the Rose* as only a Civil War novel; rather, "it is the tragedy of a people, closely bound by ties of kinship and common feeling, who refuse to dissociate 'the life of the affections' from 'what we mean by life,' in desperate conflict with other people who insist that such a dissociation is not only proper but necessary to human progress." Thus, in Davidson's view, *So Red the Rose* confronts and concerns one of the great and tragic conflicts of our times, then and now.

As a writer who had written successfully for the stage and for large magazine audiences, Young had certainly cultivated the capacity to create unforbidding, transparent, accessible prose, accessible to the imaginary general reader of the times, if not simple and easy. Young's integrity of purpose and his dedication to his art, taken together with his direct and family experience of the dimensions of southern history, serve to give his work a challenging depth and complexity. Because of his skill at crafting a clear and readable middle style, an omniscient voice to narrate a well-told story, moving steadily forward scene by realized scene, readers are in effect politely invited and ushered into the center of a felt experience. That experience is a subtle and demanding one, yielding up its essential implications, its meaning, in direct response to the intelligent engagement of the individual reader. Which is a way of saying that Mary McCarthy was at least partly right in her mixed assessment. *So Red the Rose* is appropriately "luscious," but the heart of it is as hard and cold as a broken rock.

Years later (1952), writing to Donald Davidson, who was preparing his introduction to the reprint of the novel, Young was as explicit as he could be in describing the basic intentions of his fictional rhetoric in *So Red the Rose:* "Instead of jabber and chatter and analysis and pretentious psychology or unintentional muddling I tried always for images that would convey the idea that underlay the moment. To my mind most things can be understood elementally at least by an average person, even sometimes a simple person—in a good sense. The business of a creative writer in such a case is to find what can express his idea, as a circle expresses circularity even in the moon or an orange; he is not able to rest till he finds a body for the soul of his matter."

Young's earlier novels had been set in the upcountry. In *Faulkner: A Biography,* Joseph Blotner tells us that *The Torches Flare,* for example, is "set in a thinly disguised Oxford," the Oxford where Stark Young, half a generation older than William Faulkner, grew up and went to school. For *So Red the Rose,* Young chose the Natchez area with its fine and well-known plantations and plantation houses, giving his story an elegant and resonant setting, able to evoke the physical beauty of the place before the Civil War. But there was something more that he was after also, something he stated outright in a letter (February 4, 1934) to Alabama writer Hudson Strode in which Young said his story is "laid down there in the Natchez country where the ground knows tragedy." The first lines of the epigraph selected by Young, taken from Edward FitzGerald's version of *The Rubaiyat of Omar Khayyam,* say it all:

> I sometimes think that never blows so red
> The rose as where some buried Caesar bled;
> That every hyacinth the garden wears
> Dropt in her lap from some once lovely head.

Rich garden imagery, deriving naturally from the quotidian reality of the place, is a major thread in the whole story, steady and cumulative, echoing by implication the loss of Eden.

So Red the Rose, though it includes other characters, high and low, black and white, is mainly the story of two large and interconnected plantation families—the McGehees of Montrose and the Bedfords of Portobello. McGehee is an actual family name in Stark Young's family line and, as a part of his research for the book, he had the use of many of their documents, papers, letters, and diaries. It should be noted in passing that the research is so refined, as a result of Young's method, that it does not "show" or interfere with the dramatic presentation, depending (not surprisingly for a dramatist) as much or more on scene and dialogue than on expository narration. What the intense research gave him was a subtle and powerful *authority.* The narrator/author seems to have lived through the whole experience, a sense that adds up to authenticity and credibility without distancing the reader with the smoke and mirrors of too many superficial details. The basic things—shelter, clothing, what they ate when and while they could, etc.—are all there; but it is the people and their flesh-and-blood humanity and the overwhelming impact of events that matter most. By no means saintly or even especially flawless in manner and behavior, the characters of these two families, each differently and distinctly, are shown to be decent, loving, worthwhile, and at times admirable people. We delight in their pleasures and, by the end, we are sorely wounded by their pains. Their way of life appears as neither perfect nor blameless, and yet when it is changed forever and largely lost, that loss seems irreparable, like the disappearance of a beautiful species from the taxonomy of living things. Young puts it clearly in a letter to his friend Leonidas W. Payne (February 10, 1933), even as he was writing the novel: "The book is laid in Natchez from 1860 to the autumn of 1865, no scenes in other places but echoes from places here and there during the war. Sherman, Grant and Jefferson Davis are in it and what I can't tell you about the history of the day is not worth telling! the letters and books I have read! I am making it a comment on civilization and living questions and the life of the affections and social standards, not a historical affair, but I need exact authenticity too. Pray for it. I want it to be a large, rich and beautiful canvas." *So Red the Rose* was not intended, then, to be "a historical affair," but to deal with "living questions." Neither is it exactly a war novel. The war itself comes late and suddenly and is mostly off-stage except for a few scenes when war arrives in brutal confusion with fire and sword and sudden pain and death. It is finally that image, an image of carnage, that concludes the story as the lady of Montrose, Agnes Randolph Bedford McGehee, remembers going away to the battlefield at Shiloh three years earlier, seeking, and finally finding, the body of her son, Edward. With night falling, she stands at the edge of the killing fields as the world fades to silence: "She was at Shiloh, but now she heard nothing, only the silence; then, inside her body, she heard her heart beating. Edward was among them somewhere but the others too were hers. She stood there looking out across the darkness and the field where the dead lay, as if they were all sleeping." The terrible carnage is not so much softened as it is converted, reconciled in the mind and memory of the immemorial tribal mother. The dead, on both sides, are their own monument. We know that life, the lives of the families go on. But the vision of Aunt Agnes remains: a sad, powerful, visionary ending to a story that commenced with the cheerful celebration of a birthday party.

Although Stark Young lived on until 1963 and continued to write short stories, travel pieces, drama criticism, and to translate and witness in production Chekhov's *The Cherry Orchard, The Sea Gull, The Three Sisters,* and *Uncle Vanya,* regularly traveling in Italy and across his native South, he wrote no more novels after *So Red the Rose.* He remained active in literary affairs, personally and in his voluminous correspondence. The number of literary people he was regularly in touch with is truly extraordinary, not only close friends like Allen Tate and Caroline Gordon, Ellen Glasgow, Donald Davidson, but also and including the likes of Alexander Woolcott, Julian Huxley, Francis Fergusson, Walter Kerr, Eric Bentley, Edmund Wilson, Malcolm Cowley, John Hall Wheelock, Sherwood Anderson, Thomas Wolfe, Robert Penn Warren, Charles Edward Eaton, and many others, not ignoring his fellow townsman William Faulkner. The relation between Young and Faulkner included a certain amount of competition and rivalry. Oxford was kinder to Stark Young. Young helped Faulkner in any number of ways—a place to stay in New York, a part-time job at the Doubleday bookstore, personal introductions that led to other things—but their friendship was uneasy. In letters to his mother, Faulkner always referred to Young as "Mr. Stark." Young, privately and not without a touch of sarcasm, called Faulkner "genius." Both men were gifted with talent as painters, and Young went on, later in life, to enjoy a kind of second career as a visual artist. Except for a few visits to New York and work time spent in Hollywood, Faulkner elected to stay at home. Though Young kept his place and roots in the South, he traveled widely and lived out much of his life in and around New York and died there in January of 1963. But he was buried in his homeplace of Como.

In 1951, Young published *The Pavilion*, dedicated to Allen Tate, a memoir of the first twenty-one years of his life, and he had plans of writing about the rest of his life, a memoir others were eager for because he had known so many prominent people in the theater and in the literary world. He never found the time for it. What remains now is the drama criticism, still directly witnessing a great era in American theater, and *So Red the Rose*, his finest and final novel, whose subtle artistry and surprising success were influential beyond all expectation. This new edition allows him to exercise that influence on another generation of American readers and writers.

(1992)

Foreword to *The Long Roll* by Mary Johnston

Published in 1911 by the Boston firm Houghton Mifflin Company and graced by handsome illustrations by N. C. Wyeth, Mary Johnston's *The Long Roll* was the fourth novel in a professional writing career that had begun before the turn of the century and was to include twenty-three novels, as well as other works (*Pioneers of the Old South*, 1918; and a verse play, *The Goddess of Reason*, 1907), before the author's death in 1936. *The Long Roll* received mixed notices when it appeared, after having first been serialized in the *Atlantic Monthly*. On several occasions, the novel was criticized for its failure to follow, and exploit, the tried-and-true resources of its perceived genre, the historical romance. Johnston had already earned an enviable reputation in that popular form with the extraordinary success of her second novel, *To Have and to Hold* (1900), an old-fashioned swashbuckler, if not a premature bodice-ripper, set mainly in and around the Jamestown settlement. The book sold in excess of 500,000 copies in hardcover and made her name in the literary scene. For a time thereafter, she commanded advances of $10,000 on her books, extraordinary at that time.

There was much more to Mary Johnston's art and craft than the conventions of the historical romance allowed; and even while working comfortably within that genre, she took chances and displayed other interests. Her sense of place, real and imaginary, was always vividly realized and gritty, with firmly evoked detail. And beginning even with her first novel, *Prisoners of*

Hope (1898), about pioneers in southwest Virginia, she seldom settled for conventional happy endings. Romance or not, real life took its toll in her work; even lucky survivors were scarred and bruised. Mary Johnston was simply and boldly imaginative, able to write about distant times and able, also, to create credible characters of all kinds. For example, *To Have and to Hold*, set in 1621–1622, is a first-person story told by a thirty-six-year-old man. Then and now, no critic has complained that the point of view is in any way inadequately realized. She also earned critical praise for her handling of the first-person narrative by a fictional Spaniard, Jayme de Marchena, also known as Juan Lepe, who sails on the first voyage of Columbus in her novel *1492* (1922).

One cannot escape the language, assumptions, or conventions of one's own times. Shakespeare did not; Chaucer could not; even a contemporary escape artist and literary Houdini like Kathy Acker could not. Why and how should we expect a very successful professional writer like Mary Johnston to break out of the form she had been given and had mastered? But it is clearer now, looking both backward and forward from her two novels about the Civil War, *The Long Roll* and its companion, *Cease Firing* (1912), that she regularly dared to take risks and seldom, if ever, settled for easy ways and means. It looks as if with each new novel she was working to reinvent and redesign the established form.

Even though some of the critics and reviewers of *The Long Roll* complained that her use of the conventions of the historical romance was at best cursory, others saw what Johnston was up to and praised her for it. The influential *North American Review* (11 August 1911) was unequivocal: "'The long roll' is the best fictional study of the civil war that has yet been done in America, and it achieves the impossible; it fairly makes that worn and hackneyed subject throbbingly alive." A day later, the *Saturday Review* announced: "Since Zola wrote 'La Debacle' there has been no more vivid story of war than this 'The long roll.'"

The reality in the scenes of war and combat, perhaps surprising in their accuracy and authenticity, came from several sources. First of all, Johnston had the benefit of memories and voices from two family members, to whose memory the books are dedicated—her father, John Williams Johnston, an artillery major, and her cousin, General Joseph E. Johnston. In the note "To the Reader," the author acknowledges her debts to "the historians, biographers, memoir and narrative writers, diarists, and contributors of but a vivid page or two to the magazines of the Historical Societies," adding "that many incidents which she (the author) has used were actual happenings, recorded by men and women writing of that through which they lived." She has changed the manner but not the substance, and she has used them because they were "true stories" and she wished that "breath of life within the book." *That breath of life*. She wanted a story beyond mere fiction, rooted in hard fact and real experience. We know from her papers that Mary Johnston mastered all the primary and secondary sources available at the time, and she walked the roads and explored the terrain of the battlefields to make her story as factually accurate as it could be. By the time the second volume, *Cease Firing* (1912), was published, these books had been recognized for what they were, and H. W. Mabie could write of *Cease Firing* in the *New York Times* (17 November 1912): "It takes its place beside 'The long roll': the two are our greatest stories of war."

What was this author's own life experience? Mary Johnston was born in 1870 in Buchanan, Virginia, in Boutetort County (locally pronounced Botuhtot County) in the Shenandoah Valley, nestled among the Blue Ridge Mountains and close to the James River. She was privately tutored and self-educated, and very well and widely read. She was nineteen when her mother died and she assumed parental responsibility for her five younger brothers and sisters, in addition to serving her father as hostess and housekeeper until his death in 1905. Afterward, she looked after herself and the rest of the family, earning her living as a novelist. While her father was still living, the family lived in New York City, Birmingham, and Richmond; and she traveled with her father to England, Scotland, Ireland, France, Italy, and Egypt. Beginning in 1912, after the publication of *Cease Firing*, she built and lived in a large house, Three Hills, beautifully situated on a hilltop in Bath County close to Warm Springs. She was a leader in the Equal Suffrage Movement and was involved in the formation of the Equal Suffrage League of Virginia. During the First World War, Johnston was an outspoken pacifist. She studied socialism and attended some meetings of the Socialist Party, though she never actually joined that party. A fascinated student of science as well as of psychic phenomena and forms of mysticism, she was profoundly concerned with, as she put it, "adventures in consciousness."

In the literary world, Johnston knew from her travels Thomas Hardy and J. M. Barrie. She was both friend and correspondent to Ellen Glasgow and Evelyn Thomson, and, through conferences, she came to know some of the younger generation of moderns. She was one of some thirty-three southern writers who were invited by Ellen Glasgow and Professor James Southall Wilson in the fall of 1931 to a literary gathering at the University of Virginia. Among those also present were DuBose Heyward, Paul Green, Allen Tate, Caroline Gordon, Donald Davidson, James Boyd, William Faulkner, Struthers Burt, Josephine Pinckney, and Alice Hegan Rice, author of the immensely popular *Mrs. Wiggs of the Cabbage Patch*.

On the whole, however, Johnston lived a quiet life in a quiet place; in Warm Springs to this day, the loudest noise is the splash and trickle of the steamy creeks, fed by the springs that give the hamlet its name. But as a voracious reader and a disciplined professional writer, she lived an adventurous imaginative life. Fifteen of her novels concern the life and times of Virginia. In others, she moved freely and easily in time and place: Elizabethan England and the high seas in *Sir Mortimer* (1904) and *Lewis Rand* (1908); seventeenth-century England in *The Witch* (1914); twelfth-century France in *The Fortunes of Garin* (1915); eighteenth-century Scotland in *Foes* (1918); Tudor England during the reign of Henry VII in *Silver Cross* (1922); and fifteenth-century Spain (and the ocean sea) in *1492* (1922). One of her later books, *Exile* (1927), is a utopian novel set in the future on the imaginary island of Eldorado. She is credited with two early feminist novels—*Hagar* (1913) and *The Wanderers* (1917). In all of these works, Johnston proves herself able to create large casts of credible characters with widely diverse points of view and with an appropriate and acceptable language for a wide variety of social classes and types, high and low.

All these gifts are strongly evident in *The Long Roll*. The book begins before the war and then divides itself between the early Valley campaigns and the large battles fought in the east in and around the Richmond area, ending with Chancellorsville and the death of Stonewall Jackson, and with a scene of Jackson lying in state in the Virginia Hall of Delegates in the Capitol of the Confederacy. This, then, is a narrative of the war up to what she sees as the high tide of the Confederacy and the turning point. N. C. Wyeth's frontispiece for the original edition was, appropriately, a picture of Jackson with his horse, Little Sorrel, standing on a high place, heroic, very stern, and also somehow ungainly, an awkward, heroic, and enigmatic man brooding, as it were, over the whole story that follows. From beginning to end, *The Long Roll* is a blend of real and fictional characters. Among the characters who appear and receive more than mere expository mention are Robert E. Lee, Jeb Stuart, Jefferson Davis, "Fighting Joe" Hooker, A. P. Hill, and a good many others in cameo roles.

Meanwhile, the cast of fictional characters is caught up in various personal plots and subplots that could, in another context, turn this story into a more conventional historical romance. There could be little or no suspense for the reader about the outcome of battles and the ordained end of things, but the shape of the story and the way in which it is told surprise the reader just as the characters are surprised by events. Moreover, the narrative is an implicit critique of the world of the historical romance, a world we witness being broken to pieces against the edges of hard facts. Among the fictional characters—each one with a personal story and with problems to be resolved—there is a romantic triangle: Richard Cleave, Judith Cary, and Maury Stafford, all upper-class people, each with the usual extended network of family, kinfolk, friends, and enemies. There are other important central characters—for example, Billy Maydew, the mountain man, and Allan Gold, the schoolmaster. And there is a splendidly realized cowardly low-life, Steve Dagg, a *miles gloriosus* right out of Plautus or Shakespeare, talking with a southern accent and a mountain dialect. He goes to great trouble to keep skin and bones, body and soul, intact during all situations. There are also a variety of women, and there are the slaves. All these characters have different points of view. Only the slaves speak in a phonetic dialect, as was the literary custom of the time.

Various kinds of language, rhetoric, and voices are summoned up to tell the tale. There are the voices of the different social classes and individual points of view, expressed in narration as well as in dialogue. There is a diversity of narrative rhetoric, ranging from a public, historical narrative voice, a chorus or collective vision, to the texts of real and imaginary documents; there are even song lyrics and in one case the musical notation for a bugle call. Gradually, we sense the way that the collective vision begins to overwhelm and often replace the individual (and often innocent) points of view. The problems that come from particularities of character and complexities of plot become an expendable pattern of desires and events no longer of much significance when measured against the enormity of the war. The Civil

War slowly becomes an inhuman character with a life and will and death of its own. Never completely—though it will be more complete in *Cease Firing*—the war takes over from its managers, the generals and statesmen of both sides, and even from its victims. The movement of the language of both books is from small to large, from particular to general, from the concrete toward the abstract.

Some of the language, both literary and vernacular, is dated. We are still too near in time to allow language to fade into a generalized historical past, so the language seems to be, at this stage, more like a slightly awkward version of our own. In *The Long Roll* and *Cease Firing*, we are witness to the end of the literary language of the late nineteenth century and the beginning of our own. In that sense, Johnston's work in *The Long Roll* and *Cease Firing* can be taken as transitional—certainly a precursor to the habits of modernity that derived from the shocking experience (real and imaginary) of the First World War, an experience that, with its imagery and memory, still haunts the contemporary consciousness. We tend to forget that Mary Johnston grew up among old soldiers, in a defeated society in which one out of four men between the ages of eighteen and sixty-five had been killed or permanently disabled—a society with one-armed and one-legged men everywhere. Mary Johnston knew the history of the war at first hand. She knew that to tell the truth of it, she could not discard the conventions of historical narrative, but she must also simultaneously engage the imagination of her reader. The conventions of fiction could serve this purpose. And so she helped invent a form for our time: the novel that blends fact and fiction in subtle and shifting proportions, one whose chief aim is to seek and to share the truth, outward and visible, inward and spiritual, of an experience. The whole idea of what constitutes fiction about war, and the full range of its possibilities, has been changing constantly in response to the events and complexities of the bloody and terrible twentieth century. Near its beginning, Mary Johnston, seeking to honor her father's memory and to do justice to one of the most traumatic experiences in American history, was forced to recreate and redefine the novel. In creating *The Long Roll* and *Cease Firing*, she served all of us who have come after her.

(1996)

Foreword to *Cease Firing* by Mary Johnston

When *The Long Roll* was published in 1911, an advertisement announced that it was the "first of two volumes dealing with the war between the states. With illustrations in color by N. C. Wyeth." Thus the reader of *The Long Roll* began with the awareness that this novel was only part of the whole, that the two books were meant to be linked together (or would be, for no date was mentioned for the next untitled volume) by subject matter and by design and, as well, by the use of illustrations in color by the same artist. The reader was also being warned that whatever closure occurred in *The Long Roll*, its ending could not be taken as final but must point ahead to the next novel.

What followed, a year later, was the publication of *Cease Firing*. Where *The Long Roll* is concerned with the early campaigns in the Shenandoah Valley and in and around Richmond and—among other things—follows the fighting career of Thomas Jonathan ("Stonewall") Jackson from the outset of the war until his death at Chancellorsville in 1863, *Cease Firing* begins in the West, as the Siege of Vicksburg is about to commence and continues, swiftly alternating between the West and the Virginia campaigns, following the inexorable decline of the South's fortunes and ending just before the final events at Appomattox. In addition to detailed accounting of far-flung battlefields—Gettysburg, Chickamauga, Missionary Ridge, the Wilderness, Atlanta, Franklin—we are given brief and vivid scenes set in hospitals, prison camps, the cabins of the poor, and the houses of the well-to-do. As in *The*

Long Roll, prominent historical figures on both sides appear, speak (usually in their own words), and interact amid the confusion of events. Just so, the fictional characters who dominated the first volume reappear and change before our eyes, as events replace innocence and ignorance with brutal knowledge. It is to Mary Johnston's special credit that all of her characters, the "real" as well as the fictional, see what they see and do what they do without breaking the spell of contemporaneity. Not one is a prophet able to transcend the limits of the moment. Some of them, the best and the brightest, learn something and can make some sense out of what has happened to them, and can even share that knowledge with others, but none knows what we, the readers, know. We are led into their world and share their consciousness, gradually divesting ourselves of the sure and certain knowledge of where and how things will end.

This transition is the one great advantage of using fictional characters, each with his or her own story, in a book that aims to tell the whole story of the Civil War in two volumes. For, as *Cease Firing* implacably demonstrates, it is the large story of the war that Johnston wants to tell, rather than using it, as it so often was and still is, as a kind of theatrical background against which personal stories are played out. Her fictional characters, linking together the two volumes, have lively, interesting stories, well plotted and executed, but they seem to exist mainly to give the narrative of the war a human scale and some human significance.

All are wounded, one way or another, by their experience. Some, including the principal characters, Desiree Gaillard and Edward Cary, die. Their story ends in rape and murder. Others endure. And the end of things includes a happy, if somewhat shabby, wedding and a major personal act of forgiveness and reconciliation. Not all goes badly for the survivors. There is every indication that life will go on, not as if the horrors of the war had never happened but certainly in spite of the worst that had to be endured. As we follow the lives of the fictional characters, we are invited to suppose that justice, as we wish for it, is a hit-or-miss prospect, and that Providence, though it may be at the heart of history, is much too subtle and mysterious to comprehend.

As the last bits and pieces of the "historical romance" disappear and more and more the war itself becomes the principal character of these novels, Mary Johnston uses a variety of narrative voices to tell the tale. These are often the actual voices taken from documents, memoirs, and transcripts. There is the voice of the overall, omniscient narrator, godlike, who can shift from the large and abstract picture to the sentient level of a single soldier. Present also are little scenes, like a chorus, where nameless soldiers banter with one another and brood over the shapes of what has been. There are moments of poetic narration in which the narrator comes close to creating a prose equivalent to what we would now recognize as cinematic montage:

> The bells tolled loud in the South, tolled for the women in the nighttime, tolled for the shrunken armies, tolled for the cities that waited, a vision before their eyes of New Orleans, Atlanta, Savannah, tolled for the beleaguered places where men watched in the trenches, tolled for the burned farmhouses, the burned villages, the lonely, blackened country with the gaunt chimneys standing up, tolled for famine, tolled for death, tolled for the broken-hearted, tolled for human passions let loose, tolled for anger, greed and lust, tolled for the shrunken good, tolled for the mounting ill, tolled for war! Through the South they tolled and tolled.

At times, in the midst of a battle scene, Mary Johnston goes beyond her already vividly realistic rendition of combat to edge into a kind of surrealism. Here she summons up the "Bloody Angle," using Wyeth's facing illustration (present as a color plate in the 1912 edition) functionally as an outward and visible image and a base for her own narrative poetry:

> Billy fired, bit a cartridge, loaded, fired, loaded, fired, loaded, fired, and all over and over again, then, later used his bayonet, then clubbed his musket and struck with it, lifted, struck, lifted, struck. Each distinct action carried with it a more or less distinct thought. "This is going to be hell here, presently," thought the first cartridge. "No guns and every other Yank in creation coming jumping!" *"Thunder Run!"* thought the second; *"Thunder Run, Thunder Run, Thunder Run!"* Thought the third, "I killed that man with the twisted face." Thought the fourth, "I forgot to give Dave back his tin cup." The fifth cartridge had an irrelevant vision of the schoolhouse and the water-bucket on the bench by the door. The sixth thought, "That man won't go home either!" Down the line went the word, *Bayonets!* and he fixed his bayonet, the gun bore burning his fingers as he did so. The breastwork here was log and earth. Now other bayonets appeared over it, and behind the bayonets blue caps. "I have heard

many a fuss," said the first bayonet thrust, "but never a fuss like this!" "Blood, blood!" said the second. "I am the bloody Past! Just as strong and young as I ever was! More blood!"

Johnston's careful, thoughtful imagination set her free to write some of the best combat scenes in all of American literature. How does her work stand up in comparison with other Civil War fiction? For ambition and scope—the attempt to tell the whole story of the war in two volumes—the books' chief rival, really, is not fiction at all. Shelby Foote's *The Civil War: A Narrative* does not use anything fictional, though its techniques of telling are often novelistic. *The Civil War* deliberately limits itself to hard facts and real people in their words and deeds. It aims to cover all of the war's events, east and west, on land and at sea, and it succeeds admirably. There is no place in Foote's scheme for the vestiges of "historical romance" and no need for fictional characters to humanize his tale. Foote had already written a Civil War novel, *Shiloh* (1952), equally rooted in fact, and setting an example that would be followed by other writers dealing with the subject—limiting the range and focus of the story to the one major battle or event. For *The Civil War,* Foote took as his models and ideals the great classical historians Tacitus and Thucydides, and above all the *Iliad:* "Richmond Lattimore's translation put a Greekless author in close touch with his model." Mary Johnston had no such end in view, though she certainly sought the means to tell the story of the whole war as truly as possible in fictional terms. If, in the process, she did not shatter the conventions of the "historical romance" once and for all, she did do a better job of testing them against reality than many writers before or since her time.

In the banner literary year of 1929, the year that saw the publication of William Faulkner's *The Sound and the Fury,* Thomas Wolfe's *Look Homeward, Angel,* and Ernest Hemingway's *A Farewell to Arms,* Evelyn Scott brought out *The Wave,* a novel covering the whole of the Civil War that deployed a huge cast of historical and fictional characters in a sequence of events and actions related to one another only as minute parts of a panoramic portrait of the war. "War itself is the only hero of the book," Scott said (see Peggy Bach, "On Evelyn Scott's *The Wave,*" in *Classics of Civil War Fiction,* ed. David Madden and Peggy Bach [Jackson: University Press of Mississippi, 1991]). The differences from Mary Johnston's books are, first, that here no element of the popular historical romance remains, and second, that Scott is much less interested in evoking and depicting the truths about combat. By that time, with a world war behind them, readers did not need to be forcefully reminded that war is hell.

Before Johnston's time, there had been plenty of examples of good, bad, and indifferent books dealing with the Civil War. Most of the popular fictional works were unabashed and sentimental "historical romances." On the positive side, there were exemplary poets and poems of the war— Whittier, Whitman, and Herman Melville, among others. There is every reason to believe that the avid reader Mary Johnston was familiar with their works. And in the year 1895, just as she was beginning to move toward writing her own first novel, there was the shining example of Stephen Crane's *The Red Badge of Courage: An Episode of the American Civil War*. This unique short novel, marked by its poetic language, structure, and profound psychological insight, as well as by a deliberate vagueness of time and place—almost the opposite of Johnston's gritty specificity—has more in common with the poetry of the war than its fictional representations. But it must have been an inspiration to Johnston if only in the sense that it proved that one did not need to be an actual veteran of the Civil War to write accurately about the experience, that imagination was capable of summoning up reality.

Perhaps more pertinent and useful was the example of Johnston's friend Ellen Glasgow and her Civil War novel, *The Battle-Ground*. Glasgow, like Johnston and Scott, undertook to follow the whole war, beginning to end. Deliberately not a romance, indeed written (like Mary Johnston's books a decade later) against the grain of the conventions of the popular "historical romance," *The Battle-Ground* is as concerned with the lives of women and children as it is with the lives—and deaths—of fighting men. Again, what Johnston brought to the subject that was distinctly different was her knowledge of the experience of combat, something that no other writer—except perhaps Shelby Foote in *Shiloh* and *The Civil War*—has demonstrated. Moreover, Glasgow and Johnston were starting at different points of departure, Glasgow as the very young author of three novels, two of them—*The Descendant* (1897) and *Phases of an Inferior Planet* (1898)—clearly in the naturalistic tradition; Johnston as an already established author of several highly successful "historical romances." There was an element of self-sacrifice involved in Johnston's bold attempt to bring life into a literary form. Certainly it was a risky enterprise.

Since that time, throughout our century, there has been no diminution in the fascination, shared by writers and readers, with the Civil War as subject or setting. Some of our finest novelists have written major works dealing with the Civil War. There are too many examples to be named, but surely any list of these works would include William Faulkner's *Absalom, Absalom!* (1936), which ironically appeared in the same year as Margaret Mitchell's *Gone With the Wind*, and William Faulkner's *The Unvanquished* (1938). Also from the 1930s came John Peale Bishop's *Many Thousands Gone* (1931), Stark Young's *So Red the Rose* (1934), Andrew Lytle's *The Long Night* (1936), Caroline Gordon's *None Shall Look Back* (1937), and Allen Tate's *The Fathers* (1938).

Since World War II there have been many visions and versions of the Civil War, both popular and literary, sometimes both. Besides Shelby Foote's aforementioned triumph, the three volumes of *The Civil War: A Narrative* (1958–1974), there are such outstanding examples as Foote's own *Shiloh* (1952), Mary Lee Settle's *Know Nothing* (1960); Robert Penn Warren's *Wilderness* (1961), and Stephen Becker's masterpiece, *When the War Is Over* (1969). What is noteworthy about all these works is how they focus on the war from odd and sometimes limited angles. No longer—at least in fiction—the grand epic scope; the larger story is reflected or suggested in smaller stories. We start always with a human scale. *Shiloh* is the story of a single battle. Warren's *Wilderness* has as its protagonist Adam Rosenweig, an idealistic German Jewish immigrant who finds himself working as a peddler in the midst of the Battle of the Wilderness in 1863. Mary Lee Settle's *Know Nothing*, part of her *Beulah Quintet*, follows the lives of a number of characters in the years leading up to the war, ending just as the war itself begins. Becker's story is based on the historical execution by firing squad of one Thomas Martin (May 11, 1865), a young Confederate. It brings inextricably together "real" and fictional characters in a small bitter tragedy. It would be extravagant to claim (which she never did) that Mary Johnston's *The Long Roll* and *Cease Firing* radically changed the way fiction about the Civil War was written. But it is not too much to say (perhaps not enough) that her two novels are of great importance in the tradition of American fiction about the Civil War; that, except for Evelyn Scott, she was one of the last to try to encompass the experience of the whole war in fiction; and that as a story of war—any war—*The Long Roll* and *Cease Firing* give the reader a powerful sense of being there physically during the fully imagined combat scenes. These books have earned their rediscovery, and one may hope that readers will be led to seek out other works by this gifted author.

(1996)

Foreword to *Dream Garden: The Poetic Vision of Fred Chappell*, edited by Patrick Bizarro

It is a privilege to be a kind of porter, a gatekeeper here, to swing wide the gate with a little flourish and to welcome you to this wonderful and well-earned appreciation (in various forms) of Fred Chappell. I have known both the man and his work for a good many years, going back to a day and a time at Duke University when I was a young visiting writer and Fred Chappell was some kind of student. I had the pleasure of reading some of his work and, as I recall, awarding him a prize on behalf of the local literary magazine, the *Archive*.

In my mind, anyway, I've been awarding him prizes ever since. It was not then but on another trip down to Duke when I up and asked my host, and Fred's old teacher, the great William Blackburn, a man who had taught a good many very good writers— Mac Hyman, William Styron, Reynolds Price, Anne Tyler, among others—who among them ("Mirror, mirror on the wall") was the best of all. We were both a little sloshed on Blackburn's good bourbon, else I wouldn't have dared the impertinence of asking him such a thing. His answer was sober and instantaneous: "No question about it. Fred Chappell is the most gifted and the best of the bunch. Though whether he will ever 'succeed' as a writer the way they have, I don't know."

I believe Bill Blackburn would (may well) be very happy at the measure of "success" that has come along for Ole Fred, even though, as he feared, it has not been easy. Even though, to tell the truth, a mutual friend of mine and Fred's in fact commissioned a portrait painting of my decapitated bald head on a platter, I am not John the Baptist. Nor was meant to be. But I have been tooting horns and telling people about his work for all these years. To tell some more truth, I am relieved that there is such a big crowd of us, his fans, these days, a regular marching band of his admirers. What remains to be said is what is being said herein, here and now, and what will certainly, sure enough, be said by more and more writers and reviewers and critics—readers are voting with their feet and their wallets—in times to come. For myself, I will reiterate and oversimplify my position. We have among us a very modest number of writers who, in spite of the overwhelming trend toward specialization, write both fiction and poetry. We have only a very, very few who can do both things tolerably well. Fred Chappell is among the best American poets alive, an energetic, innovative, wonderfully imaginative master artist. Likewise his novels—always from the beginning first-rate and getting better all the time, as he has been growing and changing—are among our few and finest. And do not, please, ignore or forget his marvelous short stories, of all shapes and all sizes, which (it seems to me) are among the very best examples of that form and have not been fully exposed or appreciated yet. Or the criticism, which is rigorous, intelligent, inventive, and just. A true artist leaves his mark on all he touches. Fred Chappell as teacher has exercised an enormous and benign influence on contemporary letters.

Notice that I have just described for you our preeminent man of letters. As such, he constantly teaches others, myself among them, by example and by good influence.

I reckon I know a thousand and one stories about the "real" Fred Chappell, the living and breathing, suffering and rejoicing person, the man who wrote the books. I will spare you and him, for the time being, all but one of the most recent, which will be news to him, too. Not long ago I was in New York City, engaged in an intense and difficult discussion, the give-and-take chess moves of negotiation, with an important (and moderately imperious) editor. Someone who had her doubts—they were clear in the hard light of her eyes and the high set of her jaw—about both me and my project, my ideas. She didn't actually yawn in my face but might as well have. I was losing her interest by leaps and bounds. Somehow, entirely by accident, the name of Fred Chappell came into the conversation, only for a wink and a flash, to be sure, like the sudden flight of a kingfisher. She leaned toward me and wrinkled her brow.

"Do you really know him?"

"Who?"

"Fred Chappell."

"A little. . . . Yes, ma'am, I guess I do. Fred's a friend."

She didn't actually respond with the obligatory next line (Why didn't you say so?), but her whole face changed for the better into smiles and attention.

"Tell me a little about him," she said.

And I did.

And I will be sending her a copy of this happy gathering of other voices, too. Just as soon as I have one.

(1997)

Introduction to the Modern Library Edition of *Snopes*

At the living center of the life work of William Faulkner are the novels and stories that deal with Yoknapatawpha County, that wholly imaginary and deeply imagined place, at once based on and derived from his real home country, Lafayette County, Mississippi, but nevertheless independent with its own myths and legends, its own long and shadowy history, its diverse populations, its places much like places he had known and yet altogether his own invention. And at the heart of the fictional accounting of Yoknapatawpha County stands this trilogy—*The Hamlet* (1940), *The Town* (1957), and *The Mansion* (1959)—here joined together, as he had always hoped and planned they would be, as one continuous and sequential narrative.

Since constant change, the overwhelming and universal energy of change (for the better and for the worse) is an almost obsessive theme in Faulkner's fiction, the story of the Snopes family from the Civil War until nearly the here-and-now is itself constantly changing. There is consistency, to be sure, even though the books were written years apart, interrupted by other books and projects and at otherwise very busy times of his life. Faulkner and his later editors—Saxe Commins for *The Town* and Albert Erskine for *The Mansion*—made a serious effort to reduce and to modify, if not to eliminate, discrepancies in the individual novels and indeed with many other bits and pieces of the Snopes story as it had emerged, early and late, in other novels and in many of the short stories. The author's note at the outset of

The Mansion is a kind of credo celebrating his "hopes that his entire life's work is part of a living literature, and since 'living' is motion, and 'motion' is change and alteration and therefore the only alternative to motion is unmotion, stasis, death, there will be found discrepancies and contradictions in the thirty-four-year progress of this particular chronicle."

Even so, Faulkner was perfectly consistent about his aims in the reconciliation of the Snopes material: that consistency should, in fact, work backward from the latest version. Thus a given detail in *The Mansion* can be taken as the authentic version, but by and large the factual details of the story need not match each other exactly. As he wrote to Albert Erskine: "What I am trying to say is, the essential truth of these people and their doings, is the thing; the facts are not too important."

One of the deepest sources of Faulkner's art and vision is to be found in his habitual conservation of literary material, a kind of routine recycling that allowed him (and his readers) to review and renew events, characters, places, and things—the whole experience of a story from a variety of different angles and points of view. A visionary writer by nature, he was also continually revising, in the context of new work as if freshly remembered, stories he had already told. He was thinking about the Snopes material in the early 1920s, and already by 1926 he was writing some versions of it. Because of the hypnotic impact and signature of his style (*styles*, plural, would be more accurate), it is easy to miss the wild variety of his work. As an ever-exploring craftsman, Faulkner was relentlessly, extravagantly innovative. Among all of his novels, no two are constructed in exactly the same manner or told in precisely the same way or from the same points of view. Each is a new artistic adventure, making new and sometimes surprising demands on the reader. (Faulkner is not, not even at his most complex, "hard" to read, but he insistently invites the reader to a deeper engagement in the experience of the story. To that extent he honors his readers, allowing them to bring as much as they can to the shared experience.) What relates each of the Yoknapatawpha novels, and especially the Snopes trilogy to each other, among other things, is his habit of returning to old stories and reclaiming them for a new look. He invites his reader to remember as well as to encounter events.

The Snopes trilogy, though its forward motion and action, events and plot are riddled with remembering, moves inexorably and chronologically ahead, from the late-nineteenth- and early-twentieth-century rural world of

Frenchman's Bend in *The Hamlet* through the first quarter, and then some, of our century in the county seat of Jefferson in *The Town,* ending there in 1948 in *The Mansion.* We move from the timeless world of poor farmers and sharecroppers, the "Peasants," a world not essentially different from the rural life of all recorded history, into our own times. The world that we know comes alive, comes to be, before our eyes. The automobile replaces the mule and wagon. The Memphis airport—a hundred driving miles away—not the railroad, becomes the link to the larger, wider world. And yet the past, the world of *The Hamlet,* vividly endures, linked by characters and by stories about them, stories they tell. The past persists and is forever modified by the memories and myths, the speculation and the insatiable curiosity of the central characters, some of whom are, appropriately, the chief tellers of the tale. *The Hamlet,* though it has many tales told in the quoted words of its chief characters—especially the wonderful V. K. Ratliff, itinerant salesman of sewing machines and the true custodian and preserver of the county's history and news (which become history and legend soon enough)—has an overall, omniscient narrator possessed of a kind of collective voice, a master of many voices and moods, and many points of view. There are virtuoso moments as, for example, when, in the first chapter of Book Three, "The Long Summer," the narrator gently, even sympathetically, inhabits the consciousness of Ike Snopes, the idiot in love with a cow, and even, for a moment, presents reality from the cow's point of view. Mostly the narrator offers a collective point of view (not altogether unlike that of Ratliff) or limits his focus to a deeply sympathetic, yet utterly unsentimental version of the vision of a single character. Sometimes the narrator indulges himself and talks to us in rich mouthfuls of words, as if words were paint to be flung against his canvas. Sometimes this is for fun, as when the fart of an old horse, in the opening sentence of Book Three, is described as "the rich sonorous organ-tone of its entrails." But the same high style is used to enhance events and to lift the ordinary to the level of the uncommon. See for yourself how Eula Varner is perceived and presented to us in Book Two.

The Town is entirely told by three voices: first by Charles Mallison, who was not yet born when half the events of the story took place, and who calls himself, in the second paragraph of the first chapter, the collective point of view of the town of Jefferson; by the highly educated (Harvard and Heidelberg) lawyer Gavin Stevens, an indefatigable talker who can manage some stylish mouthfuls on his own; and by his friend Ratliff, a patient listener who has learned some wisdom. The three, taken together, tell the whole story and very gradually begin to sound more and more like each other as they influence each other. In *The Mansion,* the original third-person narrator returns now to share the telling with the same three monologists from *The Town.*

Clearly, then, one of the things that the whole Snopes trilogy is "about" is storytelling, how stories come to be and come to us and how the sum and substance of them become our history—how history is made. In a larger sense, the history of Yoknapatawpha County becomes, as Faulkner planned and hoped, by action, event, allusion, and echo, a version of the history of the world. In that sense, the cumulative story of that one place is the story of every place.

The surface of these novels, this trilogy, is complex, often intricate. But the tale itself is passionately simple. It follows the almost uninterrupted rise of Flem Snopes from poverty and obscurity to power, first in the county and later in the town, where he manages also to acquire the patina of respectability, if not honor, peaking as a bank president and a deacon of the Baptist Church—a paradigm, then, of the American dream of upward mobility, except for the undeniable fact that each and every step of the way has been achieved by every conceivable kind and form of double-dealing—from simple scams worked on the illusions of simple people (never forget that Ratliff, too, falls victim at the end of *The Hamlet* and learns a lot thereby) to overt acts of blackmail, extortion, and larceny, grand and petty. Nothing is too small for the ruthless, greedy attention of Flem Snopes, and until the very end of the trilogy, he is secure in his shamelessness. Most of the swarming Snopes clan—though not all by any means; bear in mind the honorable and successful Wall Street Panic Snopes—are up to no good most of the time, fascinating and repulsive and often as funny as can be. But Flem is the master Snopes, identified like his aristocratic counterpart, Jason Compson, who has a significant cameo role, as a true son of Satan, a banal and evil man.

All by himself, Flem Snopes would be worth a trilogy or more, but the two women in his life (never mind how and why; read and find out), the fabulous Eula Varner Snopes, heir to Lillith and Helen of Troy, and her daughter, Linda, are equally remarkable creations, both doomed and tragic figures, though with a difference; the first raised to mysterious and mythical proportion, both biblical and classical, by all her beholders and a multitude of admirers; the latter more "real" to those close around her (thus to readers also).

The only two characters in the trilogy of whom we are not invited to share the inner experience of consciousness are Flem and Eula. Mysterious to others, they become the occasion for steady and unrelenting speculation. We know them only from their works and ways. They keep their secrets to the end. They remain always able to surprise us, and everyone else, fictional and real, for as long as they live. Nevertheless, we notice, suddenly and briefly, some special truths about them. In *The Town,* we learn in one flashing moment, when Eula confronts her profoundly romantic admirer, Gavin Stevens, that, mythical creature or not, she can be coldly pragmatic and ruthlessly single-minded when she thinks she has to be. She is something more and different, in truth, than anyone had imagined her to be. Flem's nefarious career, in all three novels, is so marked by success that we tend not to notice his few failures or the true source of his power over others. His powers work, like those of any confidence man, only by appealing to the greed of others. When, as in the case of the first chapter of *The Town,* the two black men, Tom Tom and Tomey's Turl, set against each other and sorely abused by Snopes, manage to get together, swallow their pride, and come to "complete federation," Snopes is beaten. We know then that he is not invulnerable.

There are so many things to celebrate about this magnificent trilogy. I have elected here to speak, in awe and honor, about only a couple of them. One is the rich variety of Faulkner's method, his endlessly inventive ways and means of telling stories. He has opened up new territories for all the writers who have come and will come after him. He has changed our ways of thinking about the power and glory of fiction. He has challenged writers and readers alike, all over the world, to bring and to give to the experience of his art nothing less than the best they have. He has demonstrated that they (we) will be well rewarded.

And I have stressed his magical capacity for characterization. The events, outrageous or quotidian, that occur in these novels are perfectly presented, executed with a timing and finesse that the finest athletes could envy. But they work, they capture our attention and sustain our involvement because they happen to characters we can care about and believe in. He presents the surface—Flem's bow tie, Ratliff's blue shirt, Stevens's corncob pipe—directly and engages us with an intense physicality. Their flesh and bones seem real enough to suffer or rejoice, and the world they move in is not so much described as felt. And, above all, no matter how foolish or flawed they may be, no matter how educated or ignorant, they are blessed with the equality of an inner life and being that renders even the least of them worthy of full attention. All of this is clear, at once poetic and explicit, in the final pages of *The Mansion* when both Stevens and Ratliff unknowingly echo the prayer of the preacher Goodyhay—"Save us, Christ, the poor sons of bitches." And the classic poor s.o.b. Mink Snopes has a final and authentic vision of himself among the dead, "himself among them, equal to any, good, as any, brave as any, being inextricable from, anonymous with all of them." Faulkner has been sometimes faulted for giving deep thoughts and feelings to common characters, but that criticism can come only from a different vision of mankind, a vision as cold and mechanical as that of Flem Snopes. Faulkner's inclusive, democratic vision of the equality of human souls shines through all his characters and makes them matter. There is much laughter in the Snopes trilogy, but there are tears also.

A great deal has been written by scholars and critics about Faulkner and about this trilogy. Some of it is extremely valuable to a full and deeper appreciation of his work. But my strong suggestion to readers coming to these novels for the first time (and there will be generations of you) is to plunge in and fare forward, allowing the experience of the story to happen as it does, without any additional mediation or guidance. Experience the story before turning to or trusting the opinions and judgments of others, myself included.

The one big exception to this rule is the biography by Joseph Blotner, preferably the revised, one-volume version of 1984, wherein the story of the creation of the Snopes novels and the public reception of each as it first appeared is followed closely and accurately and does not in any way lessen the original impact. It also seems to me likely that the words and thoughts of Faulkner himself about these books, to be found in the *Selected Letters of William Faulkner* (1977), can only serve to enhance the reader's experience.

(1994)

INTERVIEWS

Since the middle of the twentieth century and spurred on by evolving technology (the wire recorder, the tape recorder, digital recorder, video camera, etc.), the literary interview has become more or less respectable and commonplace, common enough by now to be conceived of as a kind of literary genre with its own special forms. Here are three interviews: a "conversation," sometimes called "Q and A," and two "feature" interviews in which the questions are implied and assumed.
   —G. G.

Life into Art: A Conversation with David Huddle

Recorded at the Appalachian Literary Festival, Emory and Henry College,
October 23, 1992

David Huddle, a native of southwest Virginia and a graduate of the University of Virginia, where he studied with Peter Taylor, is author of more than a dozen books of fiction, poetry, and essays. He is professor of English at the University of Vermont.
—G. G.

GEORGE GARRETT: I thought what we would do would be just wing it a little bit, as if we were having a real conversation, more of a conversation than an interview. I want to start talking about poetry and its place in your work and your life. When I was first coming along as a beginning writer, I met and got to know Glenway Wescott. He didn't show a whole lot of interest in a young student's writing, but he wanted to know if I had ever written any poetry, because he said he didn't really take any novelist or fiction writer seriously unless he had written some poetry. By the same token, I detected the notion that he didn't take you seriously if you kept on doing it, that it was a phase that you went through. And it turned out that Mr. Wescott started out with a book of poems and subsequently became a novelist. I think that his attitude was probably the attitude of that generation where lots of people had begun as poets, but we had very, very few people then, or now either, who have continued. I can think of a few—Robert Penn Warren, for example, who devoted his time to his novels and then went back to poetry. I think of you and Fred Chappell, and maybe Kelly Cherry, Richard Dillard, and a few others who write both fiction and poetry simultaneously without apparently any worry about one thing taking precedence over another. So I was wondering if there is anything you want to say about the place of poetry as more than something to pass through to write fiction?

DAVID HUDDLE: Well, in some ways I blame you for starting me in it. I think the first poems I ever wrote were at Hollins. I did it in some part because other people were doing it, and I thought I would show them I could write a poem or two. I approached that writing very casually, not very sincerely. I certainly did not have in mind to give as much of my life to poetry as I have done, and I think even the poems in my first book, *Paper Boy,* were written almost just to say I can do this, I will do this. I always felt that I was in charge of my poetry, that I was telling it what to do, and I have now come to understand that it will let me know what it wants me to do. And I will try to pay attention and be dutiful. And I count myself lucky. A switch-hitter is an appropriate metaphor, for if you can bat both left-handed and right-handed there is a chance you can do more than someone who can bat only one way. It's a voice that I need for my life. I am lucky that I can find places to publish it, because as it has served more and more of a function in my life of telling me where I am and what I am thinking about and what I need to think about, I think I have gotten a little better at writing it. I would describe myself now as maybe being a B or B+ poet. But that's fine. I certainly think I have a long way to go in terms of learning to write poetry, and I look forward to learning.

GG: There are some very special nuances about your work. You don't lose the qualities that you had in your earlier books of poems and stories; instead, you add to them. The new poems are clearly by the same voice, but they are quite different. As to your poetry's relationship to your fiction, you have found a way to conserve literary material, to use the poetry and the fiction to play off against each other. But neither is dispensable, I think. I have a feeling that if you had to dispense with one, you would end up writing poetry—what we would all like to end up doing if we could do it. Do you feel, since I mentioned Fred and Kelly Cherry and some of the other southerners of roughly your generation, do you feel that this is part of a southern tradition? It's not exactly regional, but do you think of yourself as a part of a tradition as a poet?

DH: I guess I don't in that regard. I have a fair number of poet friends who write essays and who would like to write stories. So I assume that a desire to write in other genres exists among others. John Engels here lately has been writing some short stories that demonstrate that phenomenon.

GG: Lots of writers of my generation and lots of writers elsewhere today are known as fiction writers who write some poems or poets who write some stories. I think yours is a very special case where you are known as a writer who writes poems, fiction, and essays, who covers the field and knows the field and none at the expense of the others.

DH: Again, I think it's your fault. You may be the first person I ever knew who did it, so if you are a part of a southern tradition, then I am too. Yes, I am. I followed in your footsteps in this regard. I do think that this business of a model, of somebody else who is doing it, is more important than I would at one time have acknowledged. But I have a friend, Julia Alvarez, who is from the Dominican Republic, and she mentioned as a model somebody who was writing stories about growing up in a Hispanic family. "Oh," she said when she saw somebody doing that, "I can do that." I was around you and I knew what you were working on and had read your books, so I must have said, "George does this; why don't I do that? I might enjoy doing that too." Your fault.

GG: The other thing I wanted to talk about in terms of poetry is the kind of poetry you write. In the new book, there are some poems that might be called purely lyric. There is a lovely poem—actually it's not *purely* lyric, but part of an overall story of a father and a son. There is a picture of Virginia in October that is just a gorgeous piece of lyrical language. But by and large, if I were to describe the kind of work you have done and were doing until fairly recently, I would say it was almost exclusively narrative. It told stories, whether they were long ones or short ones, or short ones that were related to each other, and it was an exploration of the spoken language. It was colloquial. It was for the ear in a way that I think really good poetry is. What are the limits of this kind of language, and its strengths?

DH: I think that one of the things that poetry made available to me was the way people talked: the way my family members talked, the way people in my hometown of Ivanhoe, Virginia, talked, the way people in southwestern Virginia talked. And that kind of talk is a pleasure to the ear; it is also a pleasure to the tongue to be able to speak in that way. We southerners certainly enjoy telling each other stories and making talk with each other, in the same way that musicians enjoy playing with each other, jazz and bluegrass musicians ad-libbing together. I'm not sure how to account for the visual aspect of it, except to say that it is an inclination of mine to make pictures with words. To move toward pictures, to move toward how things look. That has always mattered a great deal to me. I think that is a resource as a fiction writer and as a poet. I have a very simple-minded idea that I tell my students, and that is that the stories that seem to hold the most power over me are those in which I have been able to see what things look like all the way through. So I am always telling them to be more photographic, to be more painterly, so that they can show what things look like. And I'm always working to do that both in poems and stories. And that's because I am shaken by how things look. I see things that shake my bones. You do, too.

GG: What you started out doing as early as *Paper Boy* was much more rare at that point in the American scene in poetry than it is now. I think people are now moving more and more, somewhat belatedly, into the attempt to tell stories. For quite a while, American poets were off chasing other balloons and involved in other things. You have consistently gone on exploring the possibilities of narrative, and your time has come around now. You and a handful of other poets have long been doing narrative. Among those writing today, who are your models and what poets do you look to for inspiration and example?

DH: Jim Seay, whom I met at Hollins, in his first book, *Let Not Your Hart*, wrote a kind of poetry that I liked a great deal without quite adequately understanding it. It had a kind of directness and narrative quality that I very much appreciated. I think what I didn't quite understand was the wit, the literary allusiveness, the irony of Seay. I have understood that only over a long period of time. So maybe by only partially understanding his work, I set forth. He has a poem called "Kelly Dug a Hole." It's about a guy who had the skill of digging a hole straight so that when you put a plumb-bob in, you could see that it was absolutely straight. Boy, did I admire that poem. I thought that was just a wonderful poem. I liked its common qualities. I liked its celebration of work; not high work but low work, good ditch-digging work. I suppose I admired that for a long time just from hanging out with my grandfather on the farm with the farm workers who did such things as threshing wheat and baling hay and milking cows. I liked the texture of work, and I liked the notion of poetry as that low activity, that kind of enlisted-man approach to literature. So Jim really did hit me. I also heard James Dickey read at the University of Virginia just the year before I met you, and I have to say that I found that a very powerful experience on several counts. One, because it was a very macho kind of performance, a manly kind of poetry that I had never imagined being possible. And also because of his writing about animals and nature, in what seemed to me a very wild way, and portraits of wild activity that seemed to me something like what I was after when we would go out drinking late at night and driving dirt roads through the country. It was like that.

GG: "Wild to be wreckage forever."

DH: That's right. Wild to be wreckage forever. So I liked those two poets, and I guess Jim Seay still means a lot to me and James Dickey doesn't anymore. The poetry he is writing now doesn't work for me, although I still love the earlier poems. John Engels, whom I met when I went to Vermont twenty-one years ago, has been my poet companion all of these years. When I write a poem, I put it in the mail to him and wait for him to call me up and tell me what I need to do to it, and then I revise it honorably in response to what he tells me. When he writes a poem, he puts it in the mail to me, and I study up what I think I need to tell him, and I call him up and I say, "John, I think you need to cut this line," and he says, "Oh, I've already done that," and I say, "I think you need to change . . ." and he says, "I've already changed it." He has already revised it four times before I get back to him about it. But we still serve each other's needs as readers and poet companions.

GG: He probably wouldn't revise it if he didn't mail it off to you.

DH: No. He needs to send it to me. He absolutely needs to send it to me and I understand that, and I need to send my poems to him.

GG: So there is a critical paper there somewhere for someone who wants to write a complicated influence paper. Did the kind of work that was being done by James Whitehead ever have any influence on you?

DH: Well, I wish I could say it did, because everything that I have heard about James Whitehead seems to recommend him to me, but I will have to say that I have not read any of his poetry or any of his fiction.

GG: The poetry, I think, will be of great interest to you. You are poets of approximately the same age, though it's a very different world he is talking about. He's closer to Jim Seay's world in Mississippi. Anyway, I recommend him. In your poetry (and, really, it runs through everything else) there is a strong autobiographical impulse. That's something that a lot of us are still trying to find out about. And it's not an easy thing to talk about. But you have the poems and you have autobiographical elements in your literary criticism, a quality that I found to be tremendously exciting because of the kind of engagement that comes from someone's being candid about what happens to the critic at that moment and why. And you have the book jackets that report that David Huddle was in Germany and Vietnam and went to the University of Virginia and came from southwest Virginia and did that; and then the speaker in the poems and the characters in the stories do some of the same things. So these elements stress the authenticity that you get from the autobiographical. What limits do you place on yourself? What kind of inhibitions do you put on, like a coat, in your use of real experience in something that is going out to press?

DH: I think your question suggests the nature of the inhibitions. I try as much as possible not to be inhibited when I am writing something. And some of what enables me to do so is I can always say to myself, if I get into territory that I don't want anybody to read about, I will just put this away, it's not going to hurt anything for me to write it. And then after I write it, I may make some definite changes in it. There is a poem in *Paper Boy* entitled "Mrs. Green" that describes a twelve-year-old paper boy's falling in love with a young married woman whom he sees on his paper route. I changed the name of the poem from Mrs. Black, or whatever her name was, to Mrs. Green, which is not her real name, because I couldn't stand the idea of meeting up with that woman in Ivanhoe and her knowing that I had had these thoughts about her. That I wanted to walk into her kitchen.

GG: Has it ever worried you about friends or family misinterpreting? Has that bothered you at all?

DH: Yes, it has bothered me and it has bothered some members of my family, and there have been some difficulties about that. But I have to say that my family has been remarkably tolerant of me and has in many ways given me license to go ahead and use their lives in many ways for my stories. I think that is uncommonly generous of them. I know other writers whose families have denied them.

GG: Everyone has a different slant on the same event. There is one thing that I have found to be the absolute truth in dealing with families and friends: if you do write directly about them, chances are about 95 out of 100 that they won't see it. "Who was that fool in that story that you were writing about?" Then you write one that is made up and has nothing to do with anybody alive, and long faces will greet you. "How could you do that to Uncle Bill?" You can't win! I'm sure you figured that out long ago. But this is the sort of thing that writers who work closely with experience and with autobiography have to deal with. You have been successful with that because your work is not inhibited. Probably you don't use a lot of things, but that is as much a matter of good taste as it is of hurting folks. One other question: how about the personal, how about the speaker or principal character of most of the autobiographical work that you have done? Is he someone who is like the self that you present to friends and strangers, or is he different? What rules do you give yourself? I find your work particularly fascinating in that you are able to treat the self in such a way that it certainly is not embarrassing to the reader. It is very open, and we are invited to share this experience. I wonder what your thoughts are when you are writing about yourself?

DH: I wonder about that. Usually I would say that when I am making a story I don't have too much of a sense of writing about myself. I do have a sense of writing toward experience that I have probably had or that I have imagined very strongly or that I have thought about a good deal, that somehow belongs to me. But I don't have a sense of how I am going to tell my reader about David Huddle. I have a sense of going toward some experience, and I am usually after some element of a personality. I think about the story "Poison Oak," about a boy whose mother suffers from a man who puts poison oak in her bathing suit. It is very much autobiographical. It did actually happen pretty much the way the story presents it. And the boy in that story is a lot like me. But when I was writing about him, I wasn't thinking about me as much as I was thinking about this boy who had these characteristics of being interested in things and being very aware of his mother, very much in contact with her, very aware of people in town. So that there were characteristics of his personality that I felt like I was testing by putting him through that. And of course they were aspects of my personality, but I wasn't seeing them as being me but seeing them as his. As much as possible I try not to condescend to my characters. I don't always succeed with that.

GG: How about condescending to yourself? Is that a danger?

DH: Yes. Sometimes you see yourself as a fool or an idiot. And in the circumstances you should have known better. You can see that in retrospect. I am guilty of that to some extent, but I do try to give my protagonists credit for being intelligent, sensitive human beings who don't always do the right thing.

GG: Otherwise, no story. Speaking of that, I was going to ask you whether it is any different when you do a first-person story. Do you have to be more alert to create a distance from yourself and the first-person narrator?

DH: I wonder about that. I think I am a lot more comfortable with first person because then I have the quality of voice, of a person talking in a certain way. And I can take certain qualities of my way of talk, maybe my putting on the airs of professorial talk, and I can just move it over an edge, just a little more than I would ordinarily speak, and then I've got a voice that's not quite mine but that I know very well. Or I can move it down a little bit toward my kind of redneck-at-the-filling-station-getting-a-Moon-Pie voice, and that too is not my voice but I know it perfectly well. And I can just go with the voice in a way that a musician will play a phrase and go with that phrase and then put another phrase with it. And after you get it going, it will go on its own for a while. All you have to do is just sort of follow along.

GG: I have found throughout your work, from the earliest things, that there has never been any problem of empathy with a wide range of characters. I don't know what the limits are. You haven't yet tried to write about moon people. But that may come, and I am sure we would see some of that same quality if you were to move into sci-fi and fantasy. I also notice that, as you are gaining more confidence, some of the stories in *Intimates* have first-person narrators who are quite distinct. There are a couple of women first-person narrators, maybe three, all of them are quite different. All of them are, to my ear, entirely believable both in voice and in other points of perception, feeling. Are you happy working with characters who are quite different from you in a first-person story?

DH: Well, not happy, George. Never happy. In fact, scared to death, especially writing in the voice of a woman. And in these times I think that's got to be awfully bold. So I am scared about what people are going to say about *Intimates* and what reviewers are going to say about it and what my friends are going to say about it. But I think, as you know, if you are a writer and if you have any integrity, you can't go on doing what you did. I sort of wish I could. But it's just not very interesting. And it seems to me not the reason for writing. You're always on a tilt trying to do what you can't quite yet do. You learn how to do it, and once you have learned how to do it, you put it behind you and go on and do the next thing. So not happy, never happy. But I am, how shall I put it, comfortable.

GG: You are a little bit more comfortable with the challenge of this, and you might not have taken the challenge a little earlier. I have found the same thing in your use of place. Places are very important, have a very important part in your fiction. The new book *Intimates* has Seattle, New York City, Tucson, Vermont, a number of classic American places. It could have been Abingdon, it could have been Roanoke, it could have been Greenville, South Carolina. But now within your work you seem free to try a variety of places. Do you feel that way about your own work? Do you automatically think, what the hell, let's put this story in Santa Fe?

DH: Well, I guess so. I rarely write about some place that I have never been. Usually I have been there or have been close to there. I think of myself as being someone who responds to place; when I go somewhere, it affects me. I will be affected by having been at Emory and Henry College, by the light and the wind and the leaves and all of that.

GG: How soon will you be affected by that? The reason I ask is that you've caught up, in a way. Some of you will know the work of Sylvia Wilkinson, and she has always said that, try as she will, she is ten years behind in her life. Her life is dated by the time it gets into stories. We all have to start with youth. You now have people your age deeply involved in things. What is next?

DH: I guess I feel that is one reason for trying other voices, the voices of people who are not like me. If I am catching up to myself—and maybe catching up to myself in a vertical plane—maybe other voices give me horizontal possibilities. Like writing about a woman around my age attending a class reunion that I should have attended but didn't, but have a video tape of. So if I can just move over a bit and take on another life, maybe I have a way of getting more stories and more poems out of that.

GG: I notice that Hayden Carruth was right in crediting you with the sense of *linkage* in these stories, a sense of sequence in putting them together. He is right in that this is terribly important. Your stories tend to be more linked or more sequential than those that are organized in another type of collection of stories, the anthology format. Is this linkage part of the creative process as you write the story, or is it more of an organizational scheme? Are you saying, I am going to write some stories about love and relationships? Or do you say, I have been writing stories about love and relationships and they kind of come together?

DH: I think it will work differently for different books. With *The High Spirits,* I looked at the stories that I had done over a period of time and they seemed to sort of fall into this category; a few stories I had didn't fit that, and I think once I saw the category, I might have written one or two others. I actually don't think so, though. But with *Intimates,* I actually had about three stories that I had done, and then all of a sudden I looked at them and I suddenly understood something that was really at issue there, the nature of men and women and how they relate to each other in different circumstances and in different ways. And I really sort of set out and said, "Oh, yeah, that's what I'm writing about," and I wrote I don't know how many other stories.

GG: You've really done it both ways. That's interesting. And you were saying, too, something I have often thought, which is that if we are moving ahead all the time and being challenged, what we learn is how we *should have done* the book before. But it is too late and we have already moved on to something else. What have you learned from doing it both ways? Next time, will you wait around and see what happens or spring on a theme?

DH: I wonder, because I think my way of working is with one thing at a time. I can do this little piece of work, then this one, and then this one; and sometimes I can look and say I can put this with this and make that. But what I can't do is look at this whole pattern and do anything. I have written two novels that have failed, in large part because when I look at the whole big sweep of experience I write badly, I think badly. I do it badly. So what I would hope to do through this way of writing stories that work together in a novel-like way would be to come closer and closer to a book that resembles a novel. Maybe some people would call it a novel. Maybe I will be able to become a novelist by virtue of going in the back door, doing just one little piece at a time.

GG: These linked stories are very close to the contemporary practice of the novel. What writers among your peers and predecessors have influenced you? You have listed some of them: Richard Yates, Peter Taylor, André Dubus, etc. What other story writers, maybe a little younger, have had a favorable influence on you?

DH: I am voraciously eclectic about short-story writers. I like so many story writers, and I think there are so many good ones around. I like people in this group who don't like people in that group, and I like people in that group who don't like people in this group. But I love Raymond Carver. I think Raymond Carver is an important and valuable story writer, and I have learned a great deal from him. I have read André Dubus, and I think he's a wonderful and important story writer. And I don't think those two authors—one a minimalist or alleged minimalist and the other a guy who writes long, long stories—seem to go together, but I admire them both.

GG: Beyond the inspiration of admiration, do you get any practical value from the way they solve problems?

DH: I do, but I think also maybe the thing I take from both of them is the more human model of the way in which their work seems to me to address problems of great difficulty, the difficulties that human beings have living their lives. And these authors seem to me to go into these terrible places and make stories out of the most difficult and terrible circumstances. Stories that seem to me to help me with my life. In that sense, they set the first example for me, and I try to do something similar. I think with Carver there is a generosity toward human failure as his characters seem to be losers, people who have failed, who have done miserably, and yet he treats them in such a way that they have dignity, that one sees their lives as worthwhile and valuable. André Dubus is able to enter territory in which people do terrible things to each other for bad reasons, but he makes you understand them. I would say that from André Dubus I have learned some courage. I also deeply admire Eudora Welty, as I told you earlier, and Flannery O'Connor and Peter Taylor, my teacher at the University of Virginia. I admire his works for many things. If I made a list of the story writers that I admire, I bet I could come up with at least 100 or 150 story writers.

GG: In "Puttering in the Prose Garden," one of the fine essays in *The Writing Habit,* you also have a third category that you mention, which is mega-prose. There are some people in that category you like, aren't there?

DH: I particularly like Toni Cade Bambara. I think her bringing Black English into the high literary canon is just fabulous. I really love the way she uses language in her short stories. I also like very much Leonard Michaels, who writes a kind of rarefied and extremely literary story. Maybe I like his earlier work more than I do his more recent work. I have to admit I don't too much like Guy Davenport's work, which I discuss in that essay.

GG: You said "eclectic" earlier, and you really meant it. One of the things that I wanted to ask you about was this: you have been published—and happily, it seems to me—from the outset by university presses and small presses. And I have had some experience in those areas; too. I think people might be interested in hearing your views about publishing as it is today, the pros and cons of the small presses in the publishing scene.

DH: I am full of all sorts of thoughts about this. One of them is that I think I am very lucky that I have not made very much money with my writing. The biggest advance I have ever gotten was for *Intimates,* $4,000, and I still haven't gotten a thousand of that. There is in my town in Vermont a high-school teacher who just wrote a murder-mystery novel, and he got a $30,000 advance for that. This is his first book, and that's what he is getting for it. If I were that man, I might look at my work and say, "You got only $4,000; I wouldn't want to do that." On the other hand, I feel that if you make a lot of money with your work, that punishes you in several severe ways, among them being that you must write another book and you need to decide whether that's a book on which you want to make a lot of money or whether you want to write a good book. I think one of the freedoms I have by publishing in places that don't pay me very much is that I can write any way that I want to. I have the license to write whatever way I want, because I'm not making any money and the hell with it; I might as well enjoy myself. At the same time, I would like to make more money with my work than I do, and I sometimes feel that I am entitled to more money than I actually get. I was talking to John Engels about this. There is such misery involved, such little petty stuff, such as how many copies do publishers print, what blurbs do they put on the cover, how do they write the jacket copy, how well do they distribute it? All of that stuff associated with publication is such a low and petty misery. The great pleasure is to have this thing, this book. I like the looks of it, I like to hold it in my hand, I like the way the print looks on the page, I like to be able to have a book like this to give to my friends and to tell people that I published this, this is my book. And that is the major pleasure of it. David Godine makes this nice book and Gibbs Smith makes nice books, too, and they talk to me about them; they let me say how I think they should look and what ought to be in them. They give me that kind of regard, and I appreciate that.

    GG: You know publishing has changed radically in the last few years. When I first started out, I published a book with the University of Texas Press, the first collection of poetry they'd ever done, and a lot of perfectly serious poets took me aside and said don't ever publish with a university press, that's just not done. And ten years later, the university presses were the principal source of poetry publishing in America. I think there is another reason for your choices—and they would be choices. You could have chosen to go another route. You could have tried other people and commercial houses at other times. Your choice is probably the right one because these are, Godine and Gibbs Smith, for example, stable small presses in a time when presses are changing hands faster than political administrations are coming and going. You know the stories of writers who have suddenly gotten a wonderful deal with Ticknor and Fields and then discovered that it was bought by Exxon or something. New editors and the whole thing becomes different. One other thing that I don't want to overlook: your new book of essays is especially interesting for your views, which are worked out in some detail and with great subtlety, I think, on the value of teaching and learning creative writing. Here you are among the second generation of people who studied writing and taught writing. You have studied at Virginia, Hollins, and Columbia, and taught at Vermont. What advice do you have? Can you mention any of the drawbacks to the creative-writing program? We hear a lot about the disadvantages. What do you see as the real ones, if any?

    DH: Well, it could be that they offer a young writer a chance to pursue writing for career purposes or career concerns, as if those were the primary concerns. I think some of these programs, intentionally or unintentionally, encourage that, by emphasizing the publishing angle. If you go into writing with career being your primary concern, you will be suitably punished.

GG: You should be certified! What advice do you have for a young writer in the audience facing a world that may be very different from what we have known? What sort of go-and-sin-no-more advice would you have for a young writer today?

DH: Well, I guess in some ways I have the standard advice, but what seems to me the good advice is to read everything you can get your hands on. Read everything and read it attentively and generously and try to take from it what you can. And then the other thing is to try to figure out what your way is, what belongs to you as a writer. You don't know that. You can know that only by writing toward it. So it seems to me that is the direction you need always to pursue. What kind of writing is it that I want to do? What kind of writing do I need to do? And then try to make circumstances for yourself that permit you to write. In that case, you may be disappointed by many other things, but you won't be disappointed by the work. The work will always be doing something for you. It will always be sort of showing you, look here, don't you understand this; and look there, don't you understand that; and look what you can do over here. And the work will always be open to you and will be interesting to you. That seems to me to be what will keep you doing it for twenty and thirty and forty and fifty years.

GG: There is a continual process of discovery in your view of it. In a sense, you can't ever get old. You are going to die someday, but you are going to be as fresh as a writer as you were at the beginning.

DH: I hope so.

GG: I hope so too, as I took forward to reading whatever it is you do. Now I wonder if we have any questions from anybody in the audience?

QUESTION: Why do you write, and what do you expect your audience to get out of it?

DH: I think those are very legitimate questions. Some of the discussion that we had yesterday had to do with memory and imagination and how you make stories out of memory and imagination, what you know and what you can make up. I think of imagination as serving in this way. I am going to drive back to Wytheville when I leave here, and already there is a part of my mind that is sort of imagining what the interstate is going to be like, what exit I am going to take, what the weather will be like when I get to a certain point. My imagination is now sort of helping me to begin to make this trip. One of the things you do when you write stories is that you address the things in your life that are of concern to you so that you can go forward, so that you can move toward whatever is going to come next. When my father was gravely ill, I wrote a lot about my father being gravely ill because I needed to be able to address that, and my imagination helped me to do that. By making poems and stories that were about that, I was able to go forward and address it. At the same time, you need to know where you have been, which is where your memory helps you. Your memory is a way of processing where you have been so that you can keep on going forward in making this journey. It seems to me that that is what my work does for me. It keeps me from staying in the same place. It helps me move forward to the next thing in my life and in my work.

And what would I hope my audience would get out of it? I'm not sure. Some amusement, some entertainment, some pleasure. Whatever they can take from it. I am not a writer who would ever wish to persuade anybody of anything. I do not have any wisdom to offer to anyone about any aspect of human behavior. I have only these things that I have made that have helped me to move from one place to another. In my opinion, those things might help some people to move from one place to another. Maybe not the same places, maybe different, but they might be of some help in that regard.

QUESTION: As a poet, what aspects of the military did you value, and as a short-fiction writer, what kinds of people do you find interesting?

DH: Boy, those are toughies! It is going to be a great feat of synthesis if I can tie those two together. The military for me was where I realized that I could die and nobody would give a damn. They would ship my body back home, my parents would care, and my friends would care, but where I was, it wouldn't matter. And that, I guess, was a very useful piece of knowledge for me because I came from sheltering people and I was very self-indulgent and I thought the world pretty much depended on me to get along. So this thing that the army taught me, that I didn't much matter to anyone except for a few people back in Wythe County, Virginia, was a very useful thing for me to learn. I was in army intelligence, and one of the things that I received training in was report writing and essentially typing a lot. We would carry out these interviews of people, background investigations, in which I would ask, what kind of a guy you were, and whether you were stable and dependable, and what were your drinking habits, and that sort of thing. Then I would have to go back and type up the report, and I had to type it perfectly. If there were any mistakes, I had to take it out and start all over again. I hate to say it, but that particular skill gave me great patience in dealing with some of the tedium that's involved in writing poems. In writing poetry, you sometimes struggle for days to make one phrase work correctly, and if you don't have an aptitude for that, you won't get the phrase right. So I guess I learned that sitting down and getting a certain piece of written language right was something that I could do. I had a gift for it. I could do it and I even liked it. I will even admit that I liked it. It improved my typing skills.

As for the other part of the question, I'd like to say that I like all kinds of people, but that is not necessarily true. I don't know, I guess I like people who are trying to do the best they can and are having a hard time with it. And I like mean people; I like meanness. Flannery O'Connor's Misfit says, "No pleasure in life but meanness." I sort of like people who understand that. I don't know, I like all kinds of people. I like hypocritical people, I like self-righteous people. This is true.

GG: Active people. You have a lot of very active people always. The passive ones tend to get into a lot of trouble. Active people are more fun to write about anyway, because they are always doing something.

DH: Yes, these people you can move right along. Yes, indeed, these I like. But passive people interest me, too.

QUESTION: Are you happy with your work as it has developed through the years, or are there things that you would disown now and that you are unhappy with?

DH: The stories in *A Dream with No Stump Roots in It,* in some ways, seem to me clearly apprentice work in which I was learning how to do certain things. And there are failures in those that bother me. I wouldn't disown those stories, and there are things about them that I like a good deal. But there are certain stories that I no longer have any affection for, among them being "The Proof Reader." And there are aspects of some of my stories that I have trouble with. There are some happy endings of stories of mine that still seem a little bit . . . they don't persuade me. I'm not persuaded that this happy ending is possible. But for the most part, whatever of mine is printed is out there; I would stand on it. I would say that I probably could do better. I wish I could do better, but that's the best I could do at the time.

QUESTION: You have a lot of characters in the stories and poems who are the same characters, especially in *Stopping by Home* and in *Paper Boy* and in *Only the Little Bone,* and many situations that are repeated. I am very interested in the difference in the way in which working as a poet you conceive of these characters versus working as a fiction writer. Is there really a sharp distinction in the way that you approach them in a poem and in a story?

DH: One of the things you don't have to do in a poem, or in the kinds of poems that I have written so far, is that business of constructing a character, of making a personality, that you have to be doing in a story. You really do need to be making a personality and moving a personality through a certain kind of journey, and you don't have to do that in the kinds of poems that I have written so far. I think of the poems as being something like a philosophical laboratory in which I perhaps discover the nature of the problems I am particularly interested in, or the nature of the emotional knot that I am trying to get at. And once I discover that, then I can take that knowledge and go into a story and proceed with it. Most particularly, it happened in writing the poems in *Paper Boy,* in which I really didn't work too much on making a character or personality, but I got at certain experiences that I had had; then I was able to take that understanding into the stories in *Only the Little Bone.* And then construct personality and move through narrative. Did you have something else in mind?

QUESTION: You're not saying, are you, that the poems are notes toward the fiction?

DH: In some ways, *Paper Boy* served exactly that function, but that was when poetry was still not as much a part of my life as it is now. Now, there are ways in which the poems mean much more to me. Poems that matter more to me, that taught me more, that are there for their own sake, that I have not yet found a way to use in making stories.

QUESTION: Do you think your definition of mega-prose is also a definition that applies pretty much to your views of what constitutes poetry?

DH: I wonder about that. I don't know. When I think of mega-prose, I think of it as a kind of language performance in which, when a reader reads it, he is always being dazzled by language. And I don't think I will ever be that kind of a writer, except occasionally. Sometimes in a sentence, a paragraph, a stanza, or a line or two, I think a reader will experience language in an especially intense way.

QUESTION: You seem to be making overtures in that direction in "Inside the Hummingbird Aviary."

DH: Well, I wonder. I hope I'm getting better. I hope that I'm able to do more with that.

QUESTION: I wonder what you think of the comment made last night that autobiographical fiction is the highest form of art.

DH: I'm the one who said that, and it is written down in *The Writing Habit*, so I have to stand on that. Someone wrote me and said, "Come on, Huddle, do you really believe that?" And I said, yes I did, and I was ready to defend it. We carried on a correspondence in which it became clear that the kind of work he liked was very much nonautobiographical and the kind of work that I liked was pretty much autobiographical. And there was no way that I could persuade him of my values. But yes, I do think that.

QUESTION: I was trying to identify people on both sides of the line, and I'm beginning to wonder if I can really decide which of them is nonautobiographical. I thought of those on the opposite side like Proust, James Joyce, D. H. Lawrence, Doris Lessing, and a lot of other people, but on the other side there might be Shakespeare and Homer and George Garrett sometimes writing about Christopher Marlowe.

GG: It is enormously complicated because one of my reasons for thirty years of writing about Elizabethans was to get away from writing autobiographical stuff. And I find, just by living long enough, that the man behind that curtain is, in fact, more revealed in those works that are nonautobiographical than in the stories when I was telling things that had really happened to me but that could have happened to anybody. So I think there is no escape from autobiography if your inclination is in that direction, and revelation is what it is all about. You are going to be doing it if you are writing about moon people, which complicates the notion of autobiography because everything you do will be autobiography.

DH: The idea of Franz Kafka as an autobiographical writer, or "The Metamorphosis" as being a deeply autobiographical work, or "The Country Doctor" as being a deeply autobiographical work is, on the one hand, totally outrageous and, on the other hand, perfectly sensible. I suppose that's the little trick I would try to hide behind in doing the same thing. Even highly imagined works are also autobiographical. But I don't know. I would choose up sides if I had to line up, and even with writers who do both things, who write autobiographically and who write nonautobiographically, I probably would like their autobiographical work more than their nonautobiographical work. On the one hand, it's taste; on the other hand, it is sort of working through an aesthetic that suits me, that is valuable to me, that I understand, and that allows me to function.

QUESTION: What about the line between autobiography and exhibitionism?

DH: Yes, I wonder about that. I'm not sure. Just for the sake of making a case, let's say that some of Hemingway's least-successful fiction is somewhat exhibitionist in the sense that it means to demonstrate that Hemingway is more powerfully manly, a greater adventurer, than most people ever would be. That there is a kind of self-promotion, self-heroizing quality in some of that fiction. But certainly in the good Hemingway, that's not the case. All of us writers are people with unnaturally strong egos. We believe that what we have to say is at least worth writing down and sending to other people to read. So there is this temptation to present yourself as a superior human being in your work. It seems to me that serious writers resist that tendency; they are using the work to examine themselves, to test themselves, to find out things.

(1993)

Buzzards and Dodos: George Core (Editor of *Sewanee Review*) Talks with George Garrett About the Quarterlies

Shortly following his appearance on a panel about book reviewing at the annual Miami Book Fair, this interview with George Core took place in a fifteenth-story hotel room high above downtown Miami, its boarded-up storefronts and decay, its winos and druggies, mercifully out of sight. A quiet, light-filled room with a view of Biscayne Bay and Miami Beach beyond that. An occasional jet gliding toward Miami International Airport. Oddest and seemingly most incongruous of all, flocks of buzzards soaring on the air high above downtown Miami. What brings them here? Neither of us, George Core or myself, has ever seen buzzards in an urban setting, though we have both read about them as a fact of life in the cities of Third World nations.

It's all of it, high and low, a far cry from Sewanee, Tennessee, the lightly populated, ten-thousand-acre domain of the University of the South, isolated and beautiful atop a mountain, where in a gray gothic-style building the Sewanee Review *has its offices.*

We are still talking about the themes of the panel on book reviewing and the news of the day. It is, as you will soon see, the 1990s. . . .

—G. G.

"Isn't that a chilling story about Bret Easton Ellis?" Core asks. "Reading between the lines, I found that it sounds absolutely repulsive. Yet what comes across in the press is that the wife of the CEO of the company that owns Simon and Schuster is another Mrs. Doubleday suppressing a work as great as *Sister Carrie,* which is nonsense, of course. This latter-day Mrs. Doubleday tried to carry out a public service—at great expense to Simon and Schuster—but her efforts were immediately thwarted by Random House, which to its immense discredit and obvious greed is now publishing this wretched book, which might make the Marquis de Sade blush with shame.

"We are faced with the fact that reading is a dying art. People read this kind of trash, this novel, *American Psycho,* that certainly is worthy of being suppressed if anything ever has been. We are going to be in bad shape if Jesse Helms starts deciding the artistic taste of the country, but I also think we're going to be in bad shape if work as bad as this Bret Ellis novel, work that bad, *isn't* suppressed occasionally.

"It's not really being suppressed, of course; it's being rejected. But what happens is that the word *censorship* comes up and a great many people get exercised. You shouldn't censor art once it is in the public domain. But if you couldn't censor books in some form and at some stage before they are available to the public, then everything would see print in one form or another. The book reviewer ought to be prepared to say that something is rubbish. George Woodcock once said about some very bad book he reviewed for me that it was a waste of good trees."

Speaking of the earlier panel discussion, Core says: "The operative word in all that conversation was 'entertainment.' I would have been happier if they talked about being lively and entertaining, but not about simply providing entertainment for their readers. What a lot of these people don't understand is that book reviewing ought to be a department of criticism. It shouldn't be entertainment or news or something else that is ephemeral by definition.

"I think a lot of people start reading quarterlies by reading the book reviews; then they go on and read the fiction and the essays and the poetry. Some of the quarterly editors haven't figured out how important the book review is in the economy of the magazine—if for no other reason than that they have to get ads. And they have to keep getting review copies."

A native of Lexington, Kentucky, George Core was educated at Transylvania College, Vanderbilt, and Chapel Hill. He served as an officer for four years (1960–1964) in the U.S. Marine Corps. He is editor or coeditor of scholarly and critical books dealing largely with American literature. Forthcoming are *The Literalists of the Imagination: Southern Letters and the New Criticism* (Louisiana State University Press), a study of the criticism of Ransom, Tate, Brooks, Warren, and other New Critics. Some years ago, together with the novelist and critic Walter Sullivan, he wrote *Writing from the Inside* (Norton), a textbook on composition. Core has reviewed for numerous publications and was senior editor of the University of Georgia Press from 1968 to 1973, when he began editing the *Sewanee Review*.

"The experience I had at the University of Georgia Press was enormously helpful in terms of editing the magazine. I picked up a fair amount of information about design and production, on the one hand, and, on the other, promotion. But it seems to me that these are matters that everybody has to be constantly learning about. I don't pretend to be an expert. For instance, when the copyright law changed in 1978, we went to the Library of Congress, and I talked to a lawyer there who actually called me up. I found out what was going on, how to make up the copyright forms, and how to protect our authors and protect the magazine. Other magazines, like the *Yale Review* and the *New Yorker*, kept doing what they had always done as if the copyright law had never changed.

"My greatest frustration since I have been editor of the *Sewanee Review* is that we can't seem to get more subscribers. We are between three and four thousand; and the only comparable quarterlies that do better are the *Virginia Quarterly Review* and the *Hudson Review*. The *Hudson* has done well in the recent past. They were at twenty-five hundred at one point and now have about four thousand subscribers. The Morgans have been very resourceful at pushing up their subscriptions. On the other hand, there's the *Partisan Review*, which doesn't do much better through the mail, but has a very good sale on the newsstands.

"The fact is," Core continues, "we are now living in an age of the specialized magazine. I talked to one guy who has done all this body work—not on me, but on my automobile and my children's automobiles. He does antique cars on the side. I talked about doing a piece about him, and he told me that there are three antique automobile magazines. And there are all these other magazines about gourmet cooking and everything else. The literary quarterly is taking it on the chin. The heyday of the quarterlies was probably the late 1950s. And there's really nothing anybody can do culturally to create issues and make them important for the informed general reader. The thing that keeps staring me in the face is that the informed general reader is going to be as dead as the dodo in the near future."

We are soon talking about the individual quarterlies, those he admires and those he does not and, as well, features of this quarterly or another that he can praise or criticize. For example, he singles out the "Bookmarks" section of the *Georgia Review* as "a good idea," adding that "the problem is they are not reviewing enough books." He argues that the *Georgia Review* has done well in recent years, in part "because they have held down the subscription rate. It's a big fat magazine selling for a modest amount of money."

He adds: "The *Southern Review* is comparable, but the *Southern*, it seems to me, is becoming more and more academic. Unless Dave Smith turns it around, it may not be a literary quarterly anymore.

"The ones who do what, say, Peter Stitt is doing at the *Gettysburg Review*, running only essay-reviews, are making another kind of mistake. I think you need as much review coverage as you can possibly get."

About the others—to use Mailer's phrase, the other talent in the room:

"My judgment is that the *American Scholar* is a wonderfully edited quarterly and that Joseph Epstein—who is a very good short-story writer and one of our best essayists, not only a personal but a critical essayist as well—did a first-rate job. Everybody in the country who edits a quarterly was envious of his situation. He had forty or fifty thousand people, the membership of Phi Beta Kappa, taking the *American Scholar*. I doubt, frankly, that he had many more careful readers than the rest of the quarterlies; but he had an ideal situation and he did a superb job.

"I think we might devote a little consideration to the *Yale Review*. The *Yale Review* proved that it was not essential to literary life in this country under the editorship of Kai Erikson, who could not bear to bring it out on time. As a result, it was six to nine months late, and he finally had to give up altogether putting the season on the cover of the magazine. So you had to look inside and in tiny type it would say something like 'Vol. 79, No. 2, for Spring 1989, published January 1990.' I'm afraid that Professor Erikson is largely responsible for the fact that the magazine was threatened with closure, not because he didn't do a fairly decent job of editing it, but because it was not out on time. People just forgot about it.

"That's one side of it. And on the other hand, you had a president at Yale who decided that instead of putting up the necessary money for the *Yale*

Review—which is not much money for an institution that has a $3.5-billion endowment—he would instead fund a lecture series or bring in a visiting writer or something of that kind. He and his advisors simply didn't know what a quarterly does for a university.

"It's astonishing, really, that a little school like Sewanee has supported a magazine for almost one hundred years. Except for the very first few years when the magazine was funded privately (although by people who were with the university, after all), the college has always supported it and put a lot of money into it."

The problems of the *Yale Review* lead, by a simple and direct segue, to what Core calls "a very complicated matter," the recent history of the *Kenyon Review*.

"T. R. Hummer edited the *Kenyon* for about a year after having been managing editor of the *New England Review–Bread Loaf Quarterly*. Then he decided he could go back to the *NER* and left them, at the *Kenyon*, high and dry.

"Following the departure of Hummer, David Lynn was a kind of temporary editor.

"He was never given a chance to grow into the job," Core adds. "Just to hold it together until they could find somebody. Then—believe it or not—I was told that the three final candidates were all from Manhattan. I don't know who the committee members voted for, whether it was Koch or Dinkins, but the fact is that there were plenty of people elsewhere in the country who would have been at least as good and maybe better.

"So now the editor they chose, Marilyn Hacker, said that she couldn't bear to leave Manhattan until her child finished school in the Bronx, which to me is comparable to saying that you are enjoying having your house napalmed and so you will stay in it until it burns to the ground. The problem is, I don't think she can edit a magazine long-distance from Manhattan. And her first issue certainly indicated that. In her initial editorial, she was talking mainly about censorship and the NEA and about the fact that the *Kenyon* cannot possibly take a six- or seven-thousand dollar NEA grant if it means she will have to censor her authors. It seems to me that censorship is not the real issue and that it's simply a matter of terminology. It will be interesting to see what happens, but I don't think anybody can edit a magazine long-distance for a considerable period of time."

I ask Core about some of the other directions taken by quarterlies, for instance, the special issues entirely built around a specific subject published by the *Michigan Quarterly Review.*

"In theory, the *Michigan Quarterly* idea might work, but in practice, when you see those special issues on the airplane and the automobile and things of that kind, although they could be good, they just don't work out. The issue on the automobile had one very brilliant little piece in it that was about two pages long, but the rest of it was almost a dead loss.

"One thing that goes on at a lot of quarterlies is that people think you can hoke up these ideas and bring in great editors who will be interested in following up on a subject. But the truth is, every quarterly has to have an editor, a benevolent dictator—he may even have to be a savage dictator—and he can't just farm things out. He can't just pass his magazine around to everyone in the country and have them do a special issue.

"If you look at the history of literary quarterlies, beginning with Ford Madox Ford, you will see that the editor is the essential ingredient in these magazines and is in general a person who has been a benevolent tyrant."

Any exceptions to that observation?

"The only exception I can think of is in the case of Brooks and Warren. Brooks and Warren working together were such an extraordinary team that they made up a third person. You can read their textbooks and you can't tell which one is writing. And yet, if you read the criticism of either man, there is a distinct difference in style in many respects."

Since Brooks and Warren are associated with the inception and the heyday of the *Southern Review,* this leads to some consideration of that venerable and once-influential quarterly.

"In general, the way that the *Southern Review* has been edited since then bears out what I am talking about. I had Malcolm Cowley say to me one time in conversation, and not with any malice whatsoever, that the *Southern Review* was two different magazines. He was speaking, of course, of the two different editors—Lewis P. Simpson and Donald Stanford. I think the same thing is likely to be true now with Dave Smith and James Olney editing the magazine."

What about the regional situation, the place of the quarterlies, then and now, in southern letters?

"Well, for a long time there were two southern university presses and a few quarterlies that carried the whole southern literary establishment. There was the *Sewanee Review* and the *Virginia Quarterly;* there was the *Southern Review;* there was that magazine that came out of New Orleans—the *Double Dealer*. The whole literary scene in the South used to depend on the quarterlies and two university presses—LSU and North Carolina. Now we have a much better situation. We have at least a half dozen good university presses. And the South is probably characteristic of the rest of the country in that there are too damn many publications. I would hate to see any of the good ones go. But, on the other hand, if somebody came to you or me and said, what do you think about starting another quarterly, I hope we would say it is the most dismal idea we have ever heard of."

What *about* the future?

"Well, I would like to find some way of recharging our batteries, so to speak. I don't really know how to do this. I think that a magazine, when it tries to be different, is usually on the way out."

He cites the example of *Grand Street,* which he guesses is "now finished."

"It's got a new format; it's got a new editor; it's bloomed with illustrations. The writing looks much worse. It's got the first interview or two in the magazine's history. I think that it's very important for a quarterly to stick to what it has always done well. And I think literary quarterlies essentially ought to stick to literature. One of the biggest problems all of us have is that nobody reads with much intelligence. I don't know what to do about that. One of the essential aspects of the good quarterly is that your readers have got to know what you are going to do. You can have a lively magazine, but you also need to have a discernible program, one that your readers recognize and understand."

AFTERWORD

Enough time had passed since our original interview in buzzard-haunted Miami that I thought it advisable to return to the source and find out what was on George Core's mind these days (summer 2002) on the subject of the place of the quarterlies in literary America. We talked again, this time by phone. But first he kindly sent me copies of several pieces he had written for his own *Sewanee Review,* from Spring 1995 to Spring 2000, dealing with precisely some of the same subjects we had spoken of earlier on. In these pieces, he chronicled changes and ups and downs. How the *Kenyon* ("which during the years of its rebirth has demonstrated a greater propensity for making news than for publishing memorable literature") sent Marilyn Hacker home to the showers, replacing her as editor with David Lynn, "her well-qualified associate." He noted the deaths of *Poet & Critic* and *Antaeus,* the frailty of Gordon Lish's *Quarterly* and the *New England Review*. Core notes the retirement of Dabney Stuart as editor of *Shenandoah* and his replacement by poet R. T. Smith and takes note as well of the resurrection of the *Yale Review* "under the steady hand of its former poetry editor, J. D. McClatchy." He speaks of the very recent arrival at the *Georgia Review* of the itinerant T. R. Hummer. Core praises, especially, Frederick Morgan of the *Hudson Review,* who founded that quarterly in 1948 and edited it with distinction and panache until, in 1998, "he stepped aside to give the reins to his co-editor of thirty years, Paula Deitz."

Core continues: "Morgan's only three living rivals for long-term editing and influence are three distinguished editors, each of whom served more than twenty years—Lewis P. Simpson of the *Southern Review,* Charlotte Kohler of the *Virginia Quarterly Review* (probably the best quarterly editor in the U.S. in the twentieth century), and the admirable Joseph Epstein of the *American Scholar.*"

Of Epstein, Core adds a few words: "Joseph Epstein was sacked by an uncommonly pusillanimous board at Phi Beta Kappa. His sin was having high standards and living up to them. He is this country's best maker of familiar essays and one of our best critics and story writers. He is also a person who cannot brook incompetence or mediocrity. He has brought distinction to every cultural or literary pursuit in which he has been involved."

During this time, since our initial interview, several quarterlies have celebrated significant anniversaries. The *Hudson* had its fiftieth in 1998. The year 2000 witnessed the fiftieth anniversary of *Shenandoah*. Staige Blackford's *Virginia Quarterly Review* celebrated its seventy-fifth year. Core does not trouble to remind me (or them) that the *Sewanee,* having passed its hundredth birthday, is the oldest surviving quarterly in America.

Concluding, we return to the two parts of the questions we started off with: Is there still a place (and if so, what is it) for the literary quarterlies? And how are the quarterlies doing?

In answer to the first one, Core says: "As a vehicle of culture, the quarterlies seem as important as ever. They continue to provide an essential outlet for serious writers of all kinds and conditions. And don't forget that the quarterly not only judges literature through its criticism but makes literature through its fiction and poetry."

As for the other question, Core argues that, in all honesty, the outlook for the quarterlies "does not seem bleak despite urgent reports from the literary front."

"Plus ça change," I say, "plus c'est la même chose."

"You could say that, I suppose."

"If I were a real live Frenchman."

"You said it. I didn't."

(1991/2001)

An Interview with Paxton Davis (1925–1994)

This interview took place in 1989 and was done for the Dictionary of Literary Biography Yearbook *for that year. For several years, the DLB Yearbook featured an ongoing series, "Book Reviewing in America"; Davis had served as book editor of the* Roanoke Times & World-News *for more than twenty years, beginning in the 1960s, maintaining an outstanding and exemplary book page, one that has been described by writer and critic (and native of Roanoke) R. H. W. Dillard as "one of the most literate and respected in the country." [See R. H. W. Dillard, "Paxton Davis," Dictionary of Literary Biography Yearbook 1994, pp. 253–59.] A journalist and professor and head of the Department of Journalism at Washington and Lee University, Davis was also the author of ten books, beginning with the novel* Two Soldiers *(1956) and ending with a remarkable autobiographical trilogy—*Being a Boy *(1988),* A Boy's War *(1990), and* A Boy No More *(1992). Although Davis was not as well-known publicly as he might have been, his work—as writer, teacher, and critic—was much respected and admired by fellow writers and has proved to be genuinely influential. Quite aside from the modern American vices of hype, hustle, self-invention, and self-advancement, we must depend upon each other. The quality of our literature is the sum of all our voices.*

At the time of this interview, Davis had recently retired from teaching and from the newspaper except for a feisty editorial column, treating any and all subjects that interested him—politics, history, social mores, cultural and educa-

tional matters, memory, and reminiscence. He was living in the historic Virginia town of Fincastle, deep in the Shenandoah Valley.
—G. G.

Paxton Davis still writes book reviews for various papers, including the *Baltimore Sun*, the *New York Times Book Review*, and the *Washington Post Book World*. "I still review," he says, "but I don't have to anymore." He has just completed *A Boy's War*, a memoir of his time as an army sergeant in Burma from 1943 to 1946.

Davis's earlier books were published by major commercial houses— Simon and Schuster, Little Brown, Morrow, and Atheneum. But this one will be published by Blair, a small publisher in Winston-Salem, North Carolina, which earlier published the first memoir of his autobiographical trilogy, *Being a Boy*, with considerable critical and commercial success by any standards. This somewhat unusual situation becomes the occasion for us to talk a little about the increasing literary importance of small presses in recent years.

"They can focus on a book's special appeal," Davis says, "if it has one, in a way that the big publishers neither think about nor attempt. They are just as good these days at getting a book out to the book pages and sections and at getting a little special push behind it. They are every bit as good as the major publishers in this way, though they may not be as widespread."

Using this example of Blair's handling of *Being A Boy*, Davis continues: "They were very focused on the big southern papers, where I got reviewed everywhere and almost everywhere favorably." He describes as "the most bizarre thing" the fact that roughly six months after publication *Southern Living* reviewed the book on its lone book page, which consists of four five-hundred-word reviews and a color shot of the book jackets. Within three days after the issue was published, hundreds of orders for the book came in. The small presses these days—he specifically cites Algonquin, North Point, Peachtree, and the university presses—can be successful because "they have modest expectations and they can concentrate their efforts." And, of course, reviews, especially regional and local reviews, can be very influential in the success or failure of a small-press book.

We turn to his own personal history as a long-time book editor. He came to his job in 1961 with not only experience as a writer and book reviewer behind him, but also a record as a reporter for several southern papers and many years of teaching journalism at Washington and Lee:

"Louis D. Rubin, Jr. (now of Algonquin Books), is really the one who talked the Roanoke paper into creating a book page. Then, after a couple of years, he quit. They had this thing going, and it was going very successfully. He had a wide-open page, no ads of any kind on it, except maybe at Christmas. He had created something they never had before—a genuine, once-a-week Sunday book page that was serious, that attempted to do in a smaller daily the sort of thing that serious book-review media had done before and elsewhere. They asked me to do it. I had to clear it with Washington and Lee, which could be very stuffy about those things. To my surprise, they said sure, go ahead. I would finish teaching class at W & L around ten o'clock on Friday morning. Then I drove over to Roanoke—and this was before the interstate I-81 was completed and it took a little more than an hour and a half. I would work there many hours and then go back home. I was paid $25 a week in those days, and I worked hard.

"In those days, the type was still set on linotype—the hot-type process. The whole process was very cumbersome by today's standards. Today they paste them up. They were very rigid back then because you had to follow an exact mechanical schedule to get the plates made for the printing press in time, and this backs up all the way. So, what happened, I was very much involved, from the beginning, in the mechanical as well as the literary side of it. Because that's what they hired me to do. Because I was, as Louis had been, a trained newspaper person who had done not only reporting and comment, but had worked on a copy desk and knew how to write heads and how to make up a page. I had regularly reviewed for various newspapers—the *Baltimore Sun*, the *Washington Post*. And they didn't have to teach me to do anything. They wanted to hire me and not to have to worry about it anymore.

"They didn't want to spend much more money than paying me and a small amount for the secretary who opened the packages of books every week and, after I had marked them, mailed them out to our reviewers.

"I have to say I liked doing the mechanical part. It was something very pleasant. I couldn't touch the type—ever. That was forbidden unless you were a member of the union. But I stood over the stone where the page was being made up, and I could give very precise directions. I diagramed the page, what I wanted where, wrote all the heads, wrote all the cutlines, picked all the pictures, sent them to the engraver, then took the engraving back to the composing room. Then I stood over it while the compositor put the page together.

"I could make decisions. That type can't be compressed. It can be expanded a little, but with leading in the lines you can't compress it. So if something has to be omitted, you have to make a decision right then. I would always edit the reviews with that possibility in mind. I always had in my mind places where I knew I could pull a short paragraph out to make a quarter-inch.

"My point is that the mechanical side of it occupied me rather heavily always, for most of the twenty years. It didn't go into cold type—that is, electronic typesetting—until the last years, which did make that part a lot easier. But I still wrote all my own heads, did all my own cutlines, picked all my own art, wrote the identifications of all the reviewers, picked what was going on the page. Most of the time I was there, I wrote a column on the book page. And I did not write a book-news column; I wrote a review column. I reviewed a great many serious general trade books in that time in that column. It was double-columned and boxed always. That was a way of giving particular prominence to a book.

"I wanted absolute authority over every detail. That may be foolish, but I could put out precisely the page I wanted. And I think the results justified that."

He goes on to tell me something about his boss, Barton W. Morris, publisher of the Roanoke papers, and how much the book page owed to him.

"Barton was just an outstanding news executive. He picked people and then, unless they did something grievously wrong, he let them alone. And he gave me the most complete free hand and the most complete backing. So that if the advertising department or somebody else got troublesome, he always backed me up. Every time I had any problem with either the news side or the advertising side, he always backed me up. And I can't speak enough for that. Because one of the problems that book editors traditionally have had on papers everywhere is they never have the final say. Often they are outsiders, as I was, or else they are insiders who are bossed by a managing editor who doesn't give a damn about books anyway. Or maybe they decide to give the book page to some hack who's been sitting on the copy desk for twenty or thirty years and they don't know what else to do with him. Then they'll get exactly what you would expect."

But, as Davis is quick to point out, fascinating as the old days inside the newspaper business in America were (and there are *wonderful* stories of the hot-type era), and difficult as it was, in all but a few places, for book pages to thrive or even survive, it came down to the quality of reviews and reviewers, always, and to the ability of a book editor to endure other sorts of pressure. It was basically a no-win situation. As Davis puts it: "I was always accused, I thought very unfairly, by academic people of putting out too commercial a book page. I was accused by people at the paper, constantly, of having too highbrow a book page. I have to hope that means there was some kind of happy medium. This is a traditional problem, today as well, for book pages. They are certainly not part of the academic literary-journal world. They're not seeking to do that. On the other hand, they're not part of the book business either."

The pressure from the book business, from publishers, was less at the beginning of his stint than it is now.

"I don't think in those days they ever thought we [regional and local newspaper book reviewers] were a very important element in selling their books. They *couldn't* have!" But the times have changed. "Now there is a tremendous pressure to review pop books to an extent not present thirty years ago."

In any case, the key to a worthwhile book page or section lies in the quality of the reviews and the people who write them. Davis considers himself lucky. "Louis Rubin had left me a considerable number of reviewers. And I added to them or replaced them as they dropped out." He recruited from the college faculties all over the Commonwealth of Virginia. He sent them books and asked them for guidance as well: "I encouraged them, that if they knew about a book coming out, they would call me or write me, and I would get it for them. The result was that we reviewed a lot of university press books over the years, more than other papers. And that added to my bad reputation with my newspaper people. Meanwhile, my more academic readers—the faculty people at nearby Hollins College, for example—it did nothing to pacify them."

He grins in recollection of old battlefields.

Davis adds another comment about book reviewers, one that few working editors will openly admit to or discuss. "As time goes on," he says, "I think there is clearly a principle of diminishing returns in reviewing. The quality may go up for a while, as the person learns to write six hundred words effectively, but then either they become so mechanical that they're not any good in the long haul (these are the old whores, whose bylines we all see, who review year in and year out). That happens. And I saw it happen to some people who had reviewed regularly for me. Their boredom showed.

"To keep a book section or book page, you have to have a constant infusion of new reviewers. Because they get tired, they get bored, they get uninterested. They begin to slip not only in the quality of what they do, but also they become less dependable about returning copy. That's a routine problem that affects the quality of book reviewing in an invisible way. The other side is what happens to the person who is making the decisions, which in most cases is a one-person decision process. They had better be very good, or the results will show almost at once. They also have to have intuition; they have to have some kind of gestalt in their heads about what's coming out and what's ahead and what is this in the total picture.

"Book editors get tired. I am not going to pretend that I kept my level of sharpness. I kept my conscious level of commitment up to the last page I put out, but I think I got jaded. I think, finally, I saw too many books. You know how I knew this was true? When I stopped wanting to take them home every week. I realized I didn't want most of those books. Then it began to dawn on me—I was worn out with it.

"I wish I had quit five years sooner. Twenty years is too long."

What does he read now, for pleasure, now that he doesn't review books unless he feels like it?

"I find, like a lot of people who get older, that I don't read as much fiction as I once did. Partly because my eyes have betrayed me and I don't read as rapidly. But I am also not as interested. I don't know what that means.

"The novels I read are mostly entertainment—Ross Thomas, Elmore Leonard, John Le Carre. I read biography like crazy. There's a lot more of it, it seems to me, than thirty years ago. There's a lot more literary biography of varying quality."

It is an easy move to begin to talk about how things have changed in the world of book reviewing in America. What does he perceive as happening now? Are we doing better or worse?

"I think I'm reasonably objective about what they are doing and how they are doing it. For example, the *New York Times Book Review* is very good looking. It is mechanically much more orderly than it was thirty years ago. But the quantity of books reviewed has declined. The new type systems take up much more space, and then they have added so many more pictures. They have also added essays and charts and a lot of art. And the result is that they don't review as many books as they once did.

"And the *Los Angeles Times* is pretty good. But I don't have the feeling there's any consensus across the country in newspaper journalism that book reviewing is very good. It's all spotty. It's all dependent on strong local bookstores providing some kind of constituency or else an editor who doesn't give a damn whether this is popular or not. Someone who believes that one of the functions of journalism is to do this. You can't predict what you are going to see these days. It all depends on the support of the paper's management and on the type of person who takes on the job of being book editor."

Asked to be a little more specific, albeit in a general way, as to what he has noticed over the last few years, he speaks first of the book pages and sections of some of the area newspapers. He feels that the quality at the *Charlotte Observer* has declined and concludes that the Richmond papers "don't do very well." On the other hand, both Greensboro and Raleigh are doing well and getting better. "Raleigh has two facing pages, and they pay their reviewers well—as well as the *New York Times Book Review*."

What about the magazines?

"I think the whole magazine reviewing thing has gone to pot. With the possible exception of the *New Yorker,* magazine reviewing is certainly not as important as it was in the late nineteenth century or even the 1920s and 1930s. They just don't have the weight they once had.

"Some of the best reviews are in the quarterlies these days, and they are reviewing more popular books than they once did." He cites for particular praise the *Sewanee Review* and the *Virginia Quarterly Review,* adding that the *Sewanee* gave his most recent book an excellent and favorable review.

"Did it help the book?" I ask.

He laughs. "It helped my ego."

"You know," he continues, "I think one of the things we are overlooking here is something that has happened in the time I have been paying systematic attention to book reviewing. And that is the rise of the sort of celebrity author. We had Hemingway before that, yes. But this has all happened in the past few years because of television. But it is, of course, fed back to the book-publishing industry. And it is fed back to the book pages, which often want to reflect this. I don't think this was anywhere near as serious a factor when I was still working. Publishers did not put the hype on books that they now do routinely. They send out elaborate press kits and so forth. The only writer I remember from the sixties for whom they did anything like this was James Michener. It used to be, in the sixties, if I wanted to run a picture of a dust jacket, I had to take the dust jacket to the photography department and get on the schedule and get it shot. Then I would have to take the picture to the engraving people. Now it's all boiler plate. They have gotten better about things like that. But none of it seems to mean anything. Does it prove they take book reviewing seriously? The publishers evidently regard book-page space as having some kind of value."

Is it, I ask him, that the publishers have become better organized and efficient about promoting their books, getting them out to the appropriate places? He is not so sure about that. "When I quit the book page and passed it on to the present editor, Mike Mayo," Davis tells me, "I sent out a letter to all the publishers informing them of this change. About half a dozen major publishers still regularly send me review copies of their books. I get fifty or sixty books a month this way, after all this time, in Fincastle. Does this prove they are so indifferent they can't even clean up their mailing lists?"

(1986)

THREE TRIBUTES

Each year the Dictionary of Literary Biography Yearbook *publishes obituary notices of writers who have died during the past year. Together with the full obituary are short, personal, and informal "tributes" from friends and fellow writers. Here are tributes for three outstanding southern writers.*
 —G. G.

William Goyen

In fact and in flesh, *in person* as they say, we did not know each other much or well. We had worked together at a couple of writers' conferences and had met socially a few times. I remember once, to my surprise and delight, he showed up, just there, sitting in the small audience, at a poetry reading I gave one evening at Cooper Union in New York City. I didn't even know he was in town at the time. To show up at a poetry reading, even a friend's, when you don't have to and the friend won't be any the wiser, is way above and beyond the call of duty.

I remember what he looked like, of course, in photographs and in fact—tall, slender, but sturdy, well formed, handsome, and by the time I actually met him, wonderfully weather-beaten—an honest and honorable East Texas face. I remember more acutely his tact and compassion, his good humor and his real skill with people. That last surprised me. I remember once seeing him act (skillfully) as toastmaster at a banquet in Houston. He was an adept, sophisticated, yes, clever toastmaster. I was much impressed. He told jokes, presented awards, and made everyone feel good.

Occasionally we did each other routine professional favors. For example, when I had to leave Princeton for a semester, I suggested and recommended Bill as my replacement. And he got the job. I recommended him also to the people at Hollins College (where he already had such dedicated fans as Richard Dillard and Allen Wier) as a writer-in-residence, and recommended to him that he should go. He went there and was wonderful and was much loved.

So, inevitably, we shared some students over the years—Madison Smartt Bell was one of them from Princeton days. And we shared some close friends. We even shared (as friend) an editor, Sam Vaughan at Doubleday, and sometimes communicated through him.

Near the end of his life—though I had no way to know how near the end was and indeed was under a kind of hearsay impression that his health was much improved—Bill did me an enormous favor. He agreed, without reluctance, to read all the way through the huge and unwieldy manuscript of my novel *The Succession*, about which I was plagued with more than my usual quota of questions and doubts. He took precious time to read it with care and to write a response to me. Matter of fact, he wrote me a couple of letters as he went along, letters that lifted my flagging spirits and greatly encouraged me. Later, as a practical matter, he called and dictated a blurb for the book to Sam Vaughan.

I am ashamed now, of course, to have stolen time and energy from him at that time. But, nevertheless, I am happy for his attention and shall always be grateful for it.

I shall always be grateful to him for more than that, far more—for his art and his example as an artist. I came to *The House of Breath* just about the time it came out, a time when, after fooling around with writing all my life, as long as I could remember, I was finally committed (without having a clue what that commitment might mean) to the art of writing as my vocation and my life. I can't even begin, not in a few words here and maybe not in many, to tell what that book meant to me. I had just returned from a job in East Texas, all over East Texas as a matter of fact, knew something about the "reality" of which he wrote, just as, with some blood kin there, I knew something about the people, too. But the book was a profound influence. Not an influence in the conventional sense. I never even imagined myself writing like William Goyen. From the first, he was wholly admirable and wholly inimitable. But in an almost absolute sense, both his achievement, then and there and in the other, later works as they came along one by one, and his example—the example of his grace in survival as an artist of dedication and integrity, his *courage,* in good times and bad, courage that would be sorely tested and would finally triumph over fact and flesh—all these things were for me like trail signs blazed by a genuine and adventurous explorer. They were and are lights in and against the dark. In that deeper sense, he dares (almost childishly, "I dare you," wonderfully so) anyone to try and follow after him—to aim to do the right thing with one's gifts and to try to do it well.

There is no dwindling or diminishment in his story. *Arcadio* has all the power and originality and the mystery that other works, early and late, make manifest. And these days I keep close by, and reckon I will do so while I live and I can, the printed version of his talk of April 13, 1983 at New York University—"Recovering: Writing and Healing." When I first read the words, I could hear him. When I read the words and heard him, he became, as I believe he intended to be, my brother. Not mine alone, but brother to anyone with ears to hear, a brother who will not permit the easy choices of despair and silence—at least not before the true time to embrace pure silence has arrived. He will not permit me (or you, either, if you listen) to succumb to the powerful temptation to deny the holy mystery of myself and thus of others.

(1984)

Peter Taylor

I doubt that there is anyone who admires Peter Taylor's literary accomplishments more than I do or has a greater respect for his art and craft. He brought something new and wonderful to southern writing even as he sustained our finest and firmest American traditions. There is no question that the work he created, first to last, is here to stay.

The man has left us behind, slipped away into the spirit world, leaving each of us our separate memories of him.

My memory goes back more than thirty years. We first met in (of all places) New York City, doing some work for the Ford Foundation. We pretty much agreed on things and had a good time. Later on, I worked with him at some writers' conferences. He was fine to work with. I visited Greensboro a few times while he was teaching there, and I delighted in his company.

Later I had to leave Virginia for the wide world, and Peter Taylor came up from Greensboro and took over my job. To round the story off, when he retired I was chosen, partly by Peter, to replace him at Virginia; and then, entirely by accident, we ended up living next door to each other on Wayside Place. What else did we share? We both had roots in Sewanee, where he is now buried. We taught some of the same students and had a good many mutual friends. We belonged to some of the same organizations.

It is the man I mourn. The work is safely alive. I loved and admired

Peter Taylor's style—his graceful ways, his special wit and wisdom, his irrepressible sense of humor, and, above all, the courage that never failed him. I will always miss him.
Light perpetual keep him.

(1995)

Paxton Davis

I knew Paxton Davis for a little more than thirty years, starting from the days when I was teaching English at the University of Virginia and he was teaching journalism an hour and a half away at Washington and Lee. We didn't see each other all that often, not enough really, but we and our wives did get together in Virginia and in Maine. In the last few years, we would meet for a summer weekend in Warm Springs, where the loudest noise was the sound of the stream, coming from the old springs, bubbling over rocks maybe fifty yards away from the wide porch where we sat in rocking chairs and drank good bourbon and talked about everything under the sun. He was a good and loyal and generous friend. Everybody who knew him misses him.

But there is something else, quite aside from the purely personal, for which he will be and should be well remembered and deeply missed—his writing. Pax was a wonderful writer, wonderfully gifted, beautifully and strictly trained (by himself) and, unlike all too many of us, he was getting better, finer-tuned all the time. We could learn from him and we could take heart from his example. There was his books page for the *Roanoke Times & World-News* that he edited for about twenty years, beginning in 1961. Later on, there was his lively and often curmudgeonly column in that paper, which stirred up people all up and down the Shenandoah Valley and southwest Virginia. And there are the books that will last. The three most recent autobiographical books—*Being a Boy* (1988), *A Boy's War* (1990), and *A Boy No*

More (1992)—are remarkable and were remarkably successful. As writing, they are graceful and so highly refined, pared down to a subtle music of echo and evocation and innuendo, that one scarcely notices at first the magical skill of their making. They are the finest works of a writer who had already proved himself to be very, very good, good enough, had he been a different being, to allow him to write by habit, if he elected to. He had learned and developed good habits, but he kept trying to achieve something more.

Of the earlier works, my special favorites, the ones I will keep recommending to readers and writers, and here recommend to you, reader, are the lean and lovely trilogy, *A Flag at the Pole: Three Soliloquies* (1976), *Ned* (1978), and *Three Days: With Robert E. Lee at Gettysburg* (1980). He was always a spare writer, allowing himself no wasted effort or motion, just like the greatest athletes. But in these three he made a bold move toward creating the methods he perfected in the autobiographical books, able to say more and more with less and less apparent effort.

I do not know if Pax will posthumously achieve some of the honor and literary reputation he so justly deserved. Does it matter? Yes, it does, at least this much: it will be a better world if and when he does. Meanwhile, I owe him much and so do a lot of writers I know about. We are deeply beholden to him, and it is an honor to be able to say so.

(1995)

EPILOGUE

This concluding piece was originally the keynote address at the end of the 2001 convocation of the Fellowship of Southern Writers. I was honored to be asked even though (as you will notice in the opening paragraph) it comes at an unenviable position in the program as the last event, the tag end of a busy three-day conference; and it is delivered immediately following the presentation of prizes and awards and, usually, some wonderful gospel music. Hard acts to follow. As it happened, I was ill at the time of the conference, and so this talk was not delivered by me, but by proxy, by my friend, the novelist Richard Bausch.
 —G. G.

Southern Literature Here and Now: *Keynote Address for the Fellowship of Southern Writers, 2001*

In the fight game, as it was called years ago, there were three stages—the preliminaries, the main event, and the walkout bout. The preliminaries were devoted to newcomers, up-and-coming talent. The main event spoke for itself, a clash between skilled fighters, both with records, and, of course, surrounded by an environment of hype. The walkout bout was just what it announced—a match intended, at best, to distract briefly and slow down the audience, to prevent too much crowding at the exits and in the parking lot. The walkout bout, leading nowhere in particular, was devoted to old pros who had seen better days and could still more or less go through the motions.

Coming at the tag end of this very special evening, and following the unquestionable main event, the convocation of the Fellowship, I am happy to be the walkout bout. I promise to go through the motions and to be fairly brief.

If, as some people argue, the advertising commercial is really the chief art form of our time, straddling two shell-shocked centuries, then maybe my behavior will be pardonable. Just in case those people are dead wrong (and I hope and pray they are), I apologize for beginning with a commercial. I just want to say a word of thanks to the LSU Press for bringing out this handsome book, *The Cry of an Occasion,* as the first in a series of books by members of the Fellowship, this one being a gathering of fiction. The books are here and available. Many of the authors are here also and more or less available, too.

A conference like this one, a gathering of truly gifted people, can lift the spirit and bodes well for the future of southern letters. If self-esteem is a desirable quality, it is demonstrably and deservedly present here and now. And so it is perhaps my proper function to go against the grain a little bit and to conclude things on a cautionary note.

In a few generations, a fairly short time in literary history, southern literature has come a long way, from something inwardly and spiritually regional to something outwardly and visibly global, greatly influential and even (sometimes) respectable. All of us here, in our several generations, the young and the old alike, came *after* the generation of the masters, the great literary trailblazers and pioneers. Some of us, now gone from the scene—people like the late Andrew Lytle, Ralph Ellison, Brooks and Warren, and others—were a part of that fabulous generation. The rest of us stand in the shade of the trees they planted.

The South that they discovered and wrote about, with all of its faults and its vices as well as its undeniable virtues, has changed beyond recognition where it has not disappeared altogether. They, the masters, had as much to do with changing it as anyone else, as any other force. And already much that was new is growing old, taken for granted, much that was boldly original now seems almost stereotypical. We have some good reasons for satisfaction in the positive and salutary changes in southern life, "real life." And in the arts we have the satisfaction of being taken more seriously than earlier, always provided, of course, that we live up to the preconceptions of others as to what and how we should be in "real life" and in art. Like our ancestors and Blanche Dubois, we are still dependent on the kindness of strangers.

One source of strength in southern literature comes from the relatively new diversity of it, with wonderful voices that were once stifled, or anyway silent, now at last being heard and justly honored.

What seems to be missing from our newly peaceable kingdom is the critical cutting edge so evident in the generation of masters. They may have been often wrong, both in judgment and in advice and counsel, but their act of questioning the prevailing modes of thought in America was of great value in the national debates of the twentieth century. There is a sense in which the present generations of southern writers would rather be safe than sorry.

Would rather not challenge the establishment on almost any serious issue lest we be misperceived and misinterpreted to our acute disadvantage.

Isn't it true (surely a good subject for a debate) that much contemporary southern writing, while charming and aesthetically delightful, is also bland beyond belief and that it avoids any real controversy like a dread disease?

Take, as one example among many, the whole subject of the Civil War. It still haunts everything. We have a great masterpiece, Shelby Foote's *The Civil War: A Narrative,* and a multitude of other studies of all kinds, factual and fictional—good, bad, and indifferent.

The Civil War remains urgently fascinating to a very large number of readers. Recently for the *Sewanee Review* (Spring 2000) I set out, innocently enough, to write an essay-review of some of the newest and most representative books about the Civil War. This sampling of books added a mere thirty-one titles to the already more than seventy thousand books written about the war—said to be at the rate of a book a day published for every day since the war ended. Recently I discovered at our Barnes and Noble superstore an entire display table offering several dozen new books about the Civil War, all of them published in the few months since my piece in the *Sewanee Review.* Many of the earlier views and myths of that war have vanished. Certainly the story of the Lost Cause has ceased to be anything but a lost cause. Shelby Foote's narrative history gave us the hard facts, what he called "the butcher's bill" of what remains by far the worst and bloodiest in our history. Nothing else even comes close. Think rivers of blood (Henry Ward Beecher called up "oceans of blood"). Think acres of amputated arms and legs. Think of a generation of cripples. The war lasted far longer than it should have. It could, however, have lasted even longer if the Confederates had elected to continue fighting in spite of all losses or, more practically, to wage guerrilla warfare, massive terrorism for years to come. General Sherman considered that a real possibility. In a letter to Grant (April 25, 1965), he defended himself (and Grant as well) for offering terms of surrender to the enemy. "No surrender of an army not actually at the mercy of an antagonist, was ever made without 'terms,' and these always define the military status of the surrendered. . . . I now apprehend that the rebel armies will disperse; and instead of dealing with six or seven states, we will have to deal with numberless bands of desperados headed by such men as Mosby, Forrest, Red Jackson and others who know not and care not for danger and its consequences." Having seen, indeed witnessing even now in daily news from Afghanistan, Sri Lanka, Chechnya, Kashmir, the Middle East, Ireland, and Subsaharan Africa, etc., just how much trouble small bands of serious terrorists can cause for modern national states, we have to take that threat as seriously as the prescient Sherman did. And, as well, we need to remind ourselves that Lee and Johnston and Kirby Smith and Bedford Forrest and others also considered that idea and dismissed it, choosing instead an end to combat with an honorable surrender. Choosing to rejoin the Union. Choosing not to urge but to *order* their soldiers to lay down their arms and to be good citizens of the reformed Union. Thus the nation owes a debt to those Confederate leaders who chose to accept defeat and rejoin the Union and, by the way, to save many thousands of lives, on both sides, in the process.

Of course, those same leaders inspire mixed feelings, as witness the recent political quarrels concerning public statues of Bedford Forrest and others. Statues worldwide have had a hard time in our era. I recall the words of an African sculptor I met in Rome years ago who made large public statues of leaders all over the African continent and throughout the Third World. It was steady and rewarding work, but he spoke of it with some sadness. "You have to understand," he told me, "I make the statues of the leaders of these countries and they pay me very well for this. But it is a heartbreaking experience. None of them can last very long. The statues go up in the parks and squares. Then, after a little while, comes the next coup or revolution. And the first thing they do is topple and destroy the old statues and order new ones. It's a good living, but it can be discouraging."

So much for the coming and going of statues.

We now know and, quite aside from all its complex causes and purposes (all twentieth-century soldiers know that causes and purposes are among the very first things abandoned, like gas masks, in combat), we view the war as, purely and simply, a slaughterhouse.

What did it look like and feel like to those who in fact endured the experience? Mostly, except by the analogy of our own experience in the twentieth-century wars, we don't know. Like all veterans of extended and brutal combat, they found the war very hard to talk about, even to each other, until much later in life when memory had softened and suppressed itself. We believe they were like ourselves, that they began in innocence, bright-eyed and bushy-tailed, and ended like walking wounded with a thousand-yard stare. Read Shelby Foote's wonderful novel *Shiloh* and see what I mean.

Let me take the liberty here of quoting from a family diary, confessing that among the four of my great-grandfathers and one grandfather who fought in the Civil War, this one, the only one among them to keep a diary, was also the only Yankee. Colonel Oliver Hazard Palmer was the commanding officer of the 108th New York Volunteers, who fought and lived through several of the worst battles of the war. Here is part of his account of the Battle of Fredericksburg:

> I remained on the field until nearly dark and until the fighting of the day was mainly over. It was a terribly hot place. The shells were flying in every direction and plowing up the earth all around me all over as though in a whirlwind. The scene was frightful but intensely exciting. New Brigades of fresh troops were forming in line and advancing hoping to be more successful, but I knew they were doomed to disappointment and death. Broken and shattered Companies, Regiments and Brigades were falling back. Dead and wounded officers and men were being borne to the rear, some in blankets, some on the shoulders of comrades. You would see one here with one arm, another there with one leg trying to get back. Some moaning, some swearing, occasionally a poor fellow trying to save the half not yet shot away would disappear in fragments by a solid shot or amidst the smoke of an exploding shell. . . . At sundown I made my way to town to gather up fragments of my Brigade not knowing what the next day might require. Out of the 1200 men in my command in the morning I could get together at night only 400. It was a sorry sight.

Looking back from our perspective, we are entitled to ask *what if?* What if, after the first terrible battles had proved beyond doubt or question that this war was going to be a bloody slaughterhouse, a huge dance of death for both sides, what if they had seriously attempted to negotiate some kind of settlement? What if Lincoln and Davis had dedicated themselves to seeking a peace process? Would the results have been better or worse? The fighting men on both sides might well have asked what could be worse.

As writers we have to seek to tell the truth, not according to the conventions and clichés of our own traditions except insofar as we genuinely perceive them to be authentic and accurate. As for those of us who would prefer to avoid or ignore this or that topic as insensitive at best and shameful at worst, take, for example, the playing of "Dixie" in public. Take also Lincoln's remarks to a military band on the evening of April 10, 1865. He said: "I have always thought 'Dixie' one of the best tunes I ever heard. Our adversaries over the way attempted to appropriate it, but I insisted yesterday that we fairly captured it.... I now request the band to favor me with its performance."

Well then. Here we are, doing something very southern, thinking and talking about the past that is always present even as it is always changing. There is no escaping it. You cannot escape history. You cannot escape change. It seems to me, though, that there are several kinds and forms of history. One kind assumes the outcomes of events and does not feel the need, other than in ironic jest, even to consider the possibility of alternative outcomes. The weakness of this kind of remembering is the hard fact that the people actively engaged at any given time and in any given action have not a clue (beyond wishing and praying) what the outcomes may prove to be. Memory, the kissing cousin of history, is always a little askew, distorted by the presence of known outcomes. Things that were purely accidental are remembered as being inevitable.

On the other hand, narrative history, as exemplary of literary art, allows the imagination to believe or pretend, however briefly, that all outcomes are forever possible and that all the old clichés and stereotypes, true or false, are legitimately subject to scrutiny and interrogation. Narrative history assumes that truth is more a matter of dependant clauses and question marks than imperial sentences followed by exclamation points.

Early in this talk, and not without a wink and a nudge, I said that though we southern writers may not have yet fully "arrived" in the contemporary sense of the term, we have at least become, for better and worse, respectable.

Respectability beyond our borders is well within our grasp. Here, in a sentiment echoed in a recent critical essay in the *New Yorker*, is a short poem I wrote, a "flashcard," describing our situation by a specific example:

> What Professor Helen Vendler actually said in Boston
> on January 18, 1978:
> "If she had only been able to keep her health
> Flannery O'Connor might have made it in New York."

To be sure, there is no good reason for any southern writer to feel inferior to the mainstream of literature in our age. Southern writing has always been open to everything that is happening in our craft and art, to much that is new and even strange from all over the world. The past century was marked by a continuous interchange between languages and cultures. And influence and recognition work both ways. For example, the French, who have been generous to southern writing, have made cultural heroes of some of our very own, writers like William Styron and Fred Chappell and Madison Smartt Bell. As for global reputation, consider that the southern avant-garde writer R. H. W. Dillard is probably the only writer in any country and language to have received personal fan letters from both Borges and Nabokov.

For most of my lifetime, the official establishment position has been that the glories of southern literature are over and done with. There is nothing really new or interesting to report about our homeplace. This has been a favorite cliché of literary journalism, and it can make for some lively and clever copy. Meanwhile, however, two new generations of southern writers have ignored these self-appointed judges and critics, filling the second half of the twentieth century with original voices and creations. Anybody with an eye on the future is well aware of the many gifted new voices making a joyful noise and (it seems) not in the least inhibited by the towering ghosts of our literary past or by the mosquito buzzing of literary journalism in their ears. I have no idea what the future may bring or what slouching beasts are even now coming our way, but it certainly will not be the end of storytelling by southerners. There is no end of that in sight.

We do have some problems and might as well admit it. In the larger national scene, dominated by the dragon of television, we are peculiarly susceptible to the almighty power of clichés. Southern writers have always had to be intensely aware of the image we have in the rest of the country and the world. More than a few of us, some of our best and brightest, have tried to justify an attempt to be trendy as a necessary means of artistic survival. Too many of us have worried too much about the words of our mouths and the meditations of our hearts being acceptable in the national literary scene. Maybe new technology and, as well, the growth and development of our own southern publishing houses will help change things for the better.

But finally, none of the above is terribly important. What matters is that here and now we have come together to celebrate the art and the craft we live for. We are here in unusual diversity, no two of us very much alike, but happy to see each other again and hoping, against the weight of sad experience that we refuse to allow to stifle hope, that the old magic will work anew and that in the end it will send each and all of us on our way home again, singing and rejoicing.

(2001)

Acknowledgments

The author is grateful to the editors and publishers of the following publications for permission to reprint the works noted:

"Anarchy and Family: A Few Words About the Southern Tradition," *Chronicles,* March 1991.
"An American Family History We Eavesdrop While a Family Tells Its Private Stories: Review of *The Hinterlands* by Robert Morgan," *The World & I,* August 1997.
"A Life Without End Two Novels About World War II by William Hoffman," in *The Fictional World of William Hoffman,* edited by William L. Frank, University of Missouri Press, 2000.
"Liberty and the Southern Tradition," *Imprimis,* February 1992.
"Part Scam: Review of *The Encyclopedia of Southern Culture,*" *The Observer* (Charlottesville, Virginia), 17–23 August 1989.
"A Voice for the Voiceless: Review of *My Drowning* by Jim Grimsley," *The World & I,* June 1997.
"Jesse Hill Ford's Play," *Southern Quarterly,* Winter–Spring 1995.
"William Price Fox's *Dixiana Moon,*" *Dictionary of Literary Biography Yearbook: 1981,* edited by Karen L. Rood et al., Gale, 1982.
"New Market: The Cost and Waste of the War" (published as "A Civil War Battle Fought by Boys"), *The Sophisticated Traveler, New York Times,* 6 March 1994.
"The Death of Regional Writing," *The Student* (Wake Forest University), 1980.
"Soil of Hope: New and Other Voices in Southern Fiction for the Nineties," *American Notes and Queries,* October 1992. Reprinted in *Surfing Tomorrow: Essays on the Future of American Fiction,* edited by Lance Olsen, Potpourri Publications, 1995.
Review of *The Ordways* by William Humphrey, *Masterplots 1966 Annual,* edited by Frank N. Magill and Dayton Kohler, Salem Press, 1967.

Review of *Cassandra Singing* by David Madden, *Masterplots 1970 Annual*, edited by Frank N. Magill and Dayton Kohler, Salem Press, 1971.

"Crime and Punishment in Kansas: Truman Capote's *In Cold Blood*," *The Hollins Critic*, February 1966.

Review of *The Commonplace Book of William Byrd III of Westover*, edited by Kevin Berland, Jan Kirsten Gilliam and Kenneth A. Lockridge, *Washington Times*, 8 April 2001.

Review of *The Fabulous History of the Dismal Swamp Company: A Story of George Washington's Times* by Charles Royster, *Washington Times*, 14 November 1999.

Review of *A Consuming Fire: The Fall of the Confederacy in the Mind of the White Christian South*, by Eugene D. Genovese, *Washington Times*, 24 January 1997.

"No Wonder People Got Crazy As They Grew Up," review of *Bastard Out of Carolina* by Dorothy Allison, *New York Times Book Review*, 15 July 1992.

Review of *Eneas Africanus* by Harry Stillwell Edwards, *Georgia Review*, Summer 1957.

Review of *A Way of Happening: Observations of Contemporary Poetry* by Fred Chappell, *Chronicles*, October 1998.

"Gaining a Foothold in Old Jamestown with a Sovereign's Tightly Held Funds," review of *Big Chief Elizabeth* by Giles Milton, *Washington Times*, 17 December 2000.

Review of *The Sharp Teeth of Love* by Doris Betts, *Brightleaf*, October 1997.

Review of *The Big Ballad Jamboree* by Donald Davidson, *New York Times Book Review*, 12 May 1996.

Review of *White People: Stories* by Allan Gurganus, *New York Times Book Review*, 3 February 1991.

"It's True South with a Sense of Humor," review of *The Sharpshooter Blues* by Lewis Nordan, *Philadelphia Inquirer*, 3 September 1995.

Review of *Kate Vaiden* by Reynolds Price, *Chicago Tribune*, 22 June 1986.

Review of *The Collected Stories of Reynolds Price*, *New York Times Book Review*, 4 July 1993.

Review of *A Visitation of Spirits* by Randall Kenan, *Chicago Tribune*, 13 August 1989.

Review of *Nashville 1864: The Dying of the Light* by Madison Jones, *Brightleaf*, October 1997.

Review of *The Thanatos Syndrome* by Walker Percy, *Chicago Tribune*, 29 March 1987.

Review of *Celebration* by Mary Lee Settle, *Chicago Tribune*, 23 November 1986.

"Wolfe in Wolfe's Clothing," *Chronicles*, April 2000.

Review of *Peter Taylor: A Writer's Life* by Hubert A. McAlexander, *Washington Times*, 23 September 2001.

"Bow to the Bull's-Eye: Dickey's *To the White Sea*," *Philadelphia Inquirer*, 12 September 1993. Another version of this review was published by *South Carolina Review*, Spring 1994.

"A Letter from Earth," *Chronicles*, July 2000.
Foreword to *The Liberation of Lord Byron Jones* by Jesse Hill Ford, University of Georgia Press (Brown Thrasher Books Edition), 1993.
Introduction to *So Red the Rose* by Stark Young, J. S. Sanders (Southern Classics Series), 1992.
Foreword to *The Long Roll* by Mary Johnston, Johns Hopkins University Press, 1996.
Foreword to *Cease Firing* by Mary Johnston, Johns Hopkins University Press, 1996.
Foreword to *Dream Garden: The Poetic Vision of Fred Chappell*, edited by Patrick Bizzaro, Louisiana State University Press, 1997.
Introduction to *Snopes* by William Faulkner, Modern Library, 1994.
"Life into Art: A Conversation with David Huddle," *Iron Mountain Review*, Spring 1993.
"Buzzards and Dodos: George Core (Editor of the *Sewanee Review*) Talks with George Garrett About the Quarterlies," *Chronicles*, March 1991.
"An Interview with Paxton Davis (1925–1994)," *Dictionary of Literary Biography Yearbook 1989*, 1990.
"Tribute" (William Goyen), *Dictionary of Literary Biography Yearbook 1983*, 1984.
"Tribute" (Peter Taylor), *Dictionary of Literary Biography Yearbook: 1994*, 1995.
"Tribute" (Paxton Davis), *Dictionary of Literary Biography Yearbook: 1994*, 1995.